T0269733

DERSHOWITZ FAMILY SAGA

A CENTURY AND A HALF OF JEWISH LIFE IN POLAND, THROUGH AMERICA, AND INTO ISRAEL

Zecharia Dor-Shav (Dershowitz)

Foreword by Alan Dershowitz

Skyhorse Publishing

Skyhorse Publishing books may be purchased in bulk at special discounts
for sales promotion, corporate gifts, fund-raising, or educational purposes.
Special editions can also be created to specifications. For details, contact
the Special Sales Department, Sports Publishing, 307 West 36th Street,
11th Floor, New York, NY 10018 or info@skyhorsepublishing.com.

Skyhorse® and Skyhorse Publishing® are registered trademarks of Skyhorse
Publishing, Inc.®, a Delaware corporation.

Visit our website at www.skyhorsepublishing.com.

10 9 8 7 6 5 4 3 2 1

Library of Congress Cataloging-in-Publication Data is available on file.

Cover design by Brian Peterson
Front cover photo courtesy of Allen and Chanie Dershowitz

ISBN: 978-1-5107-7023-2
Ebook ISBN: 978-1-5107-7024-9

Printed in the United States of America

IN GRATITUDE

הִנֵּה אָנֹכִי שֹׁלֵחַ לָכֶם אֵת אֵלִיָּה הַנָּבִיא לִפְנֵי בּוֹא יוֹם יְקֹוָק הַגָּדוֹל וְהַנּוֹרָא
וְהֵשִׁיב לֵב־אָבוֹת עַל־בָּנִים וְלֵב בָּנִים עַל־אֲבוֹתָם....:(מלאכי ג כג)

Behold, I will send you Elijah the prophet before the coming of
the great and terrible day of the LORD. And he shall turn the
heart of the fathers to the children, and the heart of the children
to their fathers . . . (Malachi 3:23)

Thank you, God, for allowing me to finish this document, which I believe to be of importance to the family and the general public.

I wish to acknowledge the wealth of information and pictures that I received from so many members of the family, much of which has been included in this book.

I also wish to acknowledge the constructive criticism and help which I received from my wife, Lee, and from my children: Nachum, Simcha Hillel, and Etan. May this book be a source of continued interest in our roots and in the Jewish developments in which our family has shared.

Special thanks are also due to my nephew, Alan (whom we call Avi) Dershowitz, who read and commented on the book from cover to cover.

Finally, I wish to thank Julie Ganz and colleagues of Skyhorse Press and my son, Nachum, and cousin, Hillel Fendel, for their very helpful and repeated editing of the entire manuscript.

CONTENTS

FOREWORD

THIS IS A remarkable book about a remarkable family. It tells the all-too-typical story of the American Jewish experience through the eyes of one family from the late nineteenth to the early twenty-first century. But it is different from the usual immigrant story beginning with poverty and religious observance and ending with secularism and success. Justice Ruth Bader Ginsburg— whose family experienced the typical progression— once asked rhetorically, "What's the difference between a bookkeeper in the garment district and a Supreme Court Justice?" Her answer: "One generation."

This book is about my family—the Dershowitz family. And the question it asks is: "What's the difference between a working-class modern orthodox American Jewish family and a middle-class even more religiously observant family?" The answer to that atypical question that is provided in this book is: "One or two generations."

What is different about the Dershowitz experience in America is that for the most part my family has become more religious and no more successful economically since they landed in America in 1888. Every generation seems to be more observant and no wealthier than the previous generation. They have also become more Zionistic. Many of my great-grandfather's descendants now live in Israel and attend Jewish seminaries.

I am an exception. I am less religiously observant than my parents and grandparents and more economically successful. My mother, like Justice Ginsburg's mother, worked as a bookkeeper in the garment district, and it took one generation for me to become a Harvard Law Professor at age twenty-five. But I am far from the most successful member of my family. Many members of the Dershowitz clan have achieved more success—at least among the religious Jewish communities in which they live. They include eminent rabbis, great Jewish scholars, and other highly respected religious figures, who are revered and well-known in their communities.

My cousin, Rabbi Zvi Dershowitz, whom my grandfather helped rescue from the Nazis just one month before they invaded Czechoslovakia, served for more than half a century as a rabbi in some of the most important Conservative synagogues and Jewish summer camps. Among his campers was a young man named Robert Zimmerman, whom you may know as Bob Dylan. Zvi, and others of the Dershowitz family, helped Jews in the former Soviet Union exchange messages with Jews in the United States trying to help them get out, as also to smuggle in forbidden religious articles. Zvi also helped Jews get out of Iran and establish themselves in his congregation, and elsewhere, in the face of considerable difficulties and resistance. He dealt with the US government's decision to give them political asylum, leading to citizenship. His remarkable career was recounted in the Congressional Record upon his retirement, and the account is included as an appendix to this book. Others have become leading figures in Jewish education and Zionist enterprises. One of my cousins, Rabbi Dovid Fendel, is the head of a large yeshiva in Sderot, Israel, bordering on the Gaza Strip. The yeshiva's heroic stand under fire, in the IDF, and in its tireless devotion to the community during the waves of missile attacks, has had a fundamental impact on Sderot. It has been the target of many Hamas rockets—including one when I was attending

Purim services there. Under its *hesder*[1] program, it trains Israeli soldiers in Jewish studies while preparing them to defend their nation-state.

The author of this wonderful narrative is my father's youngest brother, my uncle Rabbi Professor Zecharia Dor-Shav. He Hebraized our family name to mean "the generation that returned" when he and his family made aliyah[2] to Israel half a century ago. He served with distinction as a professor at Bar-Ilan University while continuing to teach and study Jewish sources. He participated in some of Israel's most important rescue missions, including those of Soviet and Ethiopian Jewry. He recently celebrated his ninety-fifth birthday with a family Zoom call in which reminiscences were interrupted by a call from Prime Minister Benjamin Netanyahu (which I confess to facilitating).

Many books have been written about the typical American Jewish experience. This book is different in many ways and far more interesting. It begins like the others: our family living in the small polish shtetl of Pilzno, not far from Krakow. Every Jew who remained in that shtetl was murdered by the Nazis, including a

---

1 *Hesder* is an Israeli yeshiva/military service program, which combines advanced Talmudic studies with military service, usually within a religious Zionist framework.

2 *aliyah* (immigration to Israel)

sixteen-year-old Dershowitz girl and her fifteen-year-old brother. Most of our Czechoslovakia-based family was fortunate enough to leave before the Nazi era, and they helped to rescue other known personalities on the eve of the Holocaust.

The beginnings of the American Jewish immigrant story may be the same for most families, but our family moved in a very different direction. This book tells that story. It is filled with adventures, challenges, confrontations, disappointments, and successes. Readers who know my story will see its roots in the Dershowitz family history, despite my secularization. Readers who know the more observant members of the family may also recognize the intellectual and spiritual heritage we all received from our ancestors who made the decision to move to America.

At the time they made this momentous and challenging decision, America was called the "*Goldene Medina*" (the golden country) as well as the "*treifa medina*."[3] Those who stayed behind in Poland were fearful that their descendants would become treifa—nonobservant, secular, or even intermarried. The secular temptations of the Goldene Medina might be too great to resist. The saga of the Dershowitz family shows that for the most part, these skeptics were wrong. With

---

3 *treifa medinah* (non-kosher country)

a very few exceptions, the family has remained committed—albeit in somewhat different ways—to Jewish values, culture, and religion.

This is a story that every person in America—a nation of immigrants—can benefit from reading. It has left me with a sense of real pride in being a small part of this increasingly large family from Pilzno, Poland, by way of the Lower East Side, Williamsburg, Borough Park, the suburbs, and Israel. It is a Jewish American success story—with success measured in religious as well as secular terms.

—Alan Dershowitz

INTRODUCTION

IN 1988, NOTING the passage of one hundred years in the United States, the Zecharja Derschowitz clan decided to take score and bless the One on High for its happy sojourn in the United States after fleeing Galicia in the Austria-Hungary Empire in 1888. They grew and prospered in their newly adopted land, the United States. Since that time, a substantial minority of their descendants moved on to the Promised Land. The author of this work—the only surviving child of Zecharja's oldest son, Louis—is one of the fortunate ones who, in 1969, was able to make this move. Hopefully, Israel is the last stop of the biblically prophesized sojourn of the family and the Jewish people on Earth.

As one of the participants in that centennial gathering wrote in verse at the time:

> From the days in the Lower East Side,
> our branches grew far and wide.

This country was too small for some,
so, they moved East to Jerusalem.
Yet, some chose to go
north to Ontario
as they spread our family tree.
Professors and businesses, too,
vary for more than a few,
with talent in art and décor
and Rabbis and lawyers galore.
There are teachers and tutors
and high-tech computers.
It's all in our family tree.

This book is meant to chronicle the history of the family from our earliest known ancestors to the present time—from a generation or two earlier than those who arrived on the American shores in the late nineteenth century—i.e., from Yechezkel Derschowitz and, likely, a brother, Shlomo (Salmen) Deresiewicz, with confirmed and possible siblings.[1] The information is

---

1   A possible sibling is Wolf, who married Chaya Feige and had a son, Chaim Mechel, in 1865. We know of a Wolf—perhaps the same—who had a child, Rechel, in 1839 who married Abraham Schmerling. There is a possible family member, Moshe (1776–1831); another one named Chaim, who died during his first year of life in 1813; and one, Bainish, who served as a civil witness to the marriage of Rechel in 1838. Finally, we know of Solomon, who served as a civil witness to the birth

relatively complete for my branch of the family, and most definitely limited for other branches because of my inability to procure more complete information from them and their progeny at this time.

Our family traveled a path that mirrored the development of that cohort of American Jews who stem from the Polish state (established by the Piast dynasty[2] and preeminent since the tenth century), as also from the Pale of Eastern Europe. These Jews succeeded in maintaining a high level of religious observance and involvement. During the mourning period for my mother, Ida Dershowitz, each of her children was being comforted by prominent members of the many Jewish organizations with which the family was involved. In Israel, too, the family is deeply involved with many and varied bearers of developing and developed Jewish endeavors.

While each branch of the greater family as well as each person within each branch is unique and pursues

---

of Abraham Lowe to Yechezkel, in 1864. Nonetheless, since there was another, seemingly unrelated Derschowitz family in Pilzno at the time of Zecharja—as reported below—we do not know which, if any, of the above, might be from the family of that unrelated neighbor.

2   The conversion of Duke Mieszko I to Christianity paved the way for Poland to become a member of the family of Christian kingdoms. In 1000, during the Congress of Gniezno, Poland was recognized as a state by the Holy Roman Empire and the Pope. In 1025, Duke Boleslaus I the Brave was crowned King of Poland, marking the starting date for a Polish Kingdom. Wikipedia, The Kingdom of Poland.

a style of life that is personally suitable, we all remember and feel ourselves as part of the unique clan that is Dershowitz. We are like a crazy quilt, all different but, also, all part of the same quilt: we are different in our personal lives, but we feel ourselves the same when we are referencing the Jewish people as our unique religion, and when referencing our part in the Nation of Israel.

Furthermore, as a result of familiarity with many of the very prominent heads of Torah institutions in the United States, important conversations and religious rulings that are known to me from personal experience have been included. I have been most expansive regarding things gleaned from Rabbi Yitzchak Hutner of the Mesivta Yeshiva Rabbeinu Chaim Berlin, my personal rabbi.[3]

In a sense, my generation mirrors the generation of Ezra and Nehemiah that built the Second Temple, bridged the period from the First to the Second Temples, and about which is written:

וְרַבִּים מֵהַכֹּהֲנִים וְהַלְוִיִּם וְרָאשֵׁי הָאָבוֹת הַזְּקֵנִים אֲשֶׁר רָאוּ
אֶת־הַבַּיִת הָרִאשׁוֹן בְּיָסְדוֹ

---

3   When, in this document, we write of a community's master and teacher, the spelling "rabbi" is used. When writing of the head of a Hasidic dynasty, the spelling "Rebbe" is used. The word "Rebbi" is used when one has a very personal relationship with this master or teacher. In general, italics are used for the first instance of any word that does not appear in the Merriam-Webster Unabridged Dictionary. Uncommon Hebrew and Yiddish words are defined in the Glossary.

זֶה הַבַּיִת בְּעֵינֵיהֶם כַּכֶם בְּקוֹל גָּדוֹל וְרַבִּים בִּתְרוּעָה בְשִׂמְחָה לְהָרִים קוֹל

Many of the priests and Levites, family heads and Elders—who had seen the First Temple in situ—when they saw the Second Temple, cried in a loud voice and many [others] trumpeted in joy in a loud voice. (Ezra 3:12)

Many times, in the history of the Jewish People, as at the time of Ezra and Nehemiah, great tragedies were followed by great advancements. We, as a bridge between the generation of the Holocaust and the generation of the establishment of the State of Israel, the generation that saw the fall of atheist communism in the Soviet Union and the mass emigration of a significant number of its Jews, pray that our memories and experiences of destruction will yet turn into great blessing, and we will merit to rejoice in the formation of what, we hope, is the beginning of the unfolding of the final stage of our predestined mission on Earth.

This account is being written at the time of the ongoing 2020 pandemic of coronavirus disease (COVID-19). With regard to this tragedy too, I pray:

May it be that in our time, the sound of the new joy will overwhelm the memory and sound of the old.

1888–1973

1882–1955

Composition by Nachum Dershowitz

Chapter One
FAMILY ORIGINS

WE BEGIN THIS epic story with the arrival of my father, Louis/Leibish Dershowitz,[1] on the shores of the United States in 1891. He was born in Pilzno[2] in the administrative district of Tarnow, Poland (then Austria-Hungary),

---

1   His Hebrew name was Yekutiel Yehudah. Spellings of names in this work correspond to what was found in at least one of the documents examined. They often appear differently in other documents. In some instances, a transliterated Hebrew name is used, although it may be listed in the document by its English equivalent.

2   This market town, about fifty miles east of Cracow or Kraków, was once a bustling Hasidic center and is still a pilgrimage site for Hasidic Jews. The main street is Zydowska Street, meaning "Jewish Street." All that remains of the main synagogue is the central bimah ("platform," from which the Torah is read), with four tall pillars, a typical feature of Polish masonry synagogues. These are now protected by a canopy roof and stand in a park, the grounds of which were once the body of the synagogue. (From Ruth E. Gruber, "Visiting the Vestiges of Jewish Poland." *New York Times*: October 21, 1990.)

on the Sukkoth holiday, probably, September 16, 1882 (died April 6, 1955). This is deduced from a family tradition of a big holiday repast on Simchat Torah in honor of the fact that it was the day on which Leibish's brit[3] had taken place. He had arrived in the United States with his mother, Lea (née Bander) Derschowitz,[4] and several siblings on the SS Furst Bismarck, on August 8, 1891. As was the custom with many new immigrants at that time, his father—my grandfather—Zacharja[5] (July 6, 1860–April 5, 1921), had left Europe for the United States earlier, arriving in 1888 in Castle Garden, now a museum at the foot of Battery Park in Manhattan. This gave him an opportunity to establish himself in the "new land" before he brought his family. In 1891,

---

3 *brit* (covenant or circumcision)
4 The name "Derschowitz" or "Deresiewicz" is reported to be a derivative of Derzow or Derzowci (a powerful Jewish leaseholder in Galicia). "Dereszewicz," "Dershovitz," or "Derschovitz" are also reported to be derivatives of *deresz* (a roan—a reddish-gray horse). It is also reportedly derived from the name of a town, Derschowitz, in Moravia. Finally, it was also the name of a Polish patriot of the seventeenth century. We know of several people named Derschowitz in Pilzno in the 1860s, or earlier, whose family connections to us are unknown as of the present time. Other possible spellings are Dershowitz (the spelling used by the author's family in the United States), Dereschewitz, Dereschowitz, Dereszowicz, Derchowitz, Dershewitz, Dershwitz, Derszowicz, Derzawitz, Direszowicz, Direschowitz, Dorschowitz, Dorzawitz, and Desowitz. Three modern name changes are Dash, Dersh, and Dor-Shav (the author's current name, meaning "Returned Generation").
5 This is the spelling that appears on his citizenship papers.

feeling that he could now support them, he sent for his wife and their four children.

He was of Hasidic[6] origin; more specifically, Ropshitz Hasidism,[7] with modern leanings, which is to say that he dressed in modern rather than Hasidic garb. I believe that both my father's and mother's nuclear families considered themselves Ropshitz Hasidim, as both the Pilzno and Tarnobrzeg/Dzików Rebbes were of Ropshitz descent.

The earliest confirmed Dershowitz family history is the marriage of Yechezkiel Derschowitz to Chana Rivka, sometime before 1840, in the district of Tarnow (Galicia). The birth of their oldest child, Zecharja, is there recorded. His oldest son, my father Leibish, often spoke in friendly terms about the Emperor Franz Joseph

---

6 For a basic appreciation of the gist of Hasidism see: https://yivoencyclopedia.org/article.aspx/hasidism/historical_overview, and/or "https://www.chabad.org/search/keyword_cdo/kid/193/jewish/Freeman-Tzvi.htm" by Tzvi Freeman and Menachem Posner, *17 Facts Everyone Should Know About Hasidic Jews*, Chabad.org.

7 The Ropshitz (Yiddish ראָפשיץ) dynasty (rabbinical family and group) descended from Rebbe Naftali Zvi Horowitz of Ropshitz (1760–1827). Ropshitz is the name of a town in southern Poland known in Polish as Ropczyce. Many major rabbis are descendants of the Rebbes of Ropshitz, including: (1) Rebbe Eliezer Horowitz of Tarnobrzeg/Dzików (died October 19, 1860 [3 Cheshvan 5621]), son of Rebbe Naftali Tzvi; and (2) Rebbe Meir Horowitz also of Tarnobrzeg/Dzików (died June 19, 1877 [8 Tammuz 5637]), son of Rebbe Eliezer, Rabbi of Dzików, concurrent with his father's being Rebbe there, also succeeding his father as Rebbe.

(1830–1916), who reigned over the kingdom from 1848 until 1916. (A short biography of the emperor, as regards his relationship with the Jewish subjects, appears in Appendix 1.) The Austrian government created a local council in Pilzno in 1830 and admitted Jews to the town. The first Jew, Aron Ader, a barber/surgeon from Dembitz, was approved to live in the city in 1830. After him other Jews moved to Pilzno.

An additional branch of our family was in Tylicz.[8] Yakov Elimelech Deresiewicz (1841–1903), who settled there, has the name Shlomo (Salmen) inscribed on his tombstone as his father. Shlomo was likely Yechezkiel's brother. Yakov had seven daughters and four sons. One of his sons, Aron (1860–?), had a son, Solomon (Salmen, 1884–1959), who came to the United States in 1921 with his child, Abraham Eber (1916–1987), and at Ellis Island changed the family name to Dershewitz. Abraham Eber's son, Gene, has been living in Oregon since 1969.

Another son of Yakov, Shlomo Salmen (?–1938), had a son named Simon Spira[9] (1911–1983), a Bobover

---

8 Tylicz is on the Galician side of the border with Slovakia, near the resort of Krynica.

9 This surname may be of Simon's mother. In Galicia it was quite common for Jewish people to get married religiously, but not legally, bestowing them with their mother's surname. The reasons were several. Firstly, in some places there were quotas as to how many Jewish

Hasid, who married Hilda, and whose child, Eliezer, now lives in New York City. DNA testing that I and one of my known cousins, Anthony Dash, did suggests that we have a common paternal ancestor with these Dershewitz and Spira families. With a 66 percent probability, the results suggest that Yechezkel of Pilzno, and Shlomo (Salmen) Deresiewicz of Tylicz, were brothers. Their father was born sometime in the eighteenth century. We also know of one woman, Chaya Feige, who may have been Yakov Elimelech Deresiewicz's sister.

The Jews of Pilzno, My Father's Birthplace

Poland's King Kazimierz the Great decreed the founding of Pilzno in 1354. The first arrival of Jews is thought to have been in 1560, when an elder of the town, Jan Tarlo, invited them and had them settle on the outskirts of Pilzno. The earliest records, from 1564, mention three Jewish farm-owners and two Jewish tenant farmers. Official records of 1576 name the Jews then living in Pilzno: Lazarus, Josef and his wife Jahenet,

---

families were allowed to be married. Secondly, even in places where they were allowed to get married legally, many people were reluctant to do so, because one had to appear bareheaded in an office that was full of crucifixes. Sometimes, too, it was their preference to be a citizen of the mother's homeland rather than the father's, and in that way avoid being drafted into their host country's military.

and Simon, all of whom came from Tarnow. Their occupation was trade and money-lending.

At least one citizen complained to the court against the Jews, saying that they were interfering with citizens earning an honest living in trade or other business. The Jews wrote a counterplea to King Stefan Batory. Nonetheless, he ordered them evicted and forbade them from settling in the town or vicinity.

In the sixteenth century more than twenty towns obtained the "privilegia de non tolerandis Judaeis [a ban on Jews]." These included: Warsaw in 1525, Vilna in 1551, Bydgoszcz in 1556, Stryj in 1567, Tarnogrod in 1569, and Pilzno in 1577. In practice, however, the ban was inconsistently observed. In other locations, separate suburbs or "Jewish towns" were formed. The Pilzno City Council issued a new decree in 1635 prohibiting Jews even from selling in the town's market.

In 1787, a law was issued that the Jews were required to take on German family names as of January 1789. The new names were intended to promote the process of Germanization and assimilation of the Jews. For the same reason, communities and businesses were forbidden to use Hebrew or Yiddish[10] in their ledgers. They were required to keep all accounts only in German.

---

10 A Hebrew/Aramaic/German language with local variations, spoken by Ashkenazi Jews.

In 1814, the head priest of Pilzno, in his report to the bishop, mentioned that there are no Jews in Pilzno, but that they lived in neighboring villages and came to the market. "Altogether there are nine Jewish families in the parish," he wrote. Jews had an inn near the parish church in 1760, but none of them had the rights of citizens.[11]

According to the census of 1880 (eight years before my grandfather left for the United States), Pilzno had 2,128 residents, of whom 551 were Jews. The Poviat (County) of Pilzno in 1886 had 47,500 residents, of whom 44,600 were Catholic and 2,813 were Jews. In 1900, the census in Pilzno showed 2,138 residents, including 707 Jews. Just before World War II, there were 788 Jews in the town, and 1,342 in the parish. After the Germans entered Pilzno they began to isolate the Jewish population, beginning in the fall of 1939, by having them wear the Jewish star.

The early Pilzno Jews belonged to the synagogue in Tarnow, but in 1873 they organized a separate religious community with Aron Seelenfreunden[12] as leader,

---

11 Much of this information is based on: Mike Rosenzweig, Early History of the Jews in Poland, 1998. http://www.zchor.org/heritage/history.htm.
12 After my grandmother, Rochma Bleema Maultasch, who had lived in the basement apartment of our Williamsburg apartment, passed away, the family took in an ailing bedridden Rabbi Zeelenfreund and cared for him. There was also a Zeelenfreund listed in the Tarnow genealogy records as having been a civil witness to the birth of Zecharja. It may be assumed that the rabbi in my home was from this Pilzno family.

and Jacob Ader and Mendel Kornhauser as members, among others. They bought a wooden house that was transformed into a synagogue, and adjacent to it they built a mikvah.[13] In 1873 some land was purchased for a cemetery, with a brick and stone wall around it and a wooden structure at its entry for the tahorah (purification) of bodies for burial. Before the establishment of the local cemetery, Jews had buried their dead in Dembitz. In the 1890s an official report noted that "Pilzno consists of tidy wooden courts surrounded by gardens, except for the marketplace, in which there are mostly single-story brick tenements." In 1897, Mendel Kornhauser became the head of the Jewish community. After him came Rafael Ader, who was followed by Meyer Lerner. The Jews also invited a rabbi, Yisrael Adler, eventually succeeded by his nephew, Gershon Adler.[14] After him came David Singer (Adler's son-in-law), followed by Rebbe Menachem Horowitz, of Ropshitz descent. . . . Between the two world wars, the town also had a Jewish school. Aside from the synagogue, there were also several houses of prayer (shteeblach) where Jews would gather. There were not many secularly well-educated Jews.

---

13 *mikvah* (ritual bath)
14 A direct descendent of this Rabbi Adler is Yehudah Adler, who married my wife Lee's granddaughter, Yael Gottesman.

Several dozen Jews lived in the surrounding villages. They were often poor and made their livelihood from produce bought from the farmers and sold at the market. Jews who lived near main roads often had inns, with a liquor license from the state. Jews rarely farmed.[15]

Arrival in the U.S.A.

As the immigrant arrival document indicates, *Bubba*[16] Lea (1860–1942) and their first four children (Leib, Samuel, Solie, and Scheindel) arrived in the United States on the Furst Bismarck, which docked in New York on August 8, 1891. The document shows a Scholem Derschowitz arriving on the same boat. We assume that this is an inadvertent duplication of Solie, whose Hebrew name was Baruch Shlomo.

The English names they went by were Louis (my father, who married Ida Maultasch),[17] Sam (married Ida Mehr), Sol (married twice, no children), and Sadie (married Barney Hochhauser). Scheindel, listed on the manifest, may be assumed to be my Aunt Sima, whom we called Sadie. After arrival in the United States, three

---

15 Most of this information is from: JewishGen, Inc.: Pilzno, Poland.
16 *bubba* (grandmother)
17 See Appendix 3 for the history of my mother's family in Tarnobrzeg/ Dzików.

more children were born to Zecharja and Lea: Gussie (married Boris Mines), Hymie (married Anna Rubinson), and Rosie (married Joseph Fendel). Pilzno records seem to attest to one more, Esther, having been born to the family, but we have no information about her. She seems to have remained in Europe or may have died in her youth.

As can best be determined, Zecharja had seven siblings, all born ca. 1860–1870 (see Chart 1, page 32). Of them, six are known, at least five of whom immigrated to the United States. Four established families in the New York City area, and the children of the fifth,

Bubba. Photo courtesy of Zecharia Dor-Shav

Gussie, settled in the Philadelphia area. For Abraham Leib, we have no direct information about a wife or family. We do know that there was a Benjamin Deresiewicz,[18] who survived the Holocaust in Pilzno and moved to Jersey City. His father's name was Avram Leib, who may very well have been a grandchild of that Abraham Leib.

At the time of the 1900 census, the family of "Solomon" Dershowitz (should be "Zecharja"; some

---

18 See more about him in Appendix 2.

of the ages are also incorrect) and wife Lena (Lea), aged fifty, is listed as living at 127 Goerck Street,[19] on the Lower East Side of Manhattan, with their seven children: Louis, eighteen; Solomon, fourteen; Samuel, thirteen; Sadie, twelve; Hyman, eight; Gussie, six; and Rosie, four. Four of the children are listed as attending school, while Rosie is listed as too young for school. My father, Louis, and Solomon (Sol) are listed as working. On August 4, 1902, they moved to nearby 61 Lewis Street. Zecharja was then granted American citizenship, with his occupation listed as tailor. This meant he worked in a sweatshop in the garment district.

As reported by my sister, Sylvia (Dershowitz) Fuchs, in an article in the *Jewish Press* during April 1989:

> Those were the years of posted signs stating, "If you don't come to work on Saturday, don't come back to work on Monday." [For Sabbath observers, this] necessitated working for a week at a time and then moving on to another factory.

---

19 The street name was later changed to Baruch Place, but my father always spoke of it as "Garrick Street." The streets were subsequently rezoned, and some of these names no longer exist.

Lower East Side before
the construction of the
Williamsburg Bridge,
showing Baruch, Lewis, and
Cannon Streets

The Triangle Shirtwaist
Factory fire

One of Zecharja's employers was the Triangle Shirt Factory, scene of the notorious Triangle Fire.[20] From

---

20 The Triangle Shirtwaist Factory fire in New York City on March 25, 1911, was one of the deadliest industrial disasters in the history of the city and resulted in the fourth-highest loss of life from an industrial accident in United States history. It was also one of the deadliest disasters that occurred in New York City until the destruction of the World Trade Center ninety years later. The fire caused the death of 146 garment workers—123 women and twenty-three men—who died from the fire, smoke inhalation, or falling or jumping to their deaths. Managers had locked the doors of the stairwells and exits to keep the workers from leaving early. The fire led to legislation requiring improved factory safety standards. The factory's Jewish owners, Max Blanck and Isaac Harris, were subsequently acquitted in December 1911 of first-and second-degree manslaughter charges, although ultimately found liable for wrongful death in a 1913 civil suit. Primarily from Wikipedia. Photo from Wikipedia.

Bubba and Zeide. Photo courtesy
of Zecharia Dor-Shav.

Father. Photo courtesy
of Zecharia Dor-Shav

Anne Dershowitz (our cousin and brother Menashe's wife) we learn that her grandfather Shulem in Przemyśl, Poland—Zecharja's brother—received a letter from him relating that the sparing of his life was because he had not come to work at the Triangle Factory on that fateful day—which was the Sabbath.

Parallel to Lewis Street was Cannon Street, home to the *Chevrah* (Society) that the family eventually joined and of which Zecharja became president. Under his jurisdiction, burial grounds were purchased in Mt.

Hebron Cemetery in Queens. Zecharja and his four sons—Leibish (see pictures of tombstones—paternal grandparents on left; father on right), Shmeil, Shulem, and Yechezkel—have their names engraved on the right doorpost of the synagogue cemetery plot. Those Manhattan streets have undergone changes, having been overtaken by the needs of the subsequently built Williamsburg Bridge in 1903 and other neighborhood projects. Many East Side families, including that of Zecharja, moved to fashionable Williamsburg.

Photo courtesy of Zecharia Dor-Shav

Williamsburg and the Family Synagogue

The saga of Lea and Zecharja parallel, reflect, and influence at least one hundred years in the history of the

American Jewish community.[21] Initially, Zecharja established the family synagogue on Roebling Street (named after the builder of the Williamsburg Bridge). Eventually, the synagogue moved to its permanent address at 94 South 10th Street. The deed to the building stated that one side of the property was the border between the City of Brooklyn and the Town of Williamsburg.

A view of the Williamsburg Bridge

At the time of the 1910 census, the family is listed as living at 119 Canon Street, and Louis (now called Dershowitz) is no longer listed as living there—having moved out of the family home after he married my mother on October 30, 1906. Four of the Dershowitz children are listed in that census as working as framers in a

870 Driggs Avenue. Photo courtesy of Zecharia Dor-Shav

21 Sylvia Dershowitz Fuchs, *Dershowitz Family Centennial*, The Jewish Press, April 7, 1989.

purse factory; Sol was an operator in a coat factory, and Rosie was still too young to work. Not long thereafter, my parents moved to Williamsburg.

In the 1920 census, the Zecharja Derschowitz family is recorded at 94 South 10th Street in Brooklyn, a three-story brick building with a basement apartment. Louis is listed as a thirty-eight-year-old paper salesman, living at 870 Driggs Avenue with his wife, Ida, thirty-three, and their seven children: Jacob, twelve; Harry, ten; Milton, nine; Sylvia, six; Herbert, four; Mortimor (Morris), two; and Albert, eleven months. Also, Rose (Rochma Bleema) Maultasch, my maternal grandmother, and her son, my Uncle Joe, are listed at that address. I, Zachary (Zecharia Dor-Shav), am not listed in that census. I was born on December 11, 1925, in the family home.

Zecharja converted the basement apartment into the family synagogue—pictured above in the painting by a cousin, Yussel Dershowitz, with his father, my Uncle Hymie, sitting at a table.

To make sure that the family could support itself without working on the Sabbath, the synagogue was also used as a workshop. Zecharja opened his own factory by purchasing a sewing machine and a machine that put clamps on change purses. These were set up in an unused fireplace in the corner of the ladies' section. All three of his daughters eventually lived with their families in the three-family home. Rosie and the Fendel family were on the first floor, Sadie (Hochhauser) and family moved into the second floor, and Gussie (Mines) and family moved into the top floor. After Zecharja passed away, Bubba Lea continued to live with the Fendel family above the synagogue.[22] My grandparents had opened a hole in the floor of the Fendel apartment, which was right above the reading table of the synagogue, and covered it with a grate and a carpet. The grate was directly under the dining room table. When the ladies of the family wanted to pray with the minyan,[23] they had the choice of going down to the

22 Next-door lived the Fendels' other grandmother, Joe's mother, known as Bubba Fendel.

23 *minyan* (prayer quorum of ten men)

ladies' section or remaining in the Fendel dining room and uncovering the grate in the floor. That way they looked right down at the Torah scroll as it was being read and heard all the prayers.

In an advertisement in the Yiddish press, placed by Yeshiva Torah Vodaath when Zecharja died, he was called a Hasidic businessman who studied and taught Torah all his life. They also stated that he had raised large sums of money for charity. My brother, Heshy, and others have said that he was known as the "tzaddik[24] of Williamsburg."

The "president" of the synagogue was the oldest son of the family, my father, Louis (Leibish). He was also the *baal tefillah*[25] for the Yamim Noraim.[26] He had a magnificent voice; when he sang a high C, the crystal chandelier in our home would begin to vibrate.[27] As a youngster, he sang in

---

24 *tzaddik* (a righteous person who scrupulously complies with the principles of Judaism)
25 *baal tefillah* (prayer leader)
26 *Yamim Noraim* (Days of Awe, Rosh HaShanah and Yom Kippur)
27 The finest leaded crystal is dainty and resonant enough to break at volumes that some people can produce without amplification—upward of

the Attorney Street synagogue choir of Cantor Baruch
Schorr (1823–1904),[28] who my father claimed was second only to Cantor Yussele Rosenblatt (1882–1933).[29]
We, the immediate family, and other members of the
synagogue, were my father's choir. I used to get a telephone call every year from our cousin, Leah Bacon, who
told how she remembered my father's davening[30] and
that she never heard a *baal tefillah* on the Yamim Noraim
as inspiring as he. Outside evidence of the beauty and
meaningfulness of my father's davening was provided
directly from the following. One year, after an illness, I
had to spend the Yamim Noraim in the Ramada Hotel
in Jerusalem with other old or unwell people who frequented the hotel for those days. I was quietly davening
at a table with several other people when on older man
came over and gave me a kiss. I was surprised and asked
why he kissed me, and he said because he had heard my
davening and loved it. I explained to him that I learned
how to pray from my father—and then he began to cry!
I questioned him again: "Why are you crying?" and he

---

one hundred decibels (*Scientific American*, Aug. 2007).

28 Baruch Schorr died on the last day of Pesach while conducting the
holiday service. He should not be confused with Cantor Israel Schorr,
who was born in 1886 and used to sing with Yussele Rosenblatt.

29 Rosenblatt served for several years in Congregation Ohab Zedek in fashionable Harlem, New York—later serving in Borough Park, Brooklyn.

30 *daven, davening* (pray, praying)

said, "I am crying because I am a *chozer b'tshuvah* [a returnee to the faith] and never had a father from whom I could learn to pray."

The most notable thing in our home was our Sabbath table, full of good food and lively "discussion" about everything under the sun. My mother usually ate just the leftover chicken legs—but we all had everything we needed. Singing at the table was always de rigueur, and everyone participated.

During the pre–World War II period, the synagogue imported several Jewish men from Europe to serve as rabbi. It was a well-used ruse to declare each rabbi, after just a short period of time, as not suitable for our synagogue. During the pre–World War II period, the synagogue imported several scholars from Europe for the position, so that additional Jews could receive entrance visas and also be saved from the hands of the Nazis.

As noted above, during that period, the garment industry's sweatshops were the main source of income for the newcomers. Virtually all these shops worked a six-day week, with Sunday as the day of rest. The small number of people (primarily of Hasidic Galician background) who insisted on observing the Sabbath found themselves changing employers every week. Only one of the Dershowitz children, Sol, remained in the garment industry, and he nonetheless succeeded in keeping the Sabbath. The growth of the International Ladies' Garment Workers' Union[31] and other unions eventually led America to the five-day workweek. All the other Dershowitz children and their spouses went into other lines of business.

---

31 The ILGWU had a sudden upsurge in membership that came as the result of two successful mass strikes in New York City. The first, in 1909, was known as "the Uprising of the 20,000" and lasted for fourteen weeks. It was largely spontaneous, sparked by a short walkout of workers of the Triangle Shirtwaist Factory, involving only about 20 percent of the workforce. The firm locked out its employees when it learned what was happening. That, however, only prompted the rest of the workers to seek help from the union.

News of the strike spread quickly to all the New York garment workers. At a series of mass meetings, after the leading figures of the American labor movement spoke in general terms about the need for solidarity and preparedness, Clara Lemlich rose to speak about the conditions under which she and other women worked and demanded an end to talk and the calling of a strike of the entire industry. The crowd responded enthusiastically and vowed together: "If I turn traitor to the cause I now pledge, may this hand wither from the arm I now raise." This formulation, based on the traditional Jewish oath regarding the Temple, set the way for a vote for a general strike. Approximately twenty thousand out of the thirty-two thousand workers in the shirtwaist trade walked out in the next two days.

Those workers—primarily immigrants and mostly women—defied the preconceptions of more conservative labor leaders, who thought that immigrants and women could not be organized. Their slogan, "We'd rather starve quick than starve slow," summed up the depth of their bitterness against the sweatshops in which they worked. The strike was a violent one. Police routinely arrested picketers for trivial or imaginary offenses while employers hired local thugs to beat them as police looked the other way. Adapted from Wikipedia.

My father went to elementary school until only sixth grade, as he had to help the family support itself. In fact, as a nine-year-old new immigrant, he was selling flypaper on Delancey Street in Manhattan. My mother attended only four grades of school, since she arrived in America as a twelve-year-old. One of her most vivid memories was of the event, two years after her arrival, when President William McKinley died on September 14, 1901, after having been shot by an assassin. All school children were taught to sing the hymn "Nearer my God to Thee,"[32] and my mother, too, frequently sang it to me.

Eventually, my father learned how to set type and became a printer. In retrospect, it was quite an accomplishment for one who attended school only through sixth grade to be able to master spelling the English language well enough to be a printer. Other paths that some of my father's siblings and their families navigated to earn their livelihood were partner in a furniture business, Uncle Boris; salesman, Uncle Sam; peddler, Uncle Barney, who was often seen carrying two heavy suitcases

---

32 A tale surrounding the death of President William McKinley quotes his dying words as being the first few lines of the hymn. At 3:30 p.m., in the afternoon of September 14, 1901, after five minutes of silence, numerous bands across the United States played this hymn, McKinley's favorite, in his memory. It was also played by the Marine Band on Pennsylvania Avenue during the funeral procession through Washington at the end of the funeral service itself. Wikipedia.

filled with toys, trinkets, and candy as he peddled his wares from door to door. Uncle Hymie and his brother-in-law, Uncle Joseph Fendel, opened a wholesale textile business on the lower East Side, in which my brother, Harry, eventually became a partner. A cousin, Sydney Hochhauser, was also hired as their one worker. Sydney helped unionize the business. He succeeded only after some minor violence in which union goons entered the store and overturned shelves of merchandise. A picture appeared in the local press showing the mischief.

The Family Connection with Yeshiva (and Mesivta) Torah Vodaath

"Today we have opened Williamsburg as a new Bavel (Babylonia)[33]!" This statement was uttered in early 1918 at the opening of Yeshiva Torah Vodaath. In 1916, a few concerned laymen, my father included, had decided to open a yeshiva.[34]

---

33 The center of three hundred years of Mishnaic analysis in the Talmudic Academies of Babylonia, resulting in the highly authoritative Babylonian Talmud.

34 Written in 1942 by the author of this book, as coeditor of that year's *The Scroll*, High School Yearbook of Mesivta Torah Vodaath.

The wall plaque (still there today) shows the name Zecharja Dershowitz.
Photo by Kennie Dershowitz

Yeshiva and Mesivta[35] Torah Vodaath are very important in the history of the Dershowitz family, because its elementary school was conceived originally in 1916 by my father and Binyomin Wilhelm. In its early years, the school was located in the Williamsburg neighborhood of Brooklyn. As my father told it, he and Binyomin Wilhelm were dear friends and were just then beginning to raise their families. It had become fashionable for young couples to move across the East River to the City of Williamsburg,[36] and my parents and grandparents had already moved there. One day, Mr. Wilhelm said to my father that he too would love to take the ferry across the river (the Williamsburg Bridge did not yet exist) and move to Williamsburg, but "What can we do there about educating our children?" My father answered. "We can build a yeshiva there!"

---

35 High school-level yeshiva.

36 The City of Williamsburg eventually became part of the Borough of Brooklyn. Today, New York City has the second-largest number of Jews in a metropolitan area, behind only Gush Dan (the Tel Aviv Metropolitan Area) in Israel. Borough Park, Brooklyn (also known as Boro Park), is one of the largest Orthodox Jewish communities in the world. Crown Heights, Brooklyn (the home of the World Chabad movement), also has a large Orthodox Jewish community today. Wikipedia.

From that conversation, the two proceeded to contact Rabbi Zev Gold of Congregation Beth Jacob Anshe Sholom, who was a prominent local rabbi. Together they formed a board of directors and established the yeshiva as an elementary school. Here is what Binyomin wrote in his diary at that time (as cited by his great-grandson, Rabbi Zvi Belsky):

> Our business was at 81 Norfolk Street at the time. One day my friend Leibel Dershowitz, who was living in Williamsburg, came in. I asked his advice about the topic. He said, "On the contrary, move to Williamsburg and make a yeshiva."
>
> As a young man with a hot temperament, not yet in my 30s, I did not think of the difficulties that stood in my way. I quickly answered, "Fine, I will try. If Hashem[37] helps and it is successful, fine. If not, I will be forced to move back to the East Side."

Rabbi Belsky also quoted his great-grandfather when he said to my nephew, Rabbi Yitzchak Dershowitz of Lakewood, "*Reb*[38] Binyamin also said that were it not

---

37 This appellation is used for "God" when the speaker or writer wants to be cautious about the possible desecration of the Holy Name.
38 *reb* (an honorific traditionally used for Orthodox Jewish men)

for Leibel Dershowitz, there would not be a Yeshiva Torah Vodaath."

Thus, my father is credited not only with raising and giving early financial support for the founding of the yeshiva—he and his friend each donated $500 (the equivalent dollar in 2022 was $9,400)[39] for the construction of the new spacious building on Wilson Street—but also with the very idea of establishing a yeshiva in Williamsburg. Other members of the family were also active in the yeshiva at that time, and my Uncle Sam was a vice president in its early years.

The school opened with only two classes, in which my two oldest brothers, Jack and Harry, received a year of yeshiva education. They were too old for the then-currently available grade-levels. The rest of us boys were able to complete elementary school, and some of us also completed the mesivta.

Several of my brothers started school in its original location, on Keap Street in Williamsburg. Subsequently, the new building at 206 Wilson Street was opened. Four years later, the founding members of the Yeshiva offered a teaching position to Rabbi Shraga Feivel Mendlowitz. After just a few weeks, the position

---

39 The average income in 1920 was $3,200, meaning that the purchasing power of $500 was equivalent to two months of salary.

of *Menahel* (Principal of Torah Studies) opened, and it was offered to Rabbi Mendlowitz. Rabbi Dr. David Stern—who also served as Rabbi of the Young Israel Synagogue of Manhattan and was a founder of the Young Israel movement in America—became the Principal of English (secular) Studies.

A current picture of the Yeshiva building is shown [above]. Today it houses the Popover Yeshiva. Photo courtesy of Torah Vodaath archives

Rabbi Gold was elected as the Yeshivah's first president and chose to name the school after the yeshiva of Rabbi Yitzchak Yaakov Reines, where Rabbi Gold had studied in his youth.

A member of the Zionist movement from its inception in 1902, Rabbi Reines was also a founder of the Mizrachi Religious Zionist Movement. Based on a philosophy that saw no conflict between Torah and science, he had set up in Sventsyany, Lithuania, what was in reality a revolutionary type of yeshiva, called Torah U'mada (Torah and Science)—where secular subjects were taught alongside the normal yeshiva curriculum. Subsequently, he moved the yeshiva to Lida, Belarus. At that time the idea was too radical, and the school closed. Several years later, however, when Rabbi Gold helped establish Torah Vodaath, it was, indeed, just such an incorporation of Torah and secular studies.

Rabbi Mendlowitz, who insisted that he be addressed as "Mister," and not "Rabbi," remained the guiding spirit of the school from 1922 to 1948. He abandoned the modern Hebrew pronunciation that Rabbi Gold had favored for the traditional European pronunciation. Under his leadership, a mesivta was opened in 1927. Eventually, a yeshiva gedolah[40] was also opened in Monsey, New York.

Though Rabbi Mendlowitz was Hungarian in origin, he was eclectic in his teachings. As one student of his wrote:[41]

> Even while quoting freely from the writings of Rav[42] Avraham Yitzchak HaKohen Kook, Rav Shraga Feivel maintained a close friendship with and deepest respect for Reb Yoelish, the Satmar Rebbe. . . . [His] classic yeshiva

---

40 yeshiva *gedolah* (post-high school yeshiva)
41 Rabbi Judah Mischel, "In Love with Everything Holy," *Mishpacha* magazine, August 7, 2018.
42 *Rav* (Hebrew for Rabbi)

learning was complemented with shiurim[43] on Tanakh[44] and tefillah,[45] [and] the teachings of Rav Tzaddok HaKohen of Lublin with insights on the intricacies of biblical grammar, as well as Rambam's Shemonah Perakim, Rebbe Nachman's Sippurei Maasios, Chovos Halevavos, Ramchal and the Tzemach Tzedek.

In later years, a plaque hung in the entrance hall of the high school honoring my father, who, besides being a founder, had sent his seven sons to the yeshiva.

At one point in the development of the mesivta, one of the senior rashei yeshiva, Rabbi Dovid Leibowitz, had a falling-out with Rabbi Mendlowitz about the guiding philosophy of the school. Rabbi Leibowitz favored encouraging older students to remain in the school for several additional years of study so that they could acquire advanced Torah education and attain ordination as Rabbis. Rabbi Mendlowitz, on the other hand, wanted the school to produce well-educated *baalei batim*[46] who would enter the workforce at an ear-

---

43 *shiurim* (Torah lessons)
44 *Tanakh* (Hebrew Bible)
45 *tefillah*, pl. tefillot (prayer)
46 *baalei batim* (lay persons)

lier age. This led to a Din Torah,[47] which concluded with Rabbi Leibowitz leaving to form another yeshiva (Rabbinical Seminary of America, otherwise known as Yeshiva Chofetz Chaim).[48] Rabbi Shlomo Heiman remained the rosh mesivta at Torah Vodaath. The Din Torah took place in the Zecharia[49] Dershowitz Congregation.

Interestingly, in 1914, Rabbi Gold had invited Rabbi Meir Berlin (later Hebraized to Bar-Ilan), secretary of the World Mizrachi, to come to New York to organize a branch of Mizrachi in the United States. For the next forty years, Rabbi Gold

---

47 *din torah* (a presentation before a religious court)

48 As a side note, Rabbi Leibowitz died of a massive heart attack on Friday, December 5, 1941. Since his death was on a Friday, the funeral was delayed to Sunday, December 7, so as to provide proper respect for the deceased. Little did we know what would be happening on that Sunday! By the time we left the funeral, we were informed that Pearl Harbor had been attacked and that the United States was at war with the Axis of Germany, Italy, and Japan. The thousands of Yeshiva students, and I, who were at the *hesped* in the Hewes St. Synagogue in Williamsburg, were informed of the attack just as we exited, expressing the thought: (ישעיה פרק נז א) כִּי מִפְּנֵי הָרָעָה נֶאֱסַף הַצַּדִּיק, *Before the evil occurs, the righteous is taken away.*

49 By this time, he had changed the spelling of his name from Zecharja to Zecharia.

---

traveled throughout the United States and Canada organizing chapters of the Mizrachi movement and, eventually, became president of the American Mizrachi in 1932. Rabbi Berlin, who had Hebraized his name to Bar-Ilan—after whom the university in which I taught is named—was one of the signatories of the Israeli Declaration of Independence, and Bar-Ilan University was named in his honor. The pictured stamp was issued in his honor.

The Rescue of the Deresiewicz Cousins

In Chart 1, below, Zecharja and his siblings (Generation 2) are listed with the birth dates of their blood relatives. In the balance of the table, we list their children (Generation 3) and spouses (when known). Many branches of our American families have children who have emigrated on to Israel. As of the time of this writing, Shoshana—the widow of my brother Yitzchak—has celebrated the birth of her first great-great-grandchild. Our known family tree, thus, extends at least nine generations. The rescue of my father's cousins from the clutches of the Germans and the perils of the Holocaust preserved and added a significant number of souls to our family tree.

My father's grandfather, Yechezkiel, and his wife, Chana Rivka, had seven or eight children. Six of them married and established families, namely: Zecharja, Moishe, Shulem, Chaim Shmuel, Gussie, and Chaje.

DERSCHOWITZ
Yechezkiel-Chana Rivka

1840-58 Generation #1 (ca.)								
1859-70 Generation #2 (ca.)	**DERSCHOWITZ** (1859-1921) Zacharia- Leah (Bander)	**DERSCHO-WITZ** (1862) Moishe-Gittel	**DERSCHOWITZ** (1865) Shulem- Leah Brendel	**DERSHO-WITZ** Chaim Shmuel- Molly	**KORN** Gussie- Louis	**SHISSEL** (1870) Chaje-Morris	**DERSCHO-WITZ** (1864) Abraham Lowe	**DERSCHO-WITZ** Esther
1871-1975 Generation #3 (ca.)	**DERSCHOWITZ** (1882-1973) Louis- Ida (Maultasch)	**DASH** Manny-Shirley	**DERSHOWITZ** Chaim Shmuel- Rachel	Sol	Hannah	**SHISSEL** Charles		
	Katie	Katie	**DERSHOWITZ** Chaskel-Regina	Harry	Irving	**MORGEN-LENDER** Hannah-Samuel		
	DERSCHOWITZ (1885) Sol-Anne	Carrie	**DERESIEWICZ** Wolf-Lotte	Charles	Goldie	**SHISSEL** Isadore		
	DERSCHOWITZ (1886) Sam-Ida	Charlie	**DERSHOWITZ** Shlomo-Molly	Sidney	Henry	Henry		
	HOCHHAUSER (1888) Sadie-Barney	Irving	**DERSCHOWITZ** Aharon-Aurelia	Katie	Josephine	Louis		
	DERSHOWITZ (1892) Hymie-Anna	Minny	**FINDLING** Yechiel-Shprinza	Rose	Morris			
	MINES (1894) Gussie-Boris	Harry	**DERSCHOWITZ** Hershl- Malvina	Helen	Joseph			
	FENDEL (1897) Rose-Joe				Harry			
	Esther	Esther						

Chart 1– Three Generations of Family History

In addition to the children of Zecharja and Lea, we have detailed information about only one of Zecharja's siblings, Shulem Deresiewicz. He and his wife, Leah Brendel, had seven descendants. Five sons—Chaskel, Wolf, Shlomo, Aaron, and Hershel—were living with their families in Brno, Czechoslovakia, before the onset of World War II and were rescued and permitted to enter the United States thanks to efforts by my parents and other members of the family. My father worked intensively to procure immigration passes and documents assuring that they would not become a burden to the United States. Some of the prosperous members of the Dershowitz family were willing to sign affidavits promising to be financially responsible for the refugees. Other family members, who could not actually afford to do that, were willing to take the risk and also sign.

The refugees arrived on the American shores during the years 1938–1939, and some of them were put up in our home until they could find proper housing. After just a short period of time, they succeeded in establishing themselves economically. Our uncle and aunt, Sam and Ida Dershowitz, arranged housing for some of them in properties that they owned in Williamsburg. Ida managed the properties and was thus able to have some of them put up there.

Unfortunately, two of Shulem Deresiewicz's family, Chaim Shmuel and his wife, and Shprinza (Deresiewicz) Findling and her family, could not be rescued because they were Polish citizens, and America limited the number of such immigrants. Chaim Shmuel and his wife survived the early atrocities in Przemyśl[50] but were murdered later at some unknown date. Their daughter, my sister-in-law Anne, chose *Tishah B'Av*[51] as the yahrzeit[52] because of a very vivid dream she had on one Tishah B'Av, in which she saw her parents being dragged away by the Nazis. After that dream, she marked that date as the yahrzeit, as per the advice of Rabbi Moshe Feinstein.

---

50 On September 15, 1939, the Soviets took over Przemyśl. Shortly before the Germans withdrew, they burnt down the Old Synagogue, the Klois, the Tempel Synagogue on Jagiellonska Street, and parts of the Jewish quarter. *"The soldiers had fallen on the Jewish section of town that morning and had driven all the men and boys out of their houses with blows and kicks. They made them do calisthenics for several hours in the street, and now they were driving them toward the railway station and on, until they crossed the city limits. I returned home, shaken. Only in the afternoon, when I had calmed down somewhat, did I go out again to return my truck to the power station. Now a new horror met my eyes: distraught, weeping women were running toward the cemetery, for they had heard that all the Jews taken in the morning had been shot in Pikulice, the first village outside town."* (from: Bruno Shatyn, *A Private War: Surviving in Poland on False Papers, 1941–1945,* Wayne State University Press, 1985).

51 *Tishah B'Av* (the fast of the Ninth of Av, in commemoration of the destruction of both Temples in Jerusalem)

52 *yahrzeit* (annual memorial day)

Aaron's daughter, Lili Eylon, recorded the background of their survival in Brno:

It was a windy day in March 1938. We—my father Aaron, my mother Ruth, my brother Hugo (Zvi), and myself—were listening to the morning news on the radio. There were cheers coming from the ether waves. Hitler's troops had just entered Vienna. The Austrians were ecstatic with joy. They were becoming part of the great German nation!

Father looked at Mother—their faces were pale. They knew what it meant. Despite the many reactions about earlier anti-Jewish actions on the part of their friends and acquaintances, "This can't happen here," they believed. "Our country is a democracy!"

But yes! It was indeed happening.

The next morning my father made the declaration that decided our destiny. "Children," he said, facing his little family, "Europe is no longer a place for Jews."

Action followed words. Aaron knew that Zecharja, a brother of his father, had many years earlier crossed the ocean and settled in America. He donned a Sherlock Holmes cap and began the search for family. He hoped they would help him cross the ocean as well. And that's how he got to Louis, Zecharja's oldest son.

In the meantime, the Czechs were preparing for war against Germany. They had the promise of powerful allies, the British and the French, in what was called the Big Entente. There were blackout practices, and every family received gas masks.

The Czechs were not prepared for the Munich stab in the back. The big powers (Chamberlain of Britain and Daladier of France) simply abandoned little Czechoslovakia. During their talks with Hitler in Munich, Czech President Beneš was made to sit outside the closed door. Chamberlain returned to his capital waving the signed piece of paper giving Germany a big hunk of the country, the part that the Germans called Sudetenland, and shouting victoriously the unfortunate words, "I give you peace in our time!"

During the weeks that followed, in Brooklyn, cousin Louis was busy running around to the rich relatives (one, I understand, was the owner of dozens of cinema establishments in Manhattan), talking to them about affidavits—those papers with money guarantees, assuring the government that the newcomer refugees would not become burdens to the state. . . . Louis spared no effort, and although his time was precious, measured in earnings, he was assiduous in his mission to get us and the others of the family out of danger. He succeeded admirably, and that's just the beginning.

In February 1939 (one month after Hitler invaded Czechoslovakia), we disembarked in Hoboken from the Polish ship *Batory*. Louis was there and so was Esther Mines (his niece; she kissed me on the cheek and asked, "Well, how do you like America?" I did not know any English, but I got the drift of her words). She was very helpful to me later in adjusting to the American schools.

It went without saying, it was obvious to Louis, that we would stay in his house (which did not have that much extra room, but where there is a will . . .). A huge welcoming meal awaited us, and we got the feeling, after having lost a home, of being at home.

After a few days, I (a twelve-year-old at that time) was sent to stay with the Hochhausers, which began my long and deep friendship with Selma, may she rest in peace.

Louis helped us find an apartment on Division Avenue in Williamsburg. My father found work. My mother, too, plunged into the commercial world to help ends meet. My brother and I went to school (after a few months in something called C-Class where newcomers from many countries learned English), where we were placed into the regular classes.

Life picked us up by the ears and made us go along with all its joys and vicissitudes. . . .

Without the efforts of Louis Dershowitz, I would not be here to write these words.

Lili made aliyah in 1959 with her two sons, Raanan and David Eller. Raanan became a prominent flutist. David, a promising candidate for a career in Middle East studies, dreamed to become Israel's first ambassador to Egypt. Sadly, he died at the age of nineteen from a stray bullet during his last exercise at officers' school. At the tender age of fifteen, he had composed the following moving composition titled "Man":

Sandwiched between two infinities and given a scant moment to live, man must not only sit back and enjoy the pleasures of life but must leave his mark indelibly (to the maximum) for future generations.

He must work hard to make tomorrow's world a better one than he lived in.

Bearing this in mind, if every man, fired even a moment by a spark of genius, were to pass this spark on till the whole world would be on fire, one can safely say that the world of tomorrow would be as different from ours as our world differs from that of our forefathers.

Aaron's son, Zvi, was honored in the United States House of Representatives on the occasion of his eighty-fifth birthday, by Congressman Brad Sherman. (See Appendix 4 for the gist of what he said.) Two additional neighbors and friends of the Deresiewicz[53] families in Brno were rescued. They, Isaac and Simon Bacon,[54] were the highly educated children of the local shohet.[55] Both had PhD degrees at the time and were working with the Hebrew Immigrant Aid Society

---

53 Most of these cousins changed the spelling of their name to Dershowitz. Herbert, however, who was a son of Wolf, and a Professor at Columbia University, kept the original spelling.
54 Some of them changed the spelling of their name to Bakon.
55 *shohet* (ritual slaughterer)

(HIAS) in Prague. They were brought to the United States as students of Torah Vodaath, with which, as mentioned above, our family had a connection. Isaac eventually became a dean at Yeshiva University, while his brother Simon (Shimon) made aliyah and became editor of *The Jewish Bible Quarterly*, a publication of the Jewish Agency.[56]

On the occasion of Simon's ninetieth birthday (he lived to be 103 years of age), Dr. Gavriel Sivan, Chairman of the Jewish Bible Association, said of him that he transformed the Quarterly into a prestigious journal with a worldwide distribution and many distinguished contributors. He further stated (quoting Kinnim 3:6), "The older true scholars become, the more fully their mind is composed. . . . Age [didn't] wither him, nor custom stale his infinite vitality. . . . His wisdom and experience are always available to us. [He can only be likened] to those righteous elders of whom it is said: 'They are still fruitful in old-age, vigorous and fresh they continue to be' (Psalms 92:15)."

---

56 He joined the editorial board of the *Jewish Bible Quarterly* in 1975, when the journal was known as *Dor leDor*. He was appointed assistant editor in 1976, associate editor in 1978, and editor in 1987. He received private tutoring in Talmud from his father and in 1939 earned a PhD in philosophy at Masaryk University in Prague.

Lili also affirmed that there was another family called Deresiewicz in Pilzno who was not known to be related to us. I, too, met a man whose mother (née Deresiewicz) came from Pilzno; but we were not known to be related. Furthermore, in Kolbuszowa (today, a fifty-minute drive from Pilzno), located on the important trade route from Sandomierz to Przemyśl (where some of our relatives settled), there was a mohel named Wolf Derschowitz. At the end of World War II there was an Osher Dershowitz and family there. Also, one Hirsch (Herman) Deresiewicz was a prisoner in Ferramonti di Tarsia, the Italian concentration camp in Calabria.[57]

Several years ago, a non-Jewish Dershowitz from Poland wrote to ask if we might be related. Interestingly, he attached responses that he had received from another Dershowitz to whom he had written, a née Derschowitz in Arizona who wrote that she had come from Vienna. I compared that with a letter that I had earlier received from Yetty née Derschowitz, who had come to Belgium via a children's transport from Vienna and settled in Nivelles. There, she married a non-Jew but eventually became observant and visited me in my home.

---

57 See Appendix 2 for more details of the Dershowitz family under Nazi occupation.

Her letter had been forwarded to me by my nephew, Professor Alan Dershowitz, and I discovered that the stories were identical. As a result, I reconnected two half-sisters who had survived the Holocaust but didn't know about each other. They also had a relative in Israel with our same family name, albeit without a known relationship to my family.[58]

Dershowitz Family Reunions

During Chanukah 5749 (1988), in commemoration of the hundredth anniversary of the immigration to the United States of our grandfather Zecharja, the Dershowitz clan held a reunion. It was planned and undertaken by my brother Morris and his wife, Esther Dershowitz, and cousin Selma and her husband, Buddy Shulman, in West Hempstead, Long Island, New York, at the Hebrew Academy of West Hempstead (HANC), where my cousin Rabbi Meyer Fendel was principal. Some two hundred people participated in the *hakarat*

---

58 Aided by the following sources in addition to those noted separately:
1. *Pilzno and What Happened There*, by Josef Szczeklik, translated from the original Polish of Krystyna Malesa, 1994.
2. Jerald Landau, *The Book of Dembitz*, 1998—translation of sections of the Dembitz Yizkor Book published in 1950 by a group of Dembitz emigres to Israel, organized by Daniel Leibel.
3. Tarnow Archives.
4. Wikipedia: History of the Jews of Poland.

hatov (grateful acknowledgment of God's providence), and a telephone list of about four hundred descendants was distributed. Besides the food and socializing, talks and recollections by Sylvia (Dershowitz) Fuchs, Sidney (Leibi) Hochhauser, and Rabbi Zechariah Fendel were delivered, as also by Rabbi Menashe Dershowitz and Professor Alan Dershowitz. Following are recorded comments of the latter two.

From Rabbi Menashe:

We thank You Hashem for the love of Torah and mitzvoth, and the love of Israel we have received from our grandparents and parents: Mamma and Papa, Uncle Sol, Uncle Sam and Aunt Ida, Uncle Barney and Aunt Sadie, Uncle Baruch and Aunt Gussie, Uncle Hymie and Aunt Anna, Uncle Joe and Aunt Rosie, and from other relatives who are no longer with us in this life, all of blessed memory. Their spirit remains very much a part of us, through memories of their teaching and deeds. There are sayings and stories we all know—stories of sacrifice for Yiddishkeit, stories of sacrifice to save lives—lives that are with us in this room today, stories of love for fellow Jews, stories of love of Torah. I remember Uncle Sam, a"h,[59] hugging and kissing my Rebbi, Rabbi Dovid Leibowitz, zt"l,[60] after responding to his appeal for the Slabodka Yeshiva with his usual $100 donation and exclaiming enthusiastically, "I love such Jews!" referring to Rabbi Dovid's piety and scholarship.

Many of us remember Uncle Sol's favorite story about Zeide running across the street to embrace and kiss that unknown fellow with the long beard and black clothes—only to be rebuffed in irritation by what turned out to be a Greek Orthodox priest. Funny, but heart-warming and inspiring. For all they have given us during their lifetimes, and for all they have left us with today, we are ever grateful to You, Hashem.

We thank You, Hashem, for that which is expressed in this room, a family—including our extended family of Deresiewicz' descendants of Zeide's[61] brother, Great-Uncle Shulem—a wonderful family with the most diverse talents and abilities, professions, and vocations—you name it, we have it—united and inspired by

---

59 *a"h (alav hashalom*—may he rest in peace*)*
60 *zt"l* (of blessed memory*)*
61 *zeide* (grandfather)

our Jewish background, each contributing to Our People and humanity through Torah and mitzvos, good character, and idealism.

Alan made the following interesting comment, which he includes in the final chapter of his book *Chutzpah*:

As we discussed the differing nature of our Jewishness, I thought of the story I had told during my family centennial gathering about the congregation that couldn't make up its collective mind about whether to sit or stand during the recitation of the Shma Yisrael, and of my mother's addendum to the story: that at least they all recite the Shma Yisrael. Amid the often-cacophonous diversity within Judaism about practices and levels of observance, there is, after all, a broad consensus about certain fundamentals. These fundamentals may not include the daily recitation of the Shma or any other concrete observances, but they are as real as any practices or prayers. Defining these fundamentals may be difficult, but we know them when we see and hear them. Most of them are unspoken assumptions of the kind my Borough Park friends and I share. They grew out of the common historical experiences of the Jewish People, both ancient and modern. They grew out of our common values, though the means of achieving these values may be very much in dispute. They grew out of a common concern for the survival of Israel, for the rescue of Jewish communities in danger, for the survival of Judaism. These are our Shma's.

Twenty-one years later, on Chanukah 5770 (2009), a similar gathering of the Israeli branch of the Dershowitz clan was held in Jerusalem celebrating sixty years since the aliyah of Yitzchak Dershowitz and forty years since my own aliyah. There were close to three hundred participants, including infants in carriages and in their mothers' arms. The two oldest members of the family present were Dr. Shimon Bacon and Esther (Mines-Dershowitz) Chait—whose deceased husband, Rabbi Morris, established the Yeshiva Chafetz Chaim in Jerusalem in the 1960s.

Another attendee from that generation was Rabbi Meyer Fendel,[62] whose son, Rabbi Dovid—also pres-

---

62 Author of *Nine Men Wanted for a Minyan: The Hebrew Academy of Nassau County: Bringing Torah to Long Island*, 2013 and (with his son Hillel) *Singing Our Song Again: Outreach and Kiruv*, 2019, both published by American Friends of the Max and Ruth Schwartz Hesder Yeshiva of Sderot.

ent—was one of the recipients of the 2008 Moskowitz Prize for Zionism for his establishment of the Afikei Daat Hesder Yeshiva in Sderot. Most of those present were representatives of the youngest generations—including one-month-old Adina, daughter of Brachi (Steinberg-Fendel-Dershowitz) Miller of Telz-Stone.

Representatives of many "callings" were present: heads and founders of yeshivas, college professors and directors, journalists, researchers, authors, psychologists, dentists, accountants, teachers, students, soldiers, *sherut leumi* (National Service) girls, businesspeople, housewives, and many others. The group included *haredim*, Modern Orthodox, and seculars of all brands and styles.

A PowerPoint show was presented that included photographs of the ancestors and current families. It was prepared by Dr. Avigail (Bass-Fuchs-Dershowitz) Haruvi and her parents, Rabbi Dr. Jerome and Miriam Bass.

Three people spoke to represent their branches of the family: Rabbi Kutiel Dershowitz (Bnei Brak), Rabbi Dr. Samuel Dershowitz (Jerusalem), and the author of this work, Rabbi Professor Zecharia (Dershowitz) Dor-Shav (Jerusalem), as master of ceremonies.

A sample of books and other publications by members of the family were displayed. Among the most prolific authors were Professor Alan Dershowitz, Rabbi Zechariah Fendel (Dershowitz), Professor Nachum Dershowitz, Rabbi Baruch (Mines-Dershowitz) Chait, Lili (Dershowitz) Eylon, Dr. Avi Shmidman, husband of Shirah Dershowitz, Dr. Shimon Bacon, and Rabbi Hillel Fendel (Dershowitz).

Colored ID stickers were worn by the guests to identify their connection with the earlier generations. The gathering took place in the Kalati Hall in Ramat Eshkol, which just barely contained all the participants.

As Greer Fay Cashman of the *Jerusalem Post* reported (here edited somewhat for accuracy):

> Some 250 members of the Israeli branch of the greater Dershowitz family got together on the seventh night of Chanukah at the Kalati Hall in Ramot Eshkol for a series of celebrations. Absent from the festivities was the clan's most celebrated member, Professor Alan Dershowitz, the Harvard Law School professor, who frequently visits Israel; he is usually put up by the government in the Mishkenot Sha'ananim Cultural Center & Guest House in Jerusalem but was unable to attend due to prior commitments. Only one couple from the United States, Allen and Chani Dershowitz of Lakewood,

came in from abroad for the occasion. Other American members of the tribe sent their children who are studying in Israel to represent them. Joining their Jerusalem parents, siblings, aunts, uncles and cousins were Dershowitz offspring from Tel Aviv, Ra'anana, Bnei Brak, Sderot, Safed, Kiryat Malachi, Telz-Stone, Beit Shemesh, Beit El and elsewhere. The gathering marked a series of milestone anniversaries: sixty years since the first member of the family, Rabbi Yitzchak Dershowitz, made aliyah. It was, also, the fortieth anniversary of the aliyah of Rabbi Professor Zecharia (Dershowitz) Dor-Shav and family of Jerusalem. It was the 121st anniversary of the immigration to the United States of the Zecharja and Lena Derschowitz family from Pilznó, Poland (then part of the Austro-Hungarian Empire). The family can trace its history only as far back as the 1840s,[63] when Yechezkiel and Chana Rivka, parents of Zecharja and his seven siblings, were born. Five of Yechezkiel's children immigrated to America sometime between the 1880s and the 1890s.

---

63 Since then, DNA testing, see above, has added at least one generation of ancestors.

Zecharja and Lena and their seven children took an active part in establishing institutions that became the backbone of the growing Jewish presence in the United States. Among the most prominent institutions were Yeshiva Torah Vodaath, Henry Street Settlement House and the Palestine Aid Society. The oldest members of the family present at the Jerusalem reunion were Dr. Shimon Bacon of Jerusalem and Professor Zecharia Dor-Shav, who are fourth generation descendants of Yechezkiel and Chana Rivka. Members of the next three generations of the family, including one-month-old Adina Miller of Telz-Stone, whose mother is Brachi (Steinberg/Fendel/Dershowitz) Miller, also helped to fill the hall. In terms of religious identification, the family runs the gamut from haredi[64] to secular. They engage in a large range of professions, and many of them are also writers. (Greer Fay Cashman, "The Dershowitz Dynasty," *Jerusalem Post*, December 25, 2009)

To accommodate the different eating standards of the members of the family, the food brought in had to have approval of two members of the family who represented

---

64 *haredi*, (ultra-Orthodox)

different standards: Chief Rabbinate Certification and *Badatz* Certification. Since only 150 people had answered that they were coming, the food ran out completely, but it didn't affect the good cheer that we all felt. It was interesting to note that at least in one case, three children looked at one another and said, "We are classmates and didn't even know that we are fourth cousins!"

Family Goals

Generally speaking, we were raised as Orthodox Jewish all-American kids. We were taught to take responsibility for our behavior and "to live and let live." This applied to our home, in which we eight children had to live together in peace and also in the public arena. We were expected to go to school regularly, dress properly, respect our parents and elders, and never address our parents by their given names. We were to maintain the Orthodox Jewish heritage that we were blessed with by attending synagogue services at least on the Sabbaths and holidays, and praying in school or at home, three times a day during the weekdays. We were expected to be home at the family table for Sabbath meals and to participate in the preparations for the Sabbath and in singing zemiroth.[65] As children of immigrant parents, we were expected to reach higher goals than were

---

65 *zemiroth* (Sabbath songs of praise)

possible for them. We were encouraged to use the nearby public library and expected to reach a high level of education. The goal was to eventually enter the work-world and be self-supporting after marriage.

The most important thing for my mother, in terms of long-term wishes, was best expressed by the will that she wrote over the course of many years. One of the handwritten pages that appears here dem-

Hello this is a May son all of a suden 1960 I got a feeling to add a little more to my little will that is about Itchy I wish that the family should never think Just because he is away so far and so long you should all know that he is your ... brother like the rest and his children an nephew and nieces just like the others you shouldn't feell more astranged about that branch of the family just like the others which I hope and want you should all be a close nit family thats my wish love Mother

Photo courtesy of Zecharia Dor-Shav

onstrates how important it was for her that we, as a family, keep together and care for one another.

Although our economic situation was lower middle class, our parents felt that during the summer months, we children needed to spend our time being active and enjoying the sun and sea of nearby Rockaway Beach. Rental apartments that were still available on Independence Day were drastically reduced in price. We were ready to move in one or two days after July 4. For transportation we usually hired a driver with a large open truck to bring summer supplies for us and our cousins. We, the youngest boys—Meyer and the three Zecharias—would generally join the trip. We would sit on the bedding at the top of the truck. During the summer months, our beach apartment was visited by all the many friends of my siblings. Mother would frequently say, "I don't know how many people are here today. If you want to know, just count the pairs of shoes laying around."

As young kids, weather permitting, most of our time was spent on the beach, walking, swimming, and doing acrobatics. We also spent time bike riding on the boardwalk, playing tennis, baseball, and handball, and renting rowboats. Some years, we rented an apartment

On the lawn with Meyer and Zechariah Fendel, and Zecharia Mines.
Photo courtesy of Zecharia Dor-Shav

in a building on stilts, right at the edge of the beach. If it was storming and the waves came charging in under the house, we usually occupied ourselves by playing Monopoly or some other long-lasting indoor game. Of course, when we got older, Meyer and I would spend the mornings studying in a synagogue *b'chavrutah* (as a pair), or in a class with some vacationing rosh yeshiva. Some of our best learning took place during those summer classes. Meyer would also often be my litigator if someone thought that I had offended him/her.

In the evenings, we would usually walk the boardwalk or gather with other vacationing boys and girls to sing our favorite Hasidic and American folk songs while watching the fireworks display. We also frequented the Penny Arcade at Rockaway's Playland—which closed in 1987—and watched Irish tap dancing in the nearby Irish section of the beach.

One summer, when I was just twelve, my sister and her newborn twins were also spending their summer vacation nearby. One evening, I and Gracy Pollak, the daughter of family friends, were asked to babysit for them. While sitting in an adjacent room, we heard a loud hissing noise from the twins' room. We rushed in and smelled gas. The rubber pipe connecting the stovetop burners to the gas supply had fallen off the outlet in the wall! There were no automatic shut-off valves those days! Blessed be Hashem, we had the presence of mind to quickly close the gas outlet, grab the babies, and run with them out of the room. Thus, we saved their lives—and maybe saved the whole house from an explosion. Gracy and I often reminisce about this momentous encounter.

Our World War II War Effort

A compulsory draft of all males between the ages of eighteen and forty-five had been instituted.[66] Local draft boards were responsible for the classification of registrants, selection of eligibles, and delivery of selectees into military control. In Williamsburg, where we lived, as in several other sections of the city, there was an unusually large number of yeshiva students who a priori were entitled to a 4D exemption as divinity students. As a result, several local draft boards could not fill their quota of draftees. An advisory committee of rabbis and judges (the divinity board) was appointed

---

66 On September 16, 1940, the United States instituted the Selective Training and Service Act of 1940, requiring all men aged twenty-one to forty-five to register for the draft. This was the first peacetime draft in American history. Those who were selected from the draft lottery were required to serve at least one year in the armed forces. Once the United States entered World War II, draft terms were extended for the duration of the fighting. By the end of the war in 1945, 50 million men between eighteen and forty-five had registered for the draft, and 10 million had been inducted.

to establish if a potential draftee was studying Torah "only" for its own sake, and thus eligible for the draft, or to become a communal rabbi, entitled to the exemption. In my case, since my family tradition was for all of us to learn in yeshivas, the Board decided that I was likely studying for the sake of Torah and not to become a practicing rabbi. Furthermore, since I had started attending yeshiva at the tender age of five, that was seen as confirmation of my special interest in becoming a Talmudic scholar. They recommended that I not be granted a 4D exemption, and I was ordered to report for a physical examination. As it turned out, I had a hernia and was granted an exemption on that basis. (In later years such a disability was not a cause for exemption; the army simply did the required surgery.)

We all donated blood through the American Red Cross and participated in lifesaving and first aid courses. I became both a first aid and swimming instructor, subsequently giving courses to other youngsters. We also collected discarded silver wrappings from cigarette packages and donated them to the war effort.

On Monday, August 6, 1945, as a group of us exited from a bowling outing, we passed a newspaper stand with screaming headlines that at first were completely baffling. Finally, we understood the unbelievable! An American B-29 bomber had dropped the world's first deployed atomic bomb over the Japanese city of Hiroshima. We eventually learned that the explosion had wiped out 90 percent of the city and immediately killed eighty thousand people; tens of thousands more would later die of radiation exposure. Thus, we entered the atomic age. Three days later another bomb was dropped on Nagasaki, killing an additional 60,000–80,000 people. Japan sued for unconditional peace on August 15, and World War II was over.

Museums, Outings, College, University

During our spare time, on holiday vacations and especially during the summer months, we were always involved in sports, trips to parks, and outings under the auspices of Jewish organizations. We were taught to swim in the local YMHA. We went to the movies and worked as junior and senior counselors in religious summer camps. We were members of the Agudath Israel Youth movement in Williamsburg and sang in their choir.

We had season tickets for the New York World's Fair of 1939–1940 in Flushing Meadows—the second-most-expensive American World's Fair as of that time. Many countries around the world participated in it, and over 44 million people attended its exhibits in its two seasons. It was the first exposition to be based on the future; its opening slogan was "Dawn of a New Day." This future, radiating from a white cone and globe—the Trylon and Perisphere—allowed visitors to take a look at "the world of tomorrow," according to the official pamphlet. The most popular exhibit for us was the eighteen-minute ride on the conveyor system of the Futurama Exhibit built for General Motors. This was a 36,000-square-feet exhibit, designed by a famed industrial designer. It presented a stylized model of the world twenty years into the future. It was characterized by automated highways and vast suburbs, and transported us over a huge diorama of a fictional section of the United States, designed with an array of miniature highways, towns, and waterways. Also, 500,000 individually designed homes, 50,000 miniature vehicles, and a million miniature trees of diverse species. We would usually have to wait a long time on that line, permitting us to eat our lunch sandwiches before we entered. Once we were in, the elements of the diorama gradually became larger and larger as we moved through the exhibit. The ride ended with the automobiles and other elements of the exhibit becoming life-size.

We often visited the world-famous Bronx Zoo, taking one of the longest subway rides in the city to get there. We skied, ice-skated, and visited Rockefeller Center and the broadcasting studios in Manhattan.

Hitchhiking was our standard manner of travel during the summer months—either to the beach or to the Catskills. We would stand on the side of the road, prominently wearing our *kippot*,[67] and always found drivers willing to pick us up. During the summer session, while attending Brooklyn College with a major in psychology, I would hitchhike with my friends from the beach to Flatbush Avenue, adjacent to the college. I continued my education with a master's degree in education at Rutgers University and completed a PhD in psychology and education at New York University in 1964.

Mother's Miracles

Momma believed in miracles and saw them in everyday life. I guess that the first of her miracles was the story she related about herself as a two-year-old, while yet in Poland. She told us that she was noticed sitting on the edge of a well with her feet hanging down the walls of the well. Her parents were terrified that if they shouted

---

67 *kippot* (religious small head covering)

at her she might be taken aback, lose her balance, and fall into the well. They approached very quietly with no outward anxiety until they had her within grabbing distance, and clutched her to safely. Her conviction in God's watching over her and performing miracles when needed is immortalized in the inscription on her tombstone, as pictured here.

Photo courtesy of
Zecharia Dor-Shav

One Thanksgiving day, she wanted to treat all the children with ice cream, but she wanted to make a game of it. She bought the type of ice cream for each child that she knew was that child's favorite. She then assigned Heshy with the task of being the "good fairy." Each child was asked what type of ice cream he wanted, and Heshy was sent to the kitchen to fetch exactly the correct ice cream, as Mom had anticipated. After everyone got his ice cream, Mom herself wanted ice cream but had forgotten to order for herself exactly what she liked (vanilla). In any event she had one Dixie cup left that should have been half vanilla and half chocolate. She reluctantly sighed that she should have ordered vanilla for herself. When she opened the Dixie cup, lo and behold, by mistake, it had been filled with vanilla ice cream only—and so Momma also got exactly what she wanted.

Another story she told was about when Moish (Morris) was a young child and the ice cream truck came by, just after he had had a meat meal.[68] He cried so much that she gave in to him and bought him an ice cream cone. No sooner did he take the cone into his hand when a bee came and stung him, and the ice cream fell to the floor without his taking a single bite of it.

The most moving thing that she did, that I saw as a miracle, occurred when I was just about eight years old. My brother Heshy was deathly sick. He had gotten an infection in his foot while we were in Rockaway Beach for the summer, and it developed into septicemia. He was being treated in a small hospital at the beach but was not responding favorably to treatment. In desperation, they tried what was at the time an early version of the first sulfa drugs.[69] He suffered an allergic response and was in danger of dying. My mother was in anguish. She

---

68 Laws of kashrut forbid eating milk products immediately after meat.
69 Sulfa was the first of a series of "miracle drugs" that came to be invented between the 1930s and 1960s. Nonexistent testing requirements at the time led to a sulfanilamide disaster in the fall of 1937, during which at least one hundred people were poisoned with diethylene glycol. This led to the passage of the Federal Food, Drug, and Cosmetic Act in 1938 in the United States.

took me with her to the family synagogue. My cousin, Esther (Mines) Chait, was also with us. Mom stood with us in front of the Aron Kodesh,[70] "tore" open the parocheth,[71] and cried. At that moment, we all felt the presence of God. We felt that tremendous sense of awe, as my mother explained that she had been taught that by opening the parocheth, one "tears open the sky" and comes into the presence of the *Kadosh Baruch Hu*.[72] She cried, and we cried, and Heshy recovered and lived to a ripe old age. I still shudder and am overwhelmed by emotion when I mention or remember this experience. Esther said that she too always had this reaction.

---

70 *Aron Kodesh* (holy ark of the Torah scroll)
71 *parocheth* (curtain screen that covers the holy ark)
72 *Kadosh Baruch Hu* (The Holy One, blessed be He)

Chapter Two
Highlights in the Lives of My Siblings

EACH OF THE siblings in my family had a personality of his own, developed by his life experience, education, and chance. Nonetheless, I know that we were a united family with common goals regarding our family bonds. I don't remember any serious arguments among the siblings—certainly nothing that ever led to any member of the family distancing himself from his siblings. The family Sabbath table was a regular component of our lives, and all participated in the singing and lively discussions that took place around the table. Almost always, we had non-family members as guests at our table too.

One time, many years after we were all married and had grown children, three of my siblings and I were visiting our brother Menashe in Lakewood. We were sitting around the table reminiscing and singing the many family songs that we were used to singing together at our childhood Sabbath table. One of Menashe's children ran for his video camera to record this emotional reunion, so that it would be recorded for posterity.

Jack's Struggle with Piety

Jack, or Yankif, as we called him, was my oldest brother. He married Ruth Jaffe, and they had two children, Harold and Rita. Growing up in the early 1900s when America's Jewish immigrants were struggling with maintaining their religious commitments in the new country, he and some of his best friends were not closely

Photo courtesy of Zecharia Dor-Shav

following the religious values and restrictions of their parents' strictly observant homes. Stephen Birmingham published *Our Crowd* in 1968, in which he described just such abandonment of Jewish tradition at that time by a large proportion of the Jewish immigrants. Our family, however, which followed a modernized Hasidic pattern, was mostly spared this abandonment, as were most of the Galician immigrants.[1] According to one of Yankif's very good friends, the serious illness during the infancy of Harold, his oldest child, was the catalyst for bringing him back to his childhood values. As this friend told me at one of the graveside memorials, "It wasn't his marrying Ruth that brought him back, it was Harold's illness." Yankif had prayed and made a pledge to return to proper observance, "If Hashem would heal his son."

Independently, one afternoon, Momma affirmed this change when she saw him praying minhah[2] in the house when there was no one there but God and himself. Interestingly, at the wedding of one of Harold's daughters, my nephew Yitzchak Mordechai remarked about the piety of all three of Harold's children by noting, "If Yankif became a *baal teshuva*[3] because of Harold, it is understandable why Harold merited raising

---

1 My sister published an article in which she stressed the difference between our Galician crowd and the "Crowd" of Stephen Birmingham. See: Sylvia Fuchs, "Now a Word from Our Fathers," *Jewish Observer*, January 1978.

2 *minhah* (afternoon prayer service)

3 *baal teshuva* (returnee to full observance of Judaism)

such religious daughters." All of his children are pious, and one of them, Dr. Shira Shmidman, even teaches a daf yomi (daily Talmud study class) for women in her home community of Alon Shvut in Gush Etzion.

Yankif was very dedicated to the family. Employed and earning a nice salary, he purchased a Persian lamb coat for our mother as a gift. This complements another story that Esther (Mines) Chait related about him. Esther's father, our Uncle Boris, had passed away at a young age and left his wife with five young children without adequate resources (see Chapter 7). Every Friday afternoon, Yankif would go to Flam's Delicatessen shop in Williamsburg to buy halvah for the Mines family just to cheer them up.

Harry's Concern for the Family

Harry married Claire Ringel and had two children, Alan and Nathan. Harry, or Hatoo, as we called him, was surely the brother who gave most attention to our brother Yitzchak's needs after he moved to Israel. From time to time, my mother would ask the family if they could spare some money to send to Yitzchak. Harry was always the first with the most.

Photo courtesy of Zecharia Dor-Shav

He was also the brother who, after my father died and my mother moved in with Sheindy (Sylvia), made it his business to visit my mother most often.

The first automobile owned by anyone in the nuclear family was purchased by Harry and his friends. Although Ford had introduced automatic electric starters on their Model T in 1920, I remember them cranking[4] the motor of his secondhand car. Nonetheless, it was a great novelty for our family.

Harry entered into partnership with our Uncle Joe Fendel in the wholesale dry goods business. Our Uncle Hymie, who was also a partner, had left the business when his daughters, Esther and Chayala, married into the cadre of students of Torah Vodaath who had joined the *malachim.*[5] This led to Hymie and his entire family coming under the influence of the followers of Rabbi Levine, "the Malach," as described in Chapter 7.

It is not surprising, therefore, to find that Harry's oldest son, Alan, is so very family oriented. He became a Harvard Professor of Law[6] and has been called "the

---

4   The hand-crank method was commonly used to start engines, but it was inconvenient, difficult, and dangerous. The behavior of the engine during starting was not always predictable. Often, the engine would kick back, causing a sudden reverse rotation of the crank.

5   Lit. angels. See story of Hymie's family in Chapter 7.

6   In addition to his numerous law review articles and books about criminal and constitutional law, he has written, taught, and lectured about

nation's most peripatetic civil liberties lawyer" and one of its "most distinguished defenders of individual rights," "the best-known criminal lawyer in the world," "the top lawyer of last resort," "America's most public Jewish defender," and "Israel's single most visible defender—the Jewish state's lead attorney in the court of public opinion." He has always been available to any member of the family who needed his advice or help. Among his clients were a Jewish Defense League bomb maker who killed a woman, United States Nazis,

---

history, philosophy, psychology, literature, mathematics, theology, music, sports—and even delicatessens.

His writings have been praised by Truman Capote, Saul Bellow, William Styron, David Mamet, Aharon Appelfeld, A. B. Yehoshua, Elie Wiesel, Richard North Patterson, and Henry Louis Gates Jr. More than a million of his books—translated into many languages—have been sold worldwide.

In 1983, the Anti-Defamation League of the B'nai B'rith presented him with the William O. Douglas First Amendment Award for his "compassionate eloquent leadership and persistent advocacy in the struggle for civil and human rights." In presenting the award, Nobel Laureate Elie Wiesel said, "If there had been a few people like Alan Dershowitz during the 1930s and 1940s, the history of European Jewry might have been different." Professor Dershowitz has been awarded an honorary Doctor of Law by Yeshiva University, Brooklyn College, Syracuse University, Tel Aviv University, Bar-Ilan University, New York City College, and Haifa University, among other institutions of learning. He has also been the recipient of numerous academic awards, including a Guggenheim Fellowship for his work on human rights, a fellowship at The Center for The Advanced Study of Behavioral Sciences, and several Dean's Awards for his books. (Information from the Harvard Faculty Directory and others.)

the Ku Klux Klan, and porn star Harry Reems of *Deep Throat* fame. He helped defend CIA whistle-blower Frank Snepp, Soviet dissident Anatoly Sharansky, O. J. Simpson, Claus von Bülow, Patricia Hearst, Rabbi Meir Kahane,[7] pro-PLO actress Vanessa Redgrave, and spy Jonathan Pollard.[8]

He has been quoted as saying:

> I don't need the Bill of Rights; I'm a wealthy, educated, powerful, tenured professor. I'm out there protecting people who do need the Bill of Rights.[9]

Though he is primarily a criminal lawyer, his deep respect for the Constitution of the United States led him to agree to present a neutral analysis of the impeachment process regarding President Trump. He is credited with having been a significant factor in convincing several Democratic senators to vote against

---

7 A former schoolmate of Alan's, from whom the United States State Department sought to strip his American citizenship because of his election to the Israeli Knesset.

8 See Appendix 5 for a bipartisan tribute to Alan by President Bill Clinton and Senator Ted Cruz of Texas.

9 Arlene Levinson, "Dershowitz Baits the Powers That Be: Lawyer Specializes in Unpopular Causes," Associated Press, *Los Angeles Times*, August 20, 1989.

impeachment of the president in 2020. He was a leader in the fight for the right of emigration of Soviet refuseniks. As Natan Sharansky said during an interview with Sue Fishkoff in the *Jewish News of Northern California* (November 3, 2017):

> After I was arrested . . . I was in prison. An international tribunal on my behalf—to protest the accusations against me—was held in San Francisco in 1983. Alan Dershowitz and Irwin Cotler were the young human rights lawyers presenting my case [in the mock trial].

When just entering the law profession, after completing his law degree at Yale University, Alan was interviewed for the position of law clerk for Supreme Court Justice Arthur Goldberg. Everything went well, but he felt that he had to tell the justice that he was Orthodox, which meant that he couldn't work on the Sabbath. The Justice said to him, "Lee [Justice Goldberg's other law clerk] can work on Saturdays, Alan on Sundays, giving me a functioning staff seven days a week."

No surprise, then, that he was extremely moved when, in June 2019, a new Torah scroll was completed in his honor, in recognition of his selfless efforts through

Photo courtesy of Alan Dershowitz at Chabad

the Aleph Institute,[10] on behalf of Sholom Mordechai
Rubashkin with regard to his kosher slaughterhouse
and meat-packing plant in Postville, Iowa, and many
other accused individuals. The procession[11] took place

---

10 The Aleph Institute is a Jewish humanitarian organization for both
   prisoners and military personnel.
11 The dedication of a new Torah scroll is traditionally celebrated with
   great festivity. The source of this custom is the biblical account of
   King David welcoming the holy ark into his capital: "David went and
   brought up the Ark of God . . . into the City of David, with joy. . . .
   David danced with all his might before God. . . . David and all the
   House of Israel brought up the Ark of God with shouts and with the
   sound of the *shofar*." When the Torah is completed, the ink dried, and
   the final parchment panels sewn together, the Torah is wrapped in its

in front of the World Headquarters of the Chabad-Lubavitch Hasidic movement, located at 770 Eastern Parkway in the Crown Heights section of Brooklyn, followed by a festive celebration for family and friends at the Jewish Children's Museum. The Torah scroll had been commissioned by a prominent philanthropist, who, like so many others, was moved to the core by the breadth and scope of Alan's kindness, and his advocacy for the people and land of Israel. On the mantel of the Torah is embroidered the verse צֶדֶק צֶדֶק תִּרְדֹּף (*Justice, justice shall you pursue*; Deuteronomy 16, 20), which appears in the Torah reading for the Sabbath of Alan's bar mitzvah and has been his life motif.

Justice Goldberg was a houseguest in the Harry Dershowitz home for Rosh Hashanah and Yom Kippur on several consecutive years, attending prayer services

---

mantle and other adornments . . . and in a grand procession, complete with music, singing and dancing, the Torah is carried under a *chuppah* (canopy), accompanied by candles and torches to beautify the occasion. The parade commences with its owner carrying the Torah—while beneath the *chuppah*, and surrounded by his family—for the first few steps. For the remainder of the procession, family and friends are honored with walking [escorting] the Torah part of the way beneath the *chuppah*. . . . Along the parade route, all men, women and children are given the opportunity to kiss the Torah. Infants are brought to the Torah, and their cheeks softly pressed to the mantle. [Baruch S. Davidson, Dedicating a New Torah Scroll, Chabad.org]

at the Young Israel of Borough Park with Alan and his parents' family.

Upon retirement, Alan bequeathed his legal library and papers to Brooklyn College, because it was there that he "found his wings." His high school years at the Brooklyn branch of Yeshiva University were a disaster, as he recalled:

> I was a terrible student in elementary school and at Yeshiva University High School. . . . Whenever I asked what I thought was a difficult question, I was reminded that "If the question is good, then the great rabbis have asked it before you, and if the great rabbis before you didn't ask it, it is obviously a . . . question of a stupid person."[12]

Ironically, Alan continues with regard to Yeshiva University:

> My parents had . . . me apply to Yeshiva University, where most of my high school classmates would enroll. I was rejected, however, after a personal intercession against me

---

12 Alan M. Dershowitz, *Chutzpah*, Little, Brown, 1991, p. 41.

by my high school principal. . . . Several years later, when I was awarded an honorary Doctor of Laws by Yeshiva University, the president said that this was in compensation for their rejection of me as a student some thirty-five years earlier.

Alan's mother had shown the president the letter of rejection that he had received at that earlier date. It was a loss for Yeshiva University and for the Jewish community in general in that it left Alan with this bitter feeling about his earlier poor experience in elementary and high school.

In this regard, it is interesting to note an interaction I had with an uncle of Professor Ari Goldman,[13]

---

13 A Professor of Journalism at Columbia University's prestigious Graduate School of Journalism. He began as a stringer for the *New York Times* while still a student at Yeshiva and was the first Sabbath-observing reporter ever hired by the *New York Times*. Christopher Vecsey (in: *Jews and Judaism in the* New York Times, Lexington Books, 2013) writes that after beginning to cover the diversity of religions in New York City in a detached manner, and receiving a degree at Harvard Divinity School, he became engrossed in "religious relativism" and true to the "journalistic god of objectivity." Or, as Maurice Wohlgelernter (A letter to a Harvard Divinity Student, in: Koren, N. and Wohlgelernter, M. [eds.]), *Jewish Writers/Irish writers Selected Essays on the Love of words*, 1999), writes, "When denied the honor of leading the *minchah* service . . . [you] stayed home and prayed by yourself, [even though you should, probably] understand that serving as a *hazan* in a congregation dedicated to 'religious truth,' . . . is not identical . . .

another very bright yeshiva student—a nephew of Rabbi Dr. Norman Lamm, President of Yeshiva University—who eventually became a religion editor for the *New York Times* and contributor of religious articles and books to other publishers. One day, while sitting in my synagogue next to this uncle, he turned and asked me, "What is the reason that yeshiva education apparently did not achieve its primary goal with both my nephew and your nephew, Professor Alan Dershowitz?" Both of them, while proud and dedicated Jews, found other pastures for the development of their outstanding skills, and were admittedly no longer "absolute keepers of the Sabbath." Notwithstanding, Alan was the first faculty member of any university to be an official advisor to a Chabad House, as also advisor to the Chabad House in Harvard. He still works closely with Chabad in their many services to Jews all around the world. He had met and corresponded with the Lubavitcher Rebbe on several occasions. His most extensive correspondence with the Rebbe was when Chabad honored Senator Jesse Helms[14] on the occasion of an Education Day, USA, reception.

---

with your going . . . every Christmas to the Messiah Sing-in at Avery Fisher Hall."

14 Senator Helms was a leader in the conservative movement. Nicknamed "Senator No," he was perhaps best known for his opposition to civil

Alan likes to quote in public what I said to him when he presented me with a copy of his wonderful book *Justice in Genesis*. The book is profound and presents man's development of justice as an improvement over God's imperfect world. I suggested that perhaps he should change one word in the book. He responded that one word doesn't sound like too much of a problem but, "Which word would you like me to change?" I said, "I would have preferred if only the name Dershowitz had not appeared as the author." I also think that God allowed man to perfect His world, but I believe that the book failed to state that that was exactly God's purpose to begin with, when He created man. Thus, man did not best God, but rather fulfilled His original purpose.

Nathan is a law partner with his brother and has an office in the Empire State Building in Manhattan. His son, Adam, has a PhD in aeronautical and astronautical engineering, with expertise in aircraft and spacecraft systems and instrumentation, including unmanned systems (UAVs). He models and analyzes ground and flight vehicles, systems, and their accidents and analyzes

---

rights and gay rights, thus an archenemy of Alan's civil rights advocacy. Later, as Chairman of the Foreign Relations Committee of the U.S. Senate, he became a prime supporter of Israel (see below, Chapter 8: Rabbi Menachem Mendel Schneersohn).

and presents high dimensionality and complex data. Earlier in his career, he had worked in NASA's Mission Control Center on the motion control system of the International Space Station, designed and researched advanced technology solutions for mission control, and served as a member of the orbital debris analysis team for the Space Shuttle *Columbia* accident investigation. He had been trained to fly in one of the spaceflights, but health reasons closed that option and he was transferred to Mission Control.

Menashe's Love of Torah and Israel

Menashe married Anne Dershowitz and had three children: Allen, Yitzchak Mordechai, and Zecharia. In his youth, he was the Torah scholar of the family. He was recommended for *semikah*[15] by Rabbi Dovid Leibowitz (then still in Mesivta Torah Vodaath) in 1933. Although he simultaneously went to college for training as a history teacher, his main love was Torah and the Rabbinate. In fact, he was made titular owner of the large Torah library, which was purchased for the family synagogue, and was housed in it. This, eventually, caused a minor long-standing cousin dispute. My father, and brother Menashe, always said

---

15 *semikah* (rabbinical ordination)

that the library was intended for Menashe, who was the budding family Torah scholar. Other, later budding Torah scholars said that the library was bought for all of the family. Most of the books eventually went to Menashe, but some were requisitioned by other family members.

Photo courtesy of Zecharia Dor-Shav

Menashe had been in mail contact with our second cousin, Anne Dershowitz, in Przemyśl, Poland. Subsequently, he decided that she might be just right for him as a wife and decided to travel to Poland to meet her. His trip was on the French ship *Normandie*, and the whole family came to see him off. When visitors had to leave the ship, Menashe was standing on a

deck high above us all and gave a beautiful rendition of one of his favorite songs, "A Dudela." The family, below on the pier, sang as his chorus. We all sang at the top of our voices, and it was a beautiful send-off. Menashe was a wonderful *baal tefillah,* and, in fact, according to Anne, what clinched the deal for her as his future wife was how beautifully he sang zemiroth at her parents' table when he came to Poland to meet her.

They were married during June of 1939. Immediately after the wedding, he began working on their leaving Poland, since it was obvious that war was likely to break out very soon between the Nazi Axis and the Western European Allies. To accomplish this, two things were required: convincing the authorities that they were really married—not merely a ruse to bring her to the United States—and that he could support her there. For that reason, a lawyer son of the prominent Kramer family of Bensonhurst sent a wire affirming that Menashe had been appointed rabbi of the Kramer family synagogue in Bensonhurst.[16]

---

16 It turned out that a daughter of the Kramer family, Naomi, and her husband, Sy Stemp, were among the very first founding families of the West Hempstead Jewish community, hosting our cousin Rabbi Meyer Fendel, as rabbi and principal of its Hebrew Academy of Nassau County—(HANC) which was then in its infancy—as they tried to gather a minyan for the Sabbaths. Three cousins also moved

My father had already sent all pertinent papers to the State Department, which was in no hurry to process them. By August, nothing had yet arrived at the local American legation, despite the fact that this was only one month before World War II started with the German bombardment of Poland. Anne's mother had suggested that since war seemed imminent, they should flee Przemyśl and travel to Warsaw immediately. The foreign legations were situated there, and since communication and travel would obviously be disrupted at the onset of the war, they needed to be close to these legations. Following her advice, they rented a room in Warsaw from a shoe manufacturer with whom Anne's parents had had business dealings. Every day, they went to the American Consulate to inquire if the required papers had arrived. Menashe would approach the consul, while Anne waited near the door. . . . Each day, the consul would remain in his chair and say, in a dry and disinterested voice, "No, nothing has arrived." On Friday, the day that Germany invaded Poland, Anne approached the consul and said that it was clear that war would break out any minute, which would make

---

to the community within a short time: Ruth (Hochhauser) and Moish Kaufman; my brother Moish and his wife, Esther; and Selma (Hochhauser) and Buddy Schulman. Later additional cousins moved there.

getting out of Poland impossible, and "Why should my husband be trapped?" She asked that the consul instruct Menashe to leave for America immediately. To this the consul responded that he did not have authority to order anyone to leave, but he could advise them to go to a camp over which the American flag would be flying, in a town called Brzesc, where stranded Americans had been advised to gather. This, he suggested, would protect them.

Following his advice, they went immediately to the railway station to buy tickets. Very providentially, there were two towns in Poland with the same name. To distinguish between them, the second town was called "Brzesc on the River Bug." Since they did not know which of the two towns had been designated for the Americans, Menashe and Anne turned back and remained in Warsaw. It wasn't until years later that they learned that the Germans had bombed the town where the Americans were situated, even more forcefully than other places. The confusion in the names saved them.

That very night, the first bombs fell on Warsaw. The next morning, the Sabbath, Menashe and Anne went to the consulate. This time, however, the consul beamed as he got up from behind his desk and gave them the long-awaited papers. The next step was to get transit visas to Sweden. Menashe had a visa to neighboring countries, but Anne did not. Even though it meant desecrating the Sabbath, they decided to take a taxi immediately to the Latvian legation to request a transit visa. A few moments after they got into the cab, there was another air raid. The taxi stopped, and the driver ran for cover into the hallway of a nearby apartment house. Menashe bribed the driver to keep going, and eventually he did. They arrived at the Latvian legation at about noon, only to be told that no visa could be issued to Anne unless she first received a visa to enter Sweden. Latvia did not have a harbor for transatlantic ships, and they were not interested in hosting foreigners in their country indefinitely. Meanwhile, Menashe had Anne call the Swedish Consulate and request that they please remain open a bit longer to allow them time to reach there before it closed for the weekend—from about 1 p.m. on the Sabbath until Monday!

The young couple grabbed another cab, but just then, German planes resumed bombing. Again, they bribed the cabdriver and arrived at the Swedish Consulate about a half hour later. They spoke to a young man who informed them that since Anne was a citizen of a belligerent country, America would be breaking neutrality laws by letting her in, and so he could not issue the visa. Menashe and Anne pleaded with him, but he just kept picking up his pen to issue the visa and then putting it down again, saying he couldn't do it. This happened over and over, with their nerves fraying more each time. Finally, he turned to a young woman, who was joking and laughing with some men, and asked her whether he should break the rules. Clearly, he really wanted to issue the visa but did not have the authority to do so. The woman turned her head in his direction while continuing her laughing conversation and just said "no." Just then, a heavyset man entered from another office, to whom the young man immediately appealed. Fortunately, that man said, "Yes, issue it!" It was then about 12:45, and Menashe immediately instructed Anne, "Call the Latvian Consulate and ask them to wait for our arrival." The Latvians asked whether it was for a Polish or American citizen. Menashe told Anne to say "American." Blessed be Hashem, the Consulate remained open and gave her the visa that she needed. After that, they went immediately to their room to pack and quickly left for the railway station. There were no civilian trains scheduled, only trains carrying recruits—which made the stations primary bombing targets for the Germans.

Menashe and Anne, together with the families of recruits on the way to the front, could do nothing but wait. Hours later, a train arrived, which they boarded, for what was normally a seven-hour ride. This time, however, German planes appeared at one point, and the train stopped to allow the passengers and crew members to detrain. They all jumped out of the train and ran to hide.

With the planes swooping down and shooting whomever they saw, the couple hid in a small stretch of trees. Menashe and Anne were saying viddui (the confession recited before death) as they saw stretchers of wounded being carried away. Finally, when the train started to move again, Anne saw a woman carrying a baby, crying: "I can't carry it, somebody help me, please." Anne did! For hours on end, she had been very frightened—but all fear left her when the baby was placed in her arms.

They reboarded the train, but soon, the train stopped again during another bombing raid. They ran into a shallow ditch, where a man near them started laughing hysterically for no apparent reason. Anne said that she kept hearing that laughter for years afterward. They had to remain in the ditch for some six or seven hours, because the bombs had torn up the tracks. They waited until night enfolded them, and walked for what seemed like miles, until they came to where another train was supposed to be waiting. All the passengers trudged along until, at some point, one man sat down, saying that he had injured his leg while jumping out of the train and couldn't even crawl. Both Menashe and Anne were carrying a valise filled with their clothing, but they abandoned their clothing in order to help the injured man. Sadly, after a while, but before they reached the train, their strength ran out, and they could no longer support the man and had to abandon him! Anne started to cry, and all that Menashe could do was say in a sad and tired voice, "Don't cry." Eventually, Menashe and Anne reached the waiting train.

From then on, the journey was uneventful and, according to Anne, even pleasant. With them was another American with a Polish wife, who had been planning to wait out the war in Brzesc on the River Bug. People were helpful to one another. One person had somehow obtained some water, which he shared, and another shared his sandwiches. Menashe and Anne ate one bare slice of a sandwich and gave the other slice, together with the sandwich filling, to the person who had given them the water. All this drinking and eating, however, occurred only a day and a half after the beginning of the train trip. The usual seven-hour trip to Wilno had become a thirty-six-hour nightmare. In Wilno, they met up again with an American to whom they had said goodbye when they left the Yeshiva of

Mir, where they had been for *sheva brachot* [17] after their wedding. From Wilno, they went to the border-town of Zemgale. Menashe sent a telegram to our parents in America to say that they were safely out of Poland. Since the telegram was in English, an unknown tongue to the telegraph operator, his transmission was totally incomprehensible. Our parents later told them that seeing the signature and that it had come from Latvia was enough to somewhat allay their fears. The couple went from Zemgale to Riga, Latvia's capital, where they met up again with their American friends and learned where they could get kosher food.

The next objective was to get out of landlocked Latvia and into Sweden. It took just over a week to obtain tickets on a small, eighteen-passenger plane to Stockholm. On the crossing, they were hit by a minor storm, and all the passengers, including Menashe, who was an excellent traveler, became sick. Anne managed to remain sick even after they landed! While Menashe was trying to obtain Swedish money, Anne was lying on a bench shivering, covered with the jackets of all the male passengers. Most of the people were extremely nice to one another in those difficult times. Menashe succeeded in hailing a taxi to town, where

---

17 *sheva brachot* (wedding week of seven blessings)

they found an inexpensive hotel—and whom did they meet there? Again, that other American couple. The couple had arrived a day before and had already obtained all of the pertinent information they needed. Since so many people were trying to leave Europe, the problem had now become how to find passage on a U.S.-bound ship. They spent four weeks in Stockholm, but for Anne it was like going from hell to paradise, "so peaceful and so beautiful." The time in Stockholm included Rosh Hashanah. They davened in a Jewish lawyer's office with the other Americans. The davening was truly wholehearted. The day before Yom Kippur, they boarded the *Gripsholm*[18], on which

18 Picture from Dawe Collection

one hundred places had suddenly become available because cabins that had been unused for years were now opened for those fleeing from Europe. Menashe and Anne's cabin was four or six levels below the deck—but it was theirs. On the ship they were reunited with the students of the Mir yeshiva, with whom they had davened on Rosh Hashanah. During the first two days at sea, Anne traveled quite well, but, as she later said, "Oh my! The remaining eight!!"

She was so totally seasick for the whole remainder of the trip that she said she really expected to die. She was hoping, however, that she would survive at least until they arrived on shore so that her body would not be thrown into the ocean. Another passenger got so sick that he "flipped" and started to jump and yell with happiness. Why? He said that after seeing what Menashe was going through with Anne, he was overcome with joy that he was not married.

Anne later remarked that when they finally arrived in New York, "My unexpressed negative fears left me as soon as we landed." Instead of death, she met a wonderfully warm family. The morning after their arrival at 870 Driggs Avenue, Menashe woke up bouncing in bed and blessed Hashem for granting them a safe return to the good old U.S.A.

Eventually, Menashe became Jewish Chaplain of the Middletown State Homeopathic Hospital. After retirement, he joined his children and settled in Lakewood. Their son, Allen, became a successful businessman and undertook to be supportive of his brother, Rabbi Yitzchak Mordechai, who had dedicated his life to the study of Torah under Rabbi Aharon Kotler and

his descendants, who continued to run the Beis Medrash Govoha [Lakewood Yeshiva]. Even after Yitzchak Mordecai's death in 2016, Allen continues to help the family

Photo courtesy of Chavie Dershowitz

as well as many other Jewish educational institutions. He also helped found both a yeshiva and a Beis Yaakov school in the Lakewood area.

Their youngest son, Zecharia, had planned aliyah in 1969, to join us at Bar-Ilan University, as an assistant to one of the professors of political science. In the interim he became involved in student support for the "Black Power" movement, which was being prodded by Stokely Carmichael to raise its level of civil disobedience.

Stokely had immigrated to New York City in 1952, enrolled at Howard University in 1960, joined the Student Nonviolent Coordinating Committee (SNCC), and was one of the Freedom Riders who in 1961 traveled throughout the South challenging segregation laws. After graduating with honors from Howard University in 1964, he had joined SNCC for an African American voter registration drive in Lowndes County, Alabama. They organized demonstrations against military contractors and other campus recruiters, as also against draft issues regarding the Vietnam War.

The 1967 school year had started with a large demonstration against Dow Chemical Company recruitment (the company that made napalm, the flammable gel that was used on the battlefield by the United States government) at the University of Wisconsin. On October 17, a demonstration that was peaceful at first turned into a sit-in that was violently dispersed by the Madison police and riot squad, resulting in many injuries and arrests. A mass rally and a student strike then closed the university for several days. A huge March on the Pentagon of about 100,000 people, with hundreds arrested and injured, took place on October 21. After the conventional civil rights tactics of peaceful pickets apparently didn't achieve its goal, tactics were changed, and the Oakland, California, "Stop the Draft Week" in December followed, with mass hit-and-run skirmishes with the police.

Zecharia had joined other whites against discrimination of Blacks, until he found himself, and the other whites, unwelcome. It was Stokely and his Black movement group who told Zecharia, "We don't need you here, Whitey." Zecharia was deeply frustrated by his exclusion from the fight for civil rights and began to display serious moods of despair. Unfortunately, his untimely death in 1969, while we were on the boat taking us to Israel, ended his life in sadness, before he could realize his great potential as a future political scientist. Needless to say, there were many black leaders—notably Martin Luther King—who took a completely different approach at the time. King was a uniquely important ally in the fight against anti-Semitism and for a secure Israel.

If I may indulge in speculation, I suppose that the 2020 riots in Washington of ultranationalist Proud Boys, and Black violence in Minnesota, in the wake of the death of George Floyd, and the anarchists and antifa radicals who rocked Portland on New Year's Eve, and elsewhere, were similar expressions of the estrangement of some segments of the American population from the establishment. Sadly, some of these riots have targeted

Jews and Jewish institutions specifically, as representing the white establishment.

Today, too, some of these groups are distancing volunteers of other origins, who are trying to be helpful to them. Of course, there are many leaders who eschew this estrangement of Jews and other segments of society.[19] In my opinion, the politically over-correct reactions of some politicians and media people to the desecration of synagogues and destruction of properties is a complementary unfortunate reaction to the discord, as was Zecharia's despair.

---

19 See: Elan Sherod Carr, United States Special Envoy to Monitor and Combat Anti-Semitism; Prof. Alan Dershowitz; Documentary film-maker Abby Martin; Black community leaders; and others across the political spectrum who have risen to denounce it firmly and unequivocally. These Black leaders include: Derrick Johnson, the current president of the NAACP; his predecessor, the Rev. Cornell William Brooks; and Sherrilyn Ifill, president of the NAACP Legal Defense Fund, as well as Michael Blake, vice chairman of the DNC; Sen. Cory Booker; Sen. Kamala Harris; Rep. Gregory Meeks; and Rep. Ayanna Pressley . . . major national figures of the Black left [who] have raised their voices [include] Marc Lamont Hill, Brittany Packnett Cunningham, and Anthony Beckford, president of Black Lives Matter Brooklyn. (Carly Pildis, "In Light of Rising Anti-Semitism, Rethinking Black-Jewish Relations." *Tablet* magazine, January 29, 2020.) Retired NBA star Charles Barkley decried anti-Semitism and racism and called out Black sports figures and celebrities for their anti-Semitism. "We can't allow blacks to be prejudiced if we want to be respected," he said on TNT Video Services, where he serves as a studio analyst during pregame and halftime shows.

Sylvia's (Sheindy) Love of Hebrew Studies

Our only sister, Sheindy, married Joe Fuchs and had three daughters: twins Ruchama (Rushie) and Shoshana (Shushy) and Miriam Yehudit. In our society, at that time, it was uncommon for girls to be given an education in Jewish studies, other than to know how to read the siddur.[20] Nonetheless, my mother, a very bright woman lacking an education in Jewish studies, was very determined that her daughter be not deprived of such education—but Torah Vodaath had no girls' program. Fortunately, after a few years, an afternoon Hebrew school for girls was established in Williamsburg, and Sheindy was among its first students. Upon graduating from high school, she continued her Jewish studies at the Hebrew Teachers' Training School for Girls in Manhattan, founded in 1930 by Rabbi Joseph Lookstein and eventually becoming Stern College for Women, a branch of Yeshiva University. Every evening, after spending her daytime hours at Brooklyn College, she traveled to Manhattan to continue her Jewish studies. This love of

Photo courtesy of Zecharia Dor-Shav

---

20 *siddur* (prayer book)

learning led her to suggest to her fiancé, Joe Fuchs, that she would like him to get a yeshiva education in addition to the training that he was undergoing to be a Hebrew teacher. Joe, an extremely talented student, agreed but could not find a school in which to enroll at his age. He arranged with Torah Vodaath to be taught Gemara[21] by Rabbi Snyder, who was associated with the Yeshiva. Eventually, Joe became so proficient at his studies that he became the teacher of all his yeshiva-educated friends in their study group in Borough Park, which they named "The High-Low Boys."

When their twins, Rushie and Shushy, were born, they decided to make their home a Hebrew-speaking home, and only Hebrew was spoken to them. Both of them were involved in education. Today, in Israel all of the Fuchs daughters' families are involved in Jewish studies and education. This dedication also led the girls of the following generations—especially Sara Lea (Nebenzahl), daughter of Miriam—to become very proficient scholars in Torah studies. The tradition continues even with the great-grandchildren. The husband of Miriam's granddaughter Shira Nechama, Yedidiah Meyuchas, won the World Bible Competition for Adults, held in Jerusalem, in both 2017 and 2019.

---

21 *Gemara* (text of the Talmud)

Rabbi Dr. Charles (Elchanan) Cutter, Rushie's husband, served as Judaica Librarian in the Ohio State University Library and then served as head of the Judaica Department and Special Collection Librarian and Archivist of Brandeis University, until retirement.

Her Encounter with Communism

Spiked by the 1929 crash of the stock market in the United States during the 1930s, the Great Depression in America helped the Communist Party make large inroads in the thinking of college students. The party's membership reached 85,000 in 1942, just as America was entering World War II. At that time, with New Deal liberalism sweeping the country, the party became influential in many aspects of life in the United States. In addition, because they were also industrial union organizers, the Communists became a major force in several important unions. There were also many "fellow travelers" who sympathized with the aims of the party. In New York City, a stronghold of party support, Communists became actively involved in the housing struggles of many New Yorkers. At the Party's peak, some Communists were elected to the City Council of New York.

For a few decades, from the 1930s until the demise of communism as an effective political force in the 1950s, New York City was the one place where American communists came close to becoming a mass movement. In Brooklyn College, which Sheindy attended during the 1930s, the national student organization, formed by the Communist National Student League and the Socialist Student League of Industrial Democracy, claimed six hundred members. This all ended when Harry Gideonse became president of the College in 1939. He charged that the American Youth for Democracy organization was camouflaged communism, and under his leadership, Brooklyn College refused to charter them. He testified before the Senate Internal Security subcommittee that the Communists had very considerable influence in key campus activities, including the student newspaper, which was one of their favorite sources of infiltration.

Sheindy said that she had been very attracted by the atmosphere of the Student League, and were it not for the fact that the Brooklyn chapter held its meetings on the Sabbath, she would likely have become a Communist, as did many of her acquaintances.

Herbert's (Heshy) Struggles with the Brooklyn Navy Yard

Heshy was probably the most congenial of my siblings, with an easy and infectious smile. He married

Sylvia Dienstag and had two children: Rochelle (Shelly) and Jay. Shortly before World War II, in 1940, America enacted legislation permitting a universal compulsory draft for men between the ages of eighteen and forty-five. All men of those ages were required to register with the Selective Service System, so that a draft could be imposed to fill vacancies in the armed forces that

Photo courtesy of Donnie Zinkin

were not filled through voluntary means. Twelve days after Pearl Harbor, on December 19, 1941, the law was further amended, extending the term of service to the duration of the war plus six months and requiring the registration of all men from eighteen to sixty-four years of age. In the massive draft of World War II, 50 million men from the age of eighteen to forty-five were registered, 36 million classified, and 10 million inducted.[22] One of the exemptions offered was workers in defense industries,[23] and Heshy was accepted

---

22 George Q. Flynn, *The Draft, 1940–1973*. (1993). Wikipedia: Conscription in the United States.

23 Classification: 2-B—Registrant deferred because of occupation in a war industry (Defense contractor or reserved occupation).

for work as a shipfitter at the Brooklyn Navy Yard. At its peak, in 1942, the navy yard worked twenty-four hours a day and had no workfree holidays. All workers were required to work six days a week. Being a Sabbath observer, he was permitted to leave on Fridays, but with only enough time to reach home before the onset of the Sabbath. Furthermore, he was constantly being transferred from unit to unit because each unit wanted workers who would work additional hours and would be willing to take off occasional Sundays and work instead on the Sabbath—which he was not prepared to do.

Fortunately, Menashe was at that time (1940–1942) the rabbi of Congregation Adath Jeshurun in Newport News, Virginia, where he had received a citation for his work as a volunteer rabbi of the Fort Eustis army base in the area. With his intervention, Heshy transferred to the naval base of Norfolk, adjacent to Newport News. There he had the distinction of being the only Jewish defense worker who was exempt from working on the Sabbath. (Interestingly, the only other person given that privilege was a Seventh-day Adventist.) I am convinced that Heshy's uncompromising observance of the Sabbath during that difficult time was a factor in the following story about his son, Jay.

Jay's Sabbath Success with Metropolitan Insurance and Bell Telephone

In 1970, Jay applied for a supervisory position at Metropolitan Life Insurance in New York. After taking aptitude tests, he was found to be fully qualified and was invited for an interview. At the interview, his skullcap made it obvious that he was a Sabbath observer, and he was told that all such supervisory positions require 24/7 availability, even on the Sabbath. Since he would not desecrate the Sabbath for any job, he was prepared to abandon the offered position. His father, however, was adamant about not allowing Metropolitan Life "get away" with this obvious religious discrimination. He called upon the National Council of Young Israel for advice and help. They put him in contact with COLPA, the National Jewish Commission on Law and Public Affairs.[24] COLPA brought a charge

---

24 COLPA, which calls itself the Legal Arm of Observant Jewry, describes its commitment as follows: "Judaism, with its rich tradition of laws and customs, often finds itself at odds with the norms of contemporary society. From the seemingly mundane, such as dietary restrictions and the wearing of a *yarmulka* (small head covering), to the clearly profound, such as definitions of life and death, these differences can frequently cause conflict. Since 1965, COLPA has been committed to addressing and resolving these conflicts through mediation, negotiation, and, when required, litigation, as well as through legislative initiatives. From its modest beginnings, COLPA has grown into an influential body of hundreds of attorneys, social scientists, academicians and others who share a commitment to resolving these problems within the context of the law."

against Metropolitan Life to the New York City Employment Commission.[25] After hearings, a compromise was reached specifying that Metropolitan Life would change its hiring policy and offer Jay the job, in return for which he would agree not to file a claim for damages.

While this negotiation was dragging on, Jay had applied for a position with American Telephone and Telegraph Company (AT&T).[26] As was customary with many American companies at that time, they too demanded that Jay be available 24/7. COLPA immediately notified them that they, too, were in violation of New York City law. This resulted in their backing down and offering him a position with the firm. Eventually, additional offices of the company opened their doors to the hiring of Sabbath-observant Jews. Jay worked for the New York office of AT&T for ten years.

Jay was, thus, the catalyst for opening these two large companies to observant Jews, breaking a discrimination that had been common for a long period of time.

---

25 This was possibly the precursor of the EEPC (Equal Employment Practices Commission), an independent monitor of New York City's employment practices, created by a 1989 amendment to the New York City Charter.

26 With AT&T's multitude of local exchanges continuing to stretch farther and farther yearly, eventually it created a continent-wide telephone system.

In my heart of hearts, I believe that Jay merited this privilege because of his father's strict observance of the Sabbath during World War II. Two of Jay's children are rabbis, having settled in Israel and being involved in Jewish outreach and teaching in yeshivas for older students.

Shelly married Aryeh Zinkin while he was doing his medical residency. When still a teenager, and with minimal family support, he set out to create a religious life for himself. He put himself through a Jewish high school and eventually, Yeshiva University. There, in addition to developing his

Photo courtesy of Shelly Zinkin

many talents and Talmudical studies, he became captain of the yeshiva's Wrestling Association (see Appendix 6). This didn't interfere with his becoming a successful surgeon and a pillar of his New Jersey synagogue community.

During his medical residency, he once said that he felt uncomfortable with the way the professors looked at their patients, not paying attention to them as people with personal needs. I said to him, "Aryeh, write that down so that when you are a professor, you won't act that way." Many years later, he reminded me of what

I had said and told me that he was careful not to be impersonal with his patients. In fact, he used to say a prayer on the Sabbath in synagogue for Hashem to heal them. This modesty was noticed by his office nurse, who related that during the family's shiva[27] mourning period after his death. She related, "He always treated his patients with great patience and personal concern."

An award in his memory by Yeshivat Netivot Montesori stated as follows:

> Dr. Zinkin was keenly aware that to be the role model for his family . . . he would have to be unfailingly consistent in his daily Jewish observances. He was enormously involved with his synagogue . . . serving as its President. He actively considered how he could elevate his Sabbath and Yom Tov table to be an inspiration for his family and guests. Every week, without fail, he would set aside time from his flourishing medical practice and community involvement to savor the incoming Sabbath by doing the grocery shopping, helping to cook, and setting the table.

---

27 *shiva* (lit.: seven. Seven-day mourning period during which a mourner does not sit on a regular chair, but rather sits on the floor, or a low chair)

Sabbath meals in the Zinkin home were filled with zemirot and divrei Torah. When everyone else retired [Aryeh] would demonstrate his love of Torah by opening a sepher[28] and inviting his children, and later his grandchildren, to learn with him. His Pesach seder[29] was a model for how to integrate children into the rituals creatively, through questions, games and riddles.

It is interesting to note a specific occurrence that brought Aryeh to becoming a strictly observant Jew, even though he came from a family that pushed him in other directions.[30] His son Hillel described this as an indirect result of his spending a summer in a religious camp. On the way home from summer camp, he was being driven by one of the camp's directors, who suggested that Aryeh might be interested in going to Yeshiva University, where many of his campmates were going. In his usual humorous manner, Aryeh related that the driver was not driving too carefully, and he was scared to death. So that the driver would get his mind back on the driving, Aryeh just said, "yes." He conditioned it, however,

---

28 Often spelled sefer.

29 *seder* (procedural plan for the traditional Passover eve ceremonial meal)

30 His father was the personal physician of Rabbi Aharon Kotler in Lakewood, Aryeh's hometown.

on his parents' approval. Knowing, of course, that they would not approve. Which was fine with him.

When he told his parents about the director's suggestion, the parents objected with such unbridled indignation that Aryeh, like so many rebellious youngsters in such situations, said, "If you are so strongly against what I might want to do, I will go to the Yeshiva!"

Shelly's son, Effie, has been very active in working and raising money for the Tikva Children's Home, a network of children's residences and schools in Odessa. At the time of this writing, Russian bombs have fallen near the orphanage, and Odessa's chief rabbi, Shlomo Baksht and his group, who have been running the home, put its nearly 300 young inhabitants onto buses that, days later, brought them to safety in neighboring Romania.

Ten years earlier, his sister's brother-in-law, Seth Gerszberg, co-founder of fashion giant Marc Ecko Enterprises (MEE), had taken a business trip to Odessa. There, he was approached for a donation by a Chabad Hasid who was raising money for this children's residence. Seth couldn't afford it at that time and pledged that if his company turned a profit, the first $100,000 would go toward the orphanage. That initial $100,000 contribution ultimately grew to $18 million of donations by MEE and its shareholders to Tikva over the last ten years.

In one of Effie's visits to the children's home, one of the children took his hand and attached herself physically and emotionally to him. Eventually, he brought her to America and raised her like one of his own children, until her grandmother came to America and she moved out of his home.

Moish's Efforts for the Underground in Palestine

Moish married Esther Mann and had three children: Linda, Kenny,[31] and Rena. Moish was the only member of the family who was of military age during World War II and not eligible for any deferment. He had a law degree from Brooklyn Law School and was assigned to be a judge advocate lieutenant in the army. Our family proudly hung a flag on the window of our home, indicating that we had a child in the

Photo courtesy of Zecharia Dor-Shav

---

31 Kenny was born just twelve days after my father passed away and was named after him Yekutiel Yehudah (in Yiddish, *Leibish*). He remembers that my mother would sometimes call him Leib Zissel (sweet *Leibish*): "I would ask her, 'Grandma, why do you call me Leib Zissel?' She explained that Leib Zissel was the loving name she used for her husband, and since I was the first to be named after him, she would fondly see him in me, and would sometimes call me Leib Zissel too."

military service. He was always proud of his service and became an active member of the Jewish War Veterans in the United States when he returned after the war. In fact, in honor of his service to the organization, and at the family's request, they sent a bugler and honor guard to his funeral to play "Taps."[32]

During the war, Moish was assigned to serve overseas in France. He related an interesting anecdote about the time he had a furlough and went for a skiing trip to Grenoble in the French Alps. Not being too experienced in skiing, he fell. A native French skier came to help him and greeted him in Yiddish. How he knew that he was Jewish I am not sure, but Moshe said that it felt good to be greeted that way.

As an officer, he was eligible for a furlough trip to Tel Aviv on a military plane—by way of Cairo. In Tel Aviv, he visited the Weisenfeld family,[33] cousins of my mother, with whom she had had a regular

Photo provided by Morris Dershowitz

---

32 "Taps" ("Butterfield's Lullaby"), sometimes known by the lyrics of its second verse, "Day is Done," is a famous musical piece, played in the United States military during funerals, generally on bugle or trumpet.

33 See Appendix 3.

correspondence during the war years, and to whom she had sent food packages from time to time. He also used the occasion to visit Israel and brought back the photograph on the previous page of a lone person praying in the very limited space[34] that was then available for informal prayer at what was called the Wailing Wall.

He was also permitted to bring his pistol with him on the trip. Somehow, in Tel Aviv, he "lost" the pistol—as was not uncommon among American Jewish soldiers who visited Israel at that time. "Somehow" the pistol ended up with the Haganah, which was drastically in need of weapons.

Moish was active[35] in the establishment of the Jewish community of West Hempstead, Long Island,

---

34 See story of Rabbi Moshe Segal in Chapter 4.

   A Status Quo agreement issued by the mandatory authority forbade the placing of benches or chairs near the Wall. The last prior occurrence of such a ban was in 1915, but [this] Ottoman decree was soon retracted after intervention of the *Chacham Bashi* [Turkish name for the Chief Rabbi of the Jewish community, in the time of the Ottoman Empire]. In 1928 the District Commissioner of Jerusalem, Edward Keith-Roach, acceded to an Arab request to reimplement the ban. This led to a British officer being stationed at the Wall making sure that Jews were prevented from sitting. Nor were Jews permitted to separate the sexes with a screen. In practice, a flexible modus vivendi had emerged and such screens had been put up from time to time when large numbers of people gathered to pray. Wikipedia.

35 After only a few days in Tel Aviv, an unexpected call from the American army requested all the American soldiers to evacuate immediately to Cairo. As he wrote, "That was a terrific blow for me. I decided to go

and was president of its Young Israel Synagogue from 1957 to 1959. After retiring from private law practice, he was engaged as a vice president of the Jacob K. Javits Convention Center of New York—which had replaced the New York Coliseum as the city's major convention facility—as its law and general counsel. He liked to say that his job was as an "*eitzah geber*," that is, to give counsel but not to have to do any real work.

Once, during his service there, the Nation of Islam, headed by the Reverend Louis Farrakhan, sued the operators of the center for refusing to house one of its events. Moish was proud to tell how he had prevented this ignoble Muslim anti-Semite from holding a big meeting at the Center. The following conveys a glimpse of the conflict:

> The Javits Center corporation counsel, Morris Dershowitz, said that the Oct. 25 date had already been taken by another group. If the Nation of Islam "would send us a letter detailing the kind of program they're planning and the number of people they expect," he added,

---

into hiding at least until the boys [his friends] got back from Jerusalem. By doing that I missed going back that same afternoon. After I was sure that the plane had left and that there was no possibility of my leaving that night, I returned to the hotel. . . . Lest I forget, the pilot flew low and slowly over Jerusalem and Haifa and along the Jordan Valley, so I can also say that I saw those historic places."

"we would review the matter and see what other dates are available.

"We need to know how many people are coming so we can alert the police and fire departments and prepare our security adequately," Mr. Dershowitz said.

A lawyer for the Nation of Islam, Ava K. Atkinson, asserted that Mr. Dershowitz told her in a conversation last Thursday that the Nation of Islam would "not be entitled to the use of the center's facilities for any dates" because the group was "incompatible" with other organizations renting space at the center.[36]

Subsequently, the Nation of Islam referred to him as "Morris the Cat."[37] It is not surprising that Moish was so insistent not to give a podium to Louis Farrakhan. On July 4, 2020, Farrakhan delivered a three-hour speech that was streamed live on the Nation of Islam's YouTube channel, during which he said that Jews had poisoned him with "radiated seed" to test whether he was truly a man of God, and that his survival is proof that he is. Inter alia, he also said that prominent Jewish figures such

---

36 From the *New York Times* on August 21, 1987.
37 Morris the Cat is the advertising mascot for 9Lives brand cat food. It appears on its packaging and in many of its television commercials.

as [my nephew] Alan Dershowitz and former Trump administration Middle East negotiator Jason Greenblatt are Satan and emphasized that it is his job to expose Satan so that every Muslim picks up a stone against him like they do during the pilgrimage rituals in Mecca.

Morris's son, Kenny, became an electrical engineer with a specific interest in digital electronics, computers, and programming. He became part of the team that was working for a subcontractor of the 1996 Mars Global Surveyor developed by NASA's Jet Propulsion Laboratory. His group was responsible for the digital memory facility that was developed for the Mars probe, which included the Surveyor camera. The camera memory was sensitive to the sorts of high-energy space particles that can pass through the camera while it was orbiting Mars and cause bits of memory to become corrupted and ruined. Kenny was involved in the development of the circuitry needed to protect the integrity of the image data stored. After the launch he proudly told me, "We now have a Dershowitz in space."[38]

---

38 Kenny spent one of his high school years, 1970, in Israel and was a very frequent guest in our home. He credits our son, Nachum, who eventually became a professor of computer science and was at that time a computer science major at Bar-Ilan University. He had, in Kenny's words, "A very big influence on me and was the start of a lifelong interest in computers and the things they can do." Nachum would sometimes take Kenny down into the bowels of the mysterious computer center at Bar-Ilan to see all the wonders there. This was a time when computers

Yitzchak's Love of Torah and His Coming to Israel

Yitzchak (Itchy) married Shoshana (Rosa) Akker, and they had seven children: Yekutiel, Ruchama, Chaya Leah, Yaakov, Shifra, Aharon, and Sarah. He completed Mesivta Torah Vodaath during the years of the Great Depression. As was the custom then, he left the yeshiva upon graduation and worked full-time

Photo courtesy of
Zecharia Dor-Shav

during the day but participated in an evening Torah *shiur*[39] with Rabbi Yaakov Shurkin (see below for Rabbi Shurkin's influence on my own professional life). When the economic condition of the family improved and the Lakewood Yeshiva, headed by Rabbi Aharon Kotler, had opened with thirteen students, he stopped working, enrolled there, and became a lifelong yeshiva man.

He was always interested in improving himself in Torah observance. Although I was six years his younger, he once proposed that we help each other

---

were still very large mainframes, made up of rooms of equipment maintained by specialists, and would cost hundreds of thousands of dollars each. As Kenny said: "Being down there with Nachum, surrounded by what seemed so wondrous—can you imagine that?"

39 *shiur* (Torah lesson)

avoid transgressions during our youth by confessing to each other whenever we stumbled. This pact was very difficult for me emotionally and psychologically, but it helped us through our teenage years.

His success in making aliyah in 1950 was most unusual. One Purim day in the yeshiva, he and his cherished friends Rabbi Elya Svei and Rabbi Yaakov Weisburg were sitting over a bottle of wine and said, "לשנה הבאה בירושלים (Next Year in Jerusalem)!" His friends, in fact, did succeed in visiting Israel that year, but Yitzchak did not. Shortly thereafter, his dear friend Dov Shwartzman, the son-in-law of Rabbi Kotler, was about to sail to Eretz Yisrael.[40] Yitzchak, together with most of the other students of the Yeshiva who had come to escort Rabbi Dov, remained on the boat until the time for visitors to disembark.

Before the gangplank was pulled in, Yitzchak, impulsively—but perhaps with the help of his friend Yaakov Shiff, who was also traveling on the ship—concluded that this was his golden opportunity to fulfill his pledge of לשנה הבאה בירושלים! When all the other visitors disembarked, Yitzchak remained on board, saying that he could still get off with the pilot, who would be leaving the boat when it cleared the harbor area.

---

40 *Eretz Yisrael* (the biblical Land of Israel)

But he didn't!

At about midnight, when most of the passengers had gone to their cabins to retire for the night, he was still sitting on the deck. One of those still on the deck with him suggested that there were two empty bunks in his room and that perhaps Yitzchak would want to use one of them.

The invitation seemed attractive and he accompanied the passenger to his cabin. No sooner did he get settled into the bunk when someone tapped him on the shoulder and said that he thinks that Yitzchak must be in the wrong bunk because this bunk was his. The fellow who had invited him immediately responded, "Oh, Yitzchak, I think that you should be in the other bunkbed."

In the morning a crew member came around to check that everyone was in his assigned room. When he came to Yitzchak, this fellow said, "My friend here doesn't like the people in his assigned room, and I invited him to come into this free bed." That satisfied the crew member and he moved on to the next cabin.

Later that evening my mother received a call from Reb Aharon asking if she knew where Yitzchak was. The other students who had escorted Rabbi Dov obviously had told Reb Aharon that they thought Yitzchak never got off the boat. She responded, "Why are you asking me? Isn't he in the Yeshiva?" The Rav excused himself and changed the subject without telling my mother anything more. Our family learned of Yitzchak's decision to remain onboard only the next morning, when we received a ship-to-shore telegram stating that he would be arriving in Haifa in two weeks. This was our first confirmation that he had remained aboard. Of course, we had no idea that he planned to remain in Israel permanently—neither did he, I suspect.

The ship's first port of call was Piraeus, Greece, near Athens. Yitzchak, of course, could not disembark since he didn't have a passport. He arranged for a friend to mail a letter to our parents, enclosing the key to a locker in Grand Central Station in Manhattan, asking that his tefillin[41] in the locker be forwarded to him in Israel. This corroborated the fact that his sailing was a spur-of-the-moment decision.

Shortly after his arrival, he applied to the American Consulate in Israel to issue him a passport. After some difficulty, the consul legalized his stay in Israel by issuing him the passport. His was only the second American passport issued by the American Consulate in the new State of Israel. The details of how he managed to remain on the ship without being discovered by the crew is adequately described in the book

---

41 *tefillin* (phylacteries)

Williamsburg Memories,[42] authored by his friend, Dr. Gershon Kranzler.

Visiting Israel after the 1967 Six-Day War, I was in the Old City on Tishah B'Av and happened to meet a friend of his, Rabbi Frank, who told me that he was one of the people who helped Yitzchak get off the boat. He explained, "About a hundred yeshiva students danced up the gangplank to greet the arriving Rabbi Shwartzman, and one extra person, Yitzchak, danced down with them, unhindered by the border police."[43]

Yitzchak then enrolled himself in Yeshivas Hevron (Knesses Yisroel) in Jerusalem, where he was recognized as "special," being the first American who had come to the yeshiva just to study, with no plans to become a practicing rabbi. He, however, was never content with learning Torah solely for his personal advancement and felt obliged to make a concomitant effort to help others study Torah.

Israel was just then absorbing hundreds of thousands of new immigrants from North Africa and Yemen, almost all of whom were religiously observant. Ben-Gurion's Melting Pot policy was in force.[44] As a result,

---

42 Gershon Kranzler, *Williamsburg Memories*. C.I.S. Publications, 1988, pp. 55–59.
43 His son, Yekutiel, later related to one of our relatives that Yitzchak eventually paid some money to the boat company for his trip.
44 Each immigrant group, with its own unique characteristics, had to contend with the difficulties of integrating into an emerging society in a

there was great resistance to allowing religious teachers and schools to establish themselves in the *ma'abarot* (transit camps) and outlying settlements. According to Professor Eliezer Don-Yichye,[45] religious teachers were greatly outnumbered in the camps, and those who did get in were faced with sanctions if they tried to encourage religious values in their classes. Among the sanctions enforced against them, as well as against parents who tried to register their children for religious classes and schools, was the denial of economic and employment assistance. Similar pressure was applied to have the children registered in the secular school system, and for their parents to register as members of the Histadrut General Organization of Workers in Israel (whose leadership was dominated by the Mapai Party). This was also a precondition for membership in the Clalit Health Services.[46]

---

constant state of flux. Originally, this "melting pot" policy sought to establish a uniform and unified Israeli. Immigrants were pressured to adapt to the values of the dominant culture (the secular Labor Party of David Ben-Gurion and its coalition partners), whether voluntarily or in response to the demands of the new society, with the goal of fashioning themselves in accordance with the primarily secular society. Over the years, Israel's social-cultural-political discourse has changed.

45 In "The Struggle over Education in the Immigrant Camps, and its Expression in the Public Sphere", *Niv HaMidrashiya* Vol. 18–19, 5745–5746 (Hebrew).

46 The Frumkin Commission confirmed that the new arrivals were settled into an environment rife with anti-religious sentiment and condescension toward Jews from North Africa and the Middle East. The "last

Synagogues and private classes in religion were also curtailed. In some cases, the *pe'ot* (sidelocks) of the religious Yemenite children[47] were forcibly removed.

The Vaad HaYeshivot became involved, and numerous yeshiva students volunteered to be part of a group that called itself "P'eylim" (activists), who engaged in activities to rescue the spiritually poor and what they saw as maliciously religiously deprived immigrants.

---

refuge" of the Jews turned out to be far less inviting than the one that Jewish Agency representatives had portrayed in their aliyah campaign visits to Algeria, Yemen, Iraq, Morocco, etc. The scene was somewhat less Messianic and romantic, especially for those Jews who hailed from what Ben-Gurion and other Mapai members termed "primitive" lands. The overall *geist* of the State of Israel at the time attached a severe stigma to these immigrants (Frumkin Commission, *True Torah Jews*, 183 Wilson Street, Brooklyn, undated).

47 Other atrocities against the Yemenite children were reported by the *New York Times* of Feb. 20, 2019:

Known as the "Yemenite Children Affair," there are over one thousand official reported cases of missing babies and toddlers, but some estimates from advocates are as high as 4,500. Their families believe the babies were abducted by the Israeli authorities in the 1950s, and were illegally put up for adoption to childless Ashkenazi families, Jews of European descent. The children who disappeared were mostly from the Yemenite and other "Mizrahi" communities, an umbrella term for Jews from North Africa and the Middle East. While the Israeli government is trying to be more transparent about the disappearances, to this day, it denies that there were systematic abductions.

In one of the author's university classes, when this matter was under discussion, a woman from one of Israel's very respected kibbutzim stated, "I was just eighteen at the time, but was convinced by our elders that this was best for the Yemenite families as well as for the country, and I also participated in the disappearance of these children."

They encouraged the immigrants to resist the pressure and register their children in religious classes and schools to learn Torah and mitzvoth.[48] They acted with stubborn resolution and fearlessness. Together with other P'eylim, Yitzchak engaged the directors and mayors of the immigrant settlements. Mindless of the many dangers in his way—one mayor once chased Yitschak out of his office while brandishing a baseball bat—he persisted and traveled from one immigrant camp to another to persuade parents to send their children to Torah elementary and high schools and to yeshivas. When he returned to America for a year in 1950, he and his yeshiva *buddies*, Rabbi Elya Svei and Rabbi Yaakov Weisberg, helped found the American P'eylim, which undertook the support of its sister group in Israel.

An example of what they went through is provided in the following:

It was a moonless night in 1950, outside the Ein Shemer ma'abarah (transient new immigrants camp). Dark and quiet—except for the persistent thud of a shovel, as a group of teenagers took turns burrowing out a tunnel beneath the fence that surrounded the camp.

---

48 *mitzvoth/mitzvos* (Jewish Religious commandments)

As they crawled through their tunnel and emerged on the other side, no one noticed what they had done, and no one realized that a stubbornly idealistic movement to save Jewish souls had just been launched.

Just a few short years after the Holocaust, the tide of history seemed to have turned against the Torah-observant world, as the same Jewish state that served as a refuge to so many immigrants also seemed determined to strip them of any vestiges of religious observance.

A small band of bochurim[49] and yungeleit[50] battled the odds and the anti-religious establishment, taking the name of "P'eylim" and utilizing cunning subterfuge and no small measure of chutzpah. Perhaps measured, rational, experienced adults wouldn't have responded the same way, but the bochurim didn't consider long-term calculations or assess the risks and rewards. All they knew was that there was a desperate situation and they had to act fast.

The catalyst for the formation of P'eylim was actually an event seven years earlier, on Erev

---

49 Plural of *bochur*, unmarried yeshiva students.
50 *yungeleit* (mature married yeshiva students)

Purim Katan 1943, when 1,228 European children arrived in Eretz Yisrael from a refugee camp set up by the Jewish Agency in the Iranian capital of Tehran. More than half of them were children under 14, and many were from religious homes.

Known as the Yaldei Tehran,[51] most were orphans with little more than the shirts on their backs, who had witnessed the massacre of close family members. They were joined half a year later by a second group of 200 children.

The Jewish Agency, which had orchestrated the refugees' arrival in Eretz Yisrael and whose

---

51 They were under the formal protection of the Polish-government-in-exile. Of those children, between 80 and 90 percent came from religious homes, and many had studied in *chadorim* (plural of *cheder*, a private primary day school where the emphasis is placed on Jewish religious study) and Bais Yaakov schools in Poland.

The Jewish Agency ran the camp in which the children were housed with the goal of turning the children away from their previous lives as religious Jews. The food was non-kosher, and when a group of children refused to eat it, the camp director, a member of the rabidly antireligious Hashomer Hatzair movement, responded, "Let one or two die of starvation, and the rest will soon forget about kosher food." Other children were forbidden from reciting kaddish (prayer for the dead) for their parents.

So intent was the Jewish Agency on preventing the children from receiving any religious instruction from the European rabbis who were then in Teheran that it informed the Polish government-in-exile that it would forgo any funding if it insisted on religious instruction being made available.

A colleague at Bar-Ilan University, Professor Miriam Shmida, was one of their teachers in a religious school in Israel.

counselors had, for the previous six months, tried to pry them away from religious observance, planned to place them in secular kibbutzim. When the religious community learned of the plan, an uproar ensued. Chief Rabbi Yitzchak Herzog demanded that the orphans be placed in religious communities, and ultimately the Jewish Agency conceded partially: They allowed children over 14 to choose their own placements, but Agency staff would interview the younger ones and handle their placements. In the end, 298 children were placed in secular settings, 288 in national-religious institutions, and 38 in Agudah-affiliated institutions.

That battle marked the beginning of a shift in the haredi posture vis-à-vis the secular establishment. Until then, they had remained mostly hapless in the face of the pre-state governing powers' social engineering. The outrage of the Yaldei Tehran affair sparked a sense of urgency—together with the realization as to the extent of what they were up against.[52]

---

52 Excerpted from Rav Eliyahu Gut, *Stopping the Soul Snatchers*, Mishpacha, August 1, 2018, with minor editing.

At the recommendation of Bnei Brak friends, Yitzchak was introduced to Shoshana, who had been in hiding with her family[53] during World War II. She left Holland to register in a religious school and dormitory in Bnei Brak. The meeting between the two went well, and they were married in 1954. The wedding was performed by Rabbi Aharon Kotler, who was in Jerusalem at the time for the World Congress of Agudas Yisroel.[54]

Photo courtesy of
Nachum Dershowitz

Yitzchak had great bitachon (trust) that Hashem would help him if and when he could not manage on his own. Nonetheless, he always felt that he was required to do as much as he could, even if that was assuredly not enough. An outstanding example of this

---

53 The picture is of the home within which Shoshana, her family, and others were hidden. The plaque under the attic window testifies to the owner's bravery in hiding Jews from the Germans.

54 The wedding was interrupted by Jordanian shelling of the Me'ah Shearim section of Jerusalem where the wedding was taking place. Rabbi Dov Shwartzman reported that all of the guests, including Rabbi Aharon, had to take cover under the tables during the shelling. Reb Aharon shouted out in Yiddish, "Master of the World, I want to continue living so that I can learn your Torah." One member of the Agudah Congress was wounded from the shelling.

took place during his later years when he was physically unable to travel easily on public transportation. He was studying in a kollel[55] in Tel Aviv and was traveling there regularly by taxi. On one occasion, there was a strike of taxi drivers, and he could not rely on finding a cab. Since his apartment was on the fourth floor of a building with no elevator, his wife urged him to resign himself to the fact that he could not get to his kollel that day and might as well save himself the difficulty of going down the stairs to the street to look for a cab. He refused, saying, "I must do as much as I can." He went down with the hope that he would find a strike-breaking cabdriver. His trust was rewarded. When he got down to the street, just such a strike-breaker passed by. Yitzchak hailed him and traveled to his kollel.[56]

A neighbor in his building in Bnei Brak was Rabbi Yaakov Kanievsky, the Steipler Rav. Yitzchak rarely did anything without consulting the Rav for advice.

---

55 The twentieth-century novelty of married Torah scholars in large numbers, supported by charity, dedicating themselves to a life completely insulated from the work market, was not previously admired. In fact, Maimonides (Ethics of the Fathers 4:5) decries such behavior and describes it as a *chilul* (desecration of) Hashem: "This is a desecration of God's name for the masses, for they will think of the Torah as a profession like any of the professions, and he will thus render it 'the despised word of God.'" Others disagree with this position and think it inapplicable today.

56 A two-part article on Yitzchak was published twenty years after his death, by *Yated Neeman*: B. Ram and C. Zilberman, "A Head in the Heavens and a Heart of Gold," April 2006.

Toward the end of Yitzchak's life, when he was diagnosed with melanoma, he made a very quick decision to undergo the operation he needed in the United States. He left on the first available flight. Not having sufficient time to consult with the Rav, he asked his son-in-law, Rabbi Avraham Leibowitz, to inform the Steipler that he had to leave urgently to New York for surgery. Reb Avraham went to the Steipler, who was bedridden at that time and also couldn't hear well. He penned a note saying that Yitzchak had found it necessary to go to New York for surgery. The Steipler responded, "I know! His parents live there." My parents, however, had long been in the *olam haemet*[57] at that time. Reb Avraham tried to explain this to the Steipler, but he refused to modify what he had said.

Just then, I was in the United States visiting my sister Sheindy. Yitzchak came for the surgery together with his son Yekutiel, and they too stayed at my sister's home. A few days later, Yitzchak's friend, Rabbi Elya Svei, who now was the rosh yeshiva of Yeshivas Philadelphia, came to visit, and Yekutiel told him of the mysterious response of the Steipler to Yitzchak's going to New York.

I offered the explanation that he likely meant that my parents' *zechuyot* (credits) are still alive in New York

---

57 *olam haemet*; (the world of true life, i.e., after death)

(because of their dedication to Torah Vodaath and for other outstanding good deeds that they had done there), and that these would be helpful to Yitzchok in his illness. Rabbi Elya jumped from his seat and said, "Of course, of course, that is what he meant!"

Though the surgeon had told me personally that Yitzchak couldn't be expected to live for more than six months, he lived two more years after the surgery. The Yated Ne'eman newspaper reported that Rabbi Svei eulogized Yitzchak with the following:

It is not so simple, even for a person who grew up with the *hashkofoh* (theological outlook) that one should toil over Torah study his whole life, to succeed in doing so; it is actually a tremendous feat! For a person [such as Yitzchak], however, who was raised according to another *hashkofoh*, one that postulates simultaneously concerning oneself with a material *tachlis* (goal) while building himself spiritually—to do so, and eventually to also become an eminent, respected inhabitant of Bnei Brak, he must possess Herculean *kochos hanefesh* (strength of character).

. . .We do not know what real emunah (faith) is, but the Steipler Rav surely did know, and he said that Reb Yitzchak had real emunah!

Photo courtesy of Zecharia Dor-Shav

Chapter Three
My Personal History

IN MY FIRST marriage, I married Netta Kohn and had three children: Nachum, Simcha Hillel, and Etan Yekutiel Yehudah. Their maternal grandparents, Rabbi Elisha and Rivka Kohn, had escaped with Netta from Vienna after the Anschluss Österreichs[1] with Hitler. They had saved the family Sepher Torah by carrying it to the local post office in a basket of laundry, under the eyes of the Nazis, and sending it off

---

1   The annexation of Austria into Nazi Germany on March 12, 1938.

to America. Rabbi Elisha was arrested during Kristallnacht.[2] Rivka had served as a secretary at the Second Zionist Congress in Basel, Switzerland, in 1898. Nachum is a professor of computer science and was a member of the team that developed

Left to right: Nachum, Etan, Simcha Hillel. Photo courtesy of Zecharia Dor Shav

the Bar-Ilan Responsa Project, the world's largest electronic collection of Torah literature of its kind.

---

2 *Kristallnacht*, also called the November Pogrom(s), was a pogrom against Jews carried out by SA paramilitary forces [the street thugs of the Nazi Movement, who later became the SS] and civilians throughout Nazi Germany on November 9–10, 1938. The name *Kristallnacht* (Crystal Night) comes from the shards of broken glass that littered the streets after the windows of Jewish-owned stores, buildings, and synagogues were smashed.

Jewish homes, hospitals, and schools were ransacked as the attackers demolished buildings with sledgehammers. The rioters destroyed 267 synagogues throughout Germany, Austria, and the Sudetenland. Over seven thousand Jewish businesses were damaged or destroyed, and thirty thousand Jewish men were arrested and incarcerated in concentration camps. The next day, the *Times* of London observed: "No foreign propagandist bent upon blackening Germany before the world could outdo the tale of burnings and beatings, of blackguardly assaults on defenseless and innocent people, which disgraced that country yesterday."

The pretext for the attacks was the assassination of the Nazi German diplomat Ernst von Rath by Herschel Grynszpan, a seventeen-year-old German-born Polish Jew living in Paris. Analysis of German scholarly sources [puts] the death toll at hundreds [including] deaths from post-arrest maltreatment and subsequent suicides. Wikipedia, somewhat edited.

Simcha Hillel is a school psychologist in Jerusalem, and Etan is a writer, artist, publicist, and political analyst. Nachum's son, Idan, holds the Chair of Hebrew Bible and Its Exegesis in Potsdam University, after having been a Harvard Fellow for three years.

The rescued Torah scroll was brought to Israel when we came on aliyah in 1969 and was eventually placed in El David, a settlement established after the terrorist murder of twenty-seven-year-old David Rosenfeld— the husband of Netta's cousin—of Tekoa, in the Herodian National Park on July 2, 1982.[3] The task of identifying his body, which had received no fewer than 102 stab wounds, fell upon me. I also said kaddish during the year of mourning, because his children were too young at that time. Unexpectedly and at his own initiative, Ashkenazic Chief Rabbi Shlomo Goren came to eulogize David at the funeral and stated, "Anyone who

---

3 Nokdim El David was established by Tekoa residents in the memory of David Rosenfeld and another terror victim named Eli Pressman. It was a tight-packed enclave of tents, outbuildings, and windowless mobile homes in which some twenty-five people and their army escort were encamped. Today, 135 families . . . make their homes in this integrated religious-secular community village. . . . The violent birth of El David betrays a darker current at the human heart of the settlements, and it reflects, in small, the quiet war that is daily waged to sustain them. (From: Tnuat Hityashvut Amana, The Birth of a Settlement, by James R. Gaines, November 15, 1982, in People.Com.)

is killed only for the fact that he is Jewish, is assured of an eternal place in the world to come."[4]

After thirty years of marriage, we had an amicable divorce. I was often photographed in the Old City of Jerusalem, where we lived, with Rabbi Elisha leaning on my arm, he in his nineties and me in my sixties. This continued even after I had divorced his daughter. Subsequently, I married Lee (Movsovitz) Rosenzweig. Her parents, Isadore and Helene Movsovitz, both born in Savannah, Georgia, hailed from families that were amongst the earliest settlers of Savannah and Memphis during the twentieth century.

They were very active in the Orthodox synagogue, Congregation Beth Jacob. Isadore served as president for a significant period of time and was responsible for bringing in Rabbi Avigdor Slatus, ordained at the Mirrer Yeshiva Central Institute in Brooklyn, who has had a major influence on the town during the past forty years. He promoted and established a kollel and an eruv chatzerote[5] in the town, as well as a yeshiva high school for girls.[6] Lee and her first husband, Ramon

---

4 See similar: (הרוגי מלכות, אין אדם יכול לעמוד במחיצתן (פסחים נ:א)). Those killed by a wicked regime only because they are Jewish, no one can achieve their status [in the World to Come]!

5 A symbolic enclosure to permit carrying in a courtyard, community, or town on the Sabbath.

6 See Victoria Dwek, *A Story of Savannah*, Ami-Living, July 17, 2019.

Rosenzweig, with some of their friends, had established the Savannah Hebrew Day School, which started with only ten students. In many ways I feel that what Lee and her friends did in Savannah is very similar to what my parents did in New York City.

Childhood

As told to me by my mother, I came into this world on Friday, Kislev 24, 5686, about an hour before the onset of both the Sabbath and Chanukah. I was born at home, and my mother was aided by my father's *Tanta* (Aunt) Molly Dershowitz (if I remember correctly), who was a midwife. My mother put some Sabbath sanctification wine on my lips that night and saw to it that I had such sanctification wine every Friday night thereafter, until I was old enough to take responsibility for myself.

As the youngest of eight—with a six-year gap between me and my next-older brother, Yitzchak—I was probably pampered. Each of my siblings contributed to my "allowance money." I know that during World War II while my brother Moish was serving in the army in Europe, I kept a record of how much allowance money he failed to give me as a result of his being overseas. When he came home from the war, he was duly presented with a bill. I don't remember specifically, but I assume that he paid up.

When I was not yet of school age, my mother kept me out of the way while she got the others out to school, by recommending that I remain in bed until they leave, and then she would join me to hug and wrestle a bit. Only then would she allow me to get out of bed. I have heard from more than one friend of the family that as a little child, I would ride my tricycle under the dining room table.

In my mother's opinion, I was skinny and under-nourished though pictures of me as a three-year-old don't support that description. The solution, there-fore, was "force feeding." My mother fed me, and if I complained that I was full and could eat no more, she disregarded my complaints. When I screamed and cried that I was "choking" from the food being forced down my throat, she just said, "Choke, chew, and eat!" I was also given distasteful cod liver oil (in orange juice) every day for a long period of time. On the other hand, I was often taken to the corner ice-cream shop where my mother and I would get ice-cream sodas—her favorite was always a glass of straw-berry soda with a scoop of vanilla ice cream. When I came home from the yeshiva for lunch, she would give me a nickel to buy a piece of "gooey" cake from the bakery on my way back to school.

Interestingly, a friend recently asked who was my favorite teacher in the yeshiva. My immediate and spontaneous response was, "My second-grade Hebrew teacher, Rabbi Chaim Goodman." Hearing this, she exclaimed, "He was my uncle! He always said that he wanted to teach an early grade in the yeshiva because

Photo courtesy of Diana Schiowitz

that is where a child's personality and attitude toward school is established." He certainly succeeded with me.

One of the things that often terrified me during my early childhood was "choking spells" that my mother would suffer. I don't know what caused the constriction in her throat, but every so often she would start wheezing and choking, and I could only stand by, cry, and watch—praying for the wheezing to stop.

My father suffered from high blood pressure, and when he got very angry (often in the family synagogue where he was "president"), I would see his face get blazing red, and I was sure that he would burst a blood vessel. I could only plead with him to stop, but it didn't help. Usually, the issue was who should be honored with maftir[7] or something else of equally "earth-shaking" importance. Long before I was bar mitzvah, I was given the opportunity to be called to the Torah for maftir and to recite the haftarah.[8] In our family synagogue, we followed the Hasidic custom of just reading the maftir softly without attention to the *trop* (cantillation notes). The synagogue was very child-friendly and a comfortable environment for me and my age-mate cousins (Meyer and Zechariah Fendel and Zecharia Mines). The synagogue was in the basement of the family home, and when it was not in use for prayer, my cousins, who lived in the upper floors, and I often went there to play hide-and-seek. I fondly remember Aunt Rosie's dish of cocoa and sugar that was always set out for us.

As I was growing up, my sister, Sheindy, who was twelve years older than I, was often in charge of me. When she was a college student, majoring in speech, she made great efforts not to let me talk "Brooklynese." It is because of her influence that my speech is more general American dialect than most of my Brooklyn-born

---

7 *maftir* (an honorific usually given to a distinguished member of the congregation)

8 *haftarah* (a reading from the Prophets—frequently bestowed upon a bar-mitzvah celebrant)

friends. She also took me to one of her classes when they needed a subject upon whom they could demonstrate how to administer an intelligence test to a child. When I answered one of the questions in a "cute" way, all of the students started to laugh, and I was embarrassed. The professor, of course, tried to comfort me, telling me not to be upset by their laughter because they were only enjoying my answer. I responded, "I know, all college students are stupid!" I guess I had frequently heard my father say that.[9]

The Anthropologist, Professor Margaret Mead

One of my favorite museums was the American Museum of Natural History. There was hardly a vacation period that I didn't spend at least one day visiting that museum. The exhibits of culture groups brought me to a recognition of the work of Margaret Mead,[10]

---

9   Not much different from the Glazer and Moynihan (*Beyond the Melting Pot*, 1963) description of the South Italian proverb "Do not make your child better than you," which inhibited Italian children from seeking higher education. My father certainly did not inhibit our higher education, he even encouraged it, but he may sometimes have made fun of it too.

10 Her contributions to science received special recognition when, at the age of seventy-two, she was elected to the presidency of the American Association for the Advancement of Science. In 1979 she was posthumously awarded the Presidential Medal of Freedom, the United States' highest civilian honor. Photo from Wikimedia Commons.

who had become world famous for her studies of the peoples of Oceania. She held numerous curator positions at the museum from 1926 until 1969. From 1969 to 1978, she served as curator emeritus.

My acquaintance with her work led to my requesting her to serve as a mentor for my doctoral dissertation, despite the fact that she was not connected with my university. To my great pleasure, she accepted and was a helpful guide during the process. Visiting her office in the tower of the museum was always a special pleasure because, as I walked through the halls on the way to her office, I had an opportunity to see some of the stored artifacts that were not on display in the museum.

My main mentor was Professor Herman Witkin of Brooklyn College, who had designed the tilting-room tilting-chair test to determine global versus non-global perception (or cognition). The instrument was created and designed to test prospective naval pilots.[11] I used it

---

11 See Herman Witkin et al., *Psychological Differentiation*, John Wiley and Sons, New York: 1962.

to study the cognitive style of White Anglo-Saxon Protestants (WASPs) studying in a church school, and compare them with Jewish children in Hebrew Day Schools and regular public schools.

Among the additional test measures that I used was the Kohs Block Design Test of the WAIS.[12] Margaret Mead would always surprise her first-year students by administering this test to them and then asking who had finished the tasks in a relatively short amount of time and who took longer. Those who finished quickly would proudly announce the speed with which

they had solved them, and Professor Mead would respond, "You will never make good anthropologists!"

---

12 The test has been adapted for use in several IQ tests. Consistent with the original design of the test, it continues to be used extensively in research to measure executive functioning and learning. It is useful for assessing the effects of aging, drug use, and brain research, among others. In particular, the Kohs, as a relatively nonverbal test, has been used effectively in the assessment of language issues in multicultural research settings, thus reducing the impact of native tongue on the assessment of functioning. The test task is the speed in using blocks with different configurations on each side, to form a design, as pictured.

This surprising rejoinder was because experience had taught her that an anthropologist must first see the general pattern of behavior of a culture group, and only afterward dissect its details. One who saw the details too quickly never got to understand the overall pattern well. In my study, it was the WASPs who solved the problem significantly faster than the Jewish youngsters— especially the yeshiva students. Using Professor Witkin's criteria, we called the Jewish children more field-dependent. This suggested that the Jewish style of cognition was more global, i.e., they saw things in a more global context than did White Anglo-Saxon Protestant children.

As a result of this study, which was found to be equally true of Jewish children in Israel, Professor Yaakov Frankel of the Psychology Department of Bar-Ilan University and I demonstrated that the norms that had been in general use for Israeli children on the Wechsler Intelligence Scale for children (WISC) needed a correction of several standard deviations. Otherwise, very many Jewish children would be incorrectly designated as below world average in intelligence.[13]

---

13 Dershowitz, Zecharia, and Yaakov Frankel, "Jewish Culture and WISC and WAIS Test Patterns," *Journal of Consulting and Clinical Psychology* 43, 1975, 126–134.

Upon completion of the dissertation, I invited my mentors to my home for dinner. Picking up Margaret Mead in her Greenwich Village apartment to bring her to Borough Park, I drove through the Ultra-Orthodox Williamsburg neighborhood. There, seeing many adult males walking hand in hand, she remarked that such behavior was not uncommon in male-dominated cultures. In my childhood, my teacher, Rabbi Yoel Fink—who often walked the Williamsburg Bridge on a Sabbath afternoon—would take my hand and walk with me, hand in hand. Hasidic teachers often hold their students' hand when strolling, as does a chavrutah.[14]

Books were very important to her. When entering my home, she saw a book that belonged to my baby son lying on the floor. She picked it up, put it on a table, and said, "Books should be treated with respect."

My friend and neighbor, Rivka Malek, having heard that Margaret Mead was going to be our dinner guest, asked if she could play housemaid so that she could meet and hear our dinner table discussion. We gave her an apron, and there we had a maid.

When Professor Mead saw how we ritually washed our hands before eating, she followed suit and washed

---

14 *chavrutah* (a primary learning method of Talmudic study in which a small group of students—usually 2-5—analyze, discuss, and debate a shared text)

her hands in the same manner as we did. She remarked that she knew how to observe and copy local customs when they were different from her own. Professor Witkin, on the other hand, she observed, was not so successful, though he was born to an Orthodox Jewish ritual slaughterer.

After settling in Israel, I suggested inviting her to my university, to which she replied that she would be glad to come. She died, however, before this could happen. She had told me that her daughter, Mary Catherine Bateson, had lived in Israel for a year at the age of sixteen—after she had come with her mother on a visit and decided to stay for the year. She learned Hebrew well enough to enter a regular high school. Subsequently, Catherine wrote that she "fell in love with the language and with the notion that when you move into a different language you are moving into a different way of thinking, acquiring a whole new world along with a new language."

In this context, it is interesting to read (in free translation) what Rabbi Professor Samuel Mirsky of Yeshiva University wrote about Mary Bateson in the introduction to one of his books:[15]

---

15 Samuel K. Mirsky, *Culture and Civilization of Contemporary Israel*, Sura Institute, Yeshiva University, NYC: 1961. (Hebrew)

The author . . . participated in a conference sponsored by the United States Government . . . in 1961, in Georgetown University in Washington. All of the investigations and discussions were about the identity of nations and their languages, and on the need to give teachers of foreign languages a taste of the feel and experience of the nation whose language they are teaching . . . because in truth . . . one cannot separate the essence and inner reality of a speaker and his language. All who wish to understand the latter must know the former.

Professor Margaret Mead lectured at the conference on the topic, "Culture in the Teaching of a Foreign language from an Anthropological View." She said, "One should never teach a pupil, 'this is called a glass' and in another language, for example, Hebrew, it is called 'kos.' Rather, one should say, 'this is a glass and Israelis call it kos . . .'"

At the end of the lecture, she introduced her daughter Catherine . . . as a living example of one who has mastered several languages as one. [Catherine] then related an instance that she had experienced personally. Her mother and she visited Israel. Her mother was in Tel

Aviv, while she was in Haifa . . . [she remarked that] she didn't recognize Psalm 23 (The Lord is my Shephard), which she had heard many times in the church and knew by heart, when she heard it for the first time, in its native tongue, when spoken by an Israeli.

I reminded the Conference Chairman . . . that Professor Zvi Sharfstein had written many years ago about bilingualism as taught from childhood in the Hebrew Day schools in America, that it doesn't hinder but rather helps educate . . . and then he [the Conference Chairman] pointed to my son [David] then a child . . . and said, "Here is a living example [of that principle]"

In fact, that son [Professor David Mirsky] together with Yeshiva College dean, Professor Isaac Bacon convinced the [United States] government to sponsor a summer workshop for high school teachers of Hebrew, in Israel . . . for whom I was invited to give a series of lectures [which is the substance of this book].[16]

---

16 A curious confluence of people. Samuel Mirsky, then rabbi of the Young Israel of Borough Park, became the husband of my first wife's aunt; Isaac Bacon was one of the people my father brought to America in 1939; and Margaret Mead was an advisor to my doctoral dissertation.

Transferring to Mesivta Yeshiva Rabbeinu Chaim Berlin

When I completed Torah Vodaath High School in 1942, I decided to leave formal yeshiva education and advance my dream of a career as a doctor. Not wanting to leave Torah studies completely, I registered for a special night class offered for students like me. The teacher was Rabbi Yaakov Moshe Shurkin, an outstanding former student of the Chofetz Chaim, Rabbi Yisrael Meir HaCohen of Radin, with whom Rabbi Shurkin had studied for sixteen years. In the morning he served as a rosh yeshiva at Yeshiva Chaim Berlin, and at night, he taught this class in Torah Vodaath. My intention was to continue with the Rav within this informal framework for as long as I could. My brother Yitzchak, to help alleviate the family's financial difficulties, had also decided to leave the yeshiva so as to be able to work and help support the family. At night he, too, joined the class, as mentioned earlier.

Rabbi Yaakov Moshe Shurkin

After just a few weeks in the Rav's night class, he asked me why I had dropped out of the regular mesivta program. I explained that I wanted to study to become a physician. He felt that if it was feasible for me to return to a more formal yeshiva framework without interfering with the premed program I was pursuing, I could be enticed. To my everlasting gratitude, he recommended that I meet with the rosh yeshiva of Chaim Berlin, Rabbi Yitzchak Hutner.[17] This satisfied me greatly, and I followed his advice.

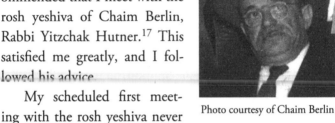

Photo courtesy of Chaim Berlin

My scheduled first meeting with the rosh yeshiva never took place. While sitting anxiously in his waiting room, Rabbi Shurkin spotted me and intervened, to spare me the possible discomfort of a "first encounter." He approached the rosh yeshiva on my behalf, came out of his office, took me by the hand, and led me to his classroom, saying that I am now a student in his class. The rosh yeshiva had accepted the fact that I would attend Rabbi Shurkin's class for morning session only and, in addition, would be permitted to miss one day completely—the day I had to attend a morning lab in college. The other days of the week, I would leave during the lunch break, just in time to catch a 2 p.m. class

---

17 In 1940, after receiving permission from Rabbi Shurkin, who was then rosh yeshiva, he began to give a class in the fourth-year post-high school program of the yeshiva. Over the years he built up the senior division and became its senior rosh yeshiva.

at the college. My brother Yitzchak also left the night class at that time.

Rabbi Shurkin was known for his very careful analysis of the Talmudic text and its interpretative commentaries. He was also known for his pithy remarks, such as his comment on the frequently used Yiddish phrase "*De velt zogt*" (the World says). He would stress that this referred to "the Torah World and not the Pitkin Avenue[18] World!" The first time I asked a question in his class that he felt was of high quality, he exclaimed, "This is why I wanted you here!"

He also said that he would never go to hear a *shiur* by Rabbi Chaim Heller, then in the Rabbi Isaac Elchanan Theological Seminary of Yeshiva University, because he might understand the questions he raised, but not the answers. Rabbi Heller was world-renowned for his contrary interpretation of verses of scripture often cited by Christian theologians in their missionary efforts. He had opened, in 1922, the Beit Midrash Elyon in Berlin, which my Rebbi and several other eventual world-famous Torah scholars attended while simultaneously studying in a university.

It was during those early years in Chaim Berlin that I became the first paid worker for the National

---

18 The street corner on which Chaim Berlin was located.

Committee for the Furtherance of Jewish Education, which had been founded in 1940 by Rabbi Yosef Yitzchak Schneersohn, the sixth Rebbe of Chabad-Lubavitch. The organization was run by Rabbi Jacob J. ("J.J.") Hecht, who organized volunteer yeshiva students to teach Jewish thought and practices to public school children within the New York City Public School System's Released Time program.[19] I was in charge of organizing volunteers from among the *beit midrash*[20] students and distributing and explaining materials that had been prepared for them by Rabbi Hecht.

Eight Years with the Baal Pachad Yitzchak

The teaching styles of my two teachers at Mesivta Rabbeinu Chaim Berlin were quite different. In contrast with Rabbi Shurkin's style, Rabbi Hutner (whom I now began to refer to as my Rebbi, or as the rosh yeshiva) gave a broader analysis. It is interesting to note that these two approaches to a Talmudic or halakhic problem were identified by Rabbi Avraham HaCohen Kook as the difference between the approach of the

---

19 A student may be released for not more than one hour a week, while school is in session, for religious education, upon a request in writing signed by the student's parents. Such religious instruction must be given off of the school grounds and be operated under the control of a duly constituted religious body.

20 *beit midrash* (senior study hall)

kohanim (priests) and that of the *dayanim* (judges).[21]

My Rebbi, the Rosh Yeshiva Rabbi Yitzchak Hutner. Photo courtesy of Chaim Berlin

He was born in Warsaw in 1906 to a family with Gerrer Hasidic ties as also with non-Hasidic Lithuanian influences. Like several other *gedolim*[22] of his generation, he had been influenced greatly by Rabbi Nosson Tzvi Finkel, the Alter (Elder) of Slabodka, a second-generation proponent of the powerful musar movement of Rabbi Yisrael Salanter, which combined musar with the scholarship of Volozhin, Belarus. The musar movement sought to help a person "find" his inner strengths. As Rabbi Salanter put it in his famous Ethical Letter, "Man is free in his imagination and bound by his intellect"—meaning that his sensory desires tempt him, but it is within the power of his mind to conquer them. He established study houses that he called "Houses of Musar," in which yeshiva students would come for a short time each day to study ethical *hashkafa* (world-view/philosophy). His advice to the student

---

21 Introduction to עין איה על אגדות חז"ל שבעין יעקב, כרך ראשון ברכות, Rabbi Tzvi Yehudah Institute, Jerusalem, 5755. (Hebrew)
22 *gedolim* (great Torah scholars)

was, "Whoever has no time [for studies of the ethics] should study them for a few minutes regularly, and he will see that he has time."[23] His goal was that every Jew must comply strictly with the ethical laws of the Choshen Mishpat (Code of Law on business dealings) in order to uphold justice and prevent injustice, no less stringently than he follows the laws pertaining to prayer and festivals. My Rebbi was a member of the group that frequented the Musar House of Slabodka.[24]

A young prodigy, he became known throughout Russia and Poland as the *Illui* (budding genius) of Warsaw. In 1925 he came to Eretz Yisrael and joined the newly formed Slabodka Yeshiva in Hebron. He remained there until the 1929 riots. It was during this period that he developed a relationship with the chief rabbi, Rabbi Avraham Kook, and his family, as he was related to the wife of Rabbi Tzvi Yehuda, Rabbi Avraham Kook's son. Narrowly escaping the 1929 massacre (he was away for that Sabbath), he returned to Europe and spent a period of time in Berlin, where he could study Torah simultaneously with university studies. There, he came under the influence of Rabbi

---

23 The Musar Movement in the Lithuanian World of Torah—the Teachings of Rabbi Yisrael Salanter zt"l, www.schechter.edu, Dec 16, 2018.
24 Sometimes spelled Slobodka.

Chaim Heller (of Bialystok and Lomz), who had advanced so rapidly in his Torah studies that from age ten, he no longer needed a teacher or rosh yeshiva at all, as he studied by himself. In 1917, he published a critical edition of the Sefer Hamitzvot of the Rambam and became the unlikely leader of numerous future intellectual giants. As mentioned above, Rabbi Heller had moved to Berlin and opened his Beit Midrash Elyon. He was there for less than a decade, but during that short span of time he had a great influence on several young modern Torah scholars of Eastern Europe who later in their careers became Torah giants. His combination of Slabodka-style learning and modern critical scholarship commanded their respect and impelled them to explore new avenues of Torah study that were less conservative than those modeled by their earlier mentors.

Among his prominent students were Rabbi Joseph B. Soloveitchik, Rabbi Menachem Mendel Schneersohn—the future Lubavitcher Rebbe—and my Rebbi.[25] The three maintained close personal relations throughout their lives, though they differed radically in their Torah hashkafa. Nevertheless, each fashioned a

---

25 See: Goldberg, H. (1986), "Between Berlin and Slobodka: The Life and Writings of Yosef Zev Lipovitz," *Tradition: A Journal of Orthodox Jewish Thought* 22(2): 47–66. Retrieved from 23259513.

unique synthesis between the Eastern European world-view and a Western way of thinking. This enabled them to serve successfully as unique spiritual leaders after each had immigrated to the United States.[26] Rabbi Heller was later invited to join the faculty of the Rabbi Isaac Elchanan Theological Seminary and lectured for a number of years on all facets of Torah knowledge.

While Rabbi Soloveitchik and Rabbi Schneersohn each completed a university degree, my Rebbi dropped out before completing any degree. Nonetheless, evidence of his combination of Torah and secular knowledge can perhaps be exemplified by a few expressions he used in an interview with Professor William Helmreich.[27] During the course of the interview, my Rebbi quoted from Winston Churchill and Chaim Nachman Bialik and said such things as "sex used to be romantic" and "we had to know languages." Evidence of his synthesizing Torah values and the secular history of the times is apparent from his discourse on the way he felt the Holocaust should be viewed:

---

26 Wikipedia: Rabbi Yitzchak Hutner.

27 Interviews conducted by Professor Helmreich with various rashei yeshiva in conjunction with his publication of *The World of the Yeshiva: An Intimate Portrait of Orthodox Jewry.* Collier Macmillan, New York City: 1982.

It should be needless to say at this point that since the churban [destruction] of European Jewry was a tochacha[28] phenomenon, an enactment of the admonishment and rebuke which Klal Yisroel [the Congregation of Israel] carries upon its shoulders as an integral part of being the Am Hanivchar—God's chosen ones—we have no right to interpret these events as any kind of specific punishment for specific sins. The tochacha is a built-in aspect of the character of Klal Yisroel until Moshiach [the Messiah] comes and is visited upon Klal Yisroel at the Creator's will and for reasons known and comprehensible only to Him. One would have to be a prophet or a Talmudic sage, to claim knowledge[29] of the specific reasons for what befell us and tramples in vain upon the bodies of the kedoshim who died [for the sanctity of God's name], and misuses the power to interpret and understand Jewish history.[30]

---

28 Lit. admonition. The sections in Chapter 26 of Leviticus and 28 of Deuteronomy, which highlight the consequences of a failure by the People of Israel to follow God's laws and keep His commandments.

29 This doesn't free other intellectuals, of course, from productive discourse in an attempt to gain understanding.

30 A translation by Chaim Feuerman and Yaakov Feitman, " 'Holocaust'—A Study of the Term, and the Epoch It Is Meant to Describe, from a discourse by Rabbi Yitzchok Hutner," *Jewish Observer.* Agudath Israel of America New York, pp. 3–9.

The rosh yeshiva was an educator par excellence. For many of us, he succeeded in modifying our entire understanding of the holidays, especially Chanukah, and created a totally novel perspective and appreciation of them. Furthermore, he gave very many of us the feeling that we were, individually, very special *talmidim*[31] to him. How he did this with hundreds of students was, I believe, dependent upon many things, but mostly on the fact that he fostered two main conditions identified by our Sages as crucial to the development of one's maximum potential: creative thought and shimush (being attendant upon the rabbi).

Chaim Berlin attracted students of many levels and strains of religious fulfillment. There were students who were of Hasidic background and those of Mitnaged (intellectual opponents of the Hasidic movement) background. There were Bnei Akiva devotees and there were Agudath Israel devotees. Many of my study partners took prominent positions in Jewish life after they left. I remember the group of members of the Bnei Akiva (at that time, Shomer HaDati) youth movement who gave a Torah scroll as a gift to one of their number as a wedding present—and were persuaded by the rosh yeshiva that having such

---

31 *talmidim* (students)

a holy object in the home required special holiness in the home and that it would be better not to store it there. There were students who opened yeshivas for newly observant students and others who opened their schools to Russian and Persian immigrants. There was Rabbi Yaakov Perlow, who in 1998 was appointed president of the Agudath Israel of America, where he led its Moetzes Gedolei HaTorah (Council of Torah Giants). The family of his grandmother were founders of the Agudath Israel in Poland. The day before he died as a result of the COVID-19 plague one week before Passover, he penned a magnificent letter, as head of the Moetzes, stressing the need to follow the health rules of the medical experts:

It is obvious that every person is obligated to obey the instructions of the government and medical professionals. Jewish families must be exceedingly careful not to err in issues which could endanger people, Heaven forbid.

May the Holy One, Blessed be He, compassionately bestow upon us support, kindness, and mercy; may He end our distress and deliver us and all of the Jewish people from this plague, and may He listen with favor to the song of Hallel and the telling of the Haggadah, and accept our mitzvos with love; and may we merit to celebrate Pesach in Yerushalaim, where we will be able to thank Hashem for our redemption of body and soul. Amen!

The rosh yeshiva put great effort into our achieving maximum development. In 1942, to maximize opportunities for creative thought, he purchased the very large and well-known book collection of Professor Nathan Isaacs of Harvard. His discourses on the holiday of Shavuot stressed the difference between תלמדו (study) and עמלות (toil) in Torah. To release the creative power of our Torah study, we were made to understand that we must strive to duplicate the conditions of the original assemblage at Sinai. Our study, we were taught, should be under an aura of אימה ויראה רתת וזיע (lofty, quaking, terrifying, and turbulent—see *B'rakhot* 22a). The eight years that I spent with this goal in mind had a tremendous effect upon my personal development.

He was not satisfied with the usual teacher-student relationship and wanted his talmidim to truly experience attending upon the master,[32] but didn't

---

32 *B'rachot* 7b.

push it. We were inspired by the teachings of the midrash on Kings I 19, 21. The verse does not say that the Prophet Eliyahu "taught" Elisha, but rather that Elisha "attended" upon Eliyahu,[33] teaching us that being attendant upon the master is greater than studying with him.[34] He dealt with each student as was appropriate for him but never discouraged such attendance when a *talmid* showed a serious intent of offering it. To those of us seeking this meaningful personal relationship, he offered guidance in the matter, and even taught it directly. I don't think that intellectual prowess played a role in who received this guidance, but only a sincere desire on the part of the talmid to establish this cherished Rebbi-talmid relationship.

Of course, there were those of us not seeking this relationship. He didn't force himself upon us, but he was keen in recognizing behavior attesting to such a desire where it did exist. Some students sought the great fountain of knowledge and brilliance of the rosh yeshiva. Others were seeking, additionally, the unique lessons in Jewish thought that he offered. A smaller group, but numbering many hundreds over the course of years, sought to find in the rosh yeshiva a

---

33 ''וילמדהו' לא נאמר, אלא ''וישרתהו'', מכאן אמרו: גדולה שמושה של תורה יותר מלמודה.
34 *Yalkut Shimoni*, Kings II 224.

Rebbe—similar, but much different, from the Hasidic Rebbe who would often accommodate a negation of the Hasid's own personality, judgment, or way of thinking in favor of the Rebbe. The rosh yeshiva quickly notified those of us who showed such a Hasidic tendency that they wouldn't get support from him for that type of behavior.

All day long, he was available to the students. We would knock at the door of his impressive office, receive permission to enter, and be invited, generally, to sit opposite him at his large desk. Such informal contact in his "inner sanctum" was penetrating and stimulating. It encouraged a much broader prospect of what we were supposed to be getting from our Master, i.e., an all-encompassing worldview. As one who sought to be myself and yet live the experience of a *talmid muvhak* (a disciple of a primary master)—if that is possible today—I offer some personal experiences.

After many meetings in his office, it happened once that after concluding the matter for which I had entered, I turned to leave. He advised me that when one exits his Rebbi's room, it is appropriate not to turn his back on the Rebbi. This suggestion was surprising to me, but it helped me develop a relationship that became so much deeper and more meaningful. When I had advanced to being among the יוצקי מים על ידיו (those who pour water upon his hands; see Kings II 3:11) before the meal, he explained his acceptance of such attendance by quoting the Sages: One who denies his talmid the opportunity of being attendant upon him, is as one who withholds kindness from him (כל המונע תלמידו מלשמשו כאילו מונע ממנו חסד).[35]

Another talmid describes how the rosh yeshiva brought him into this Rebbi-talmid relationship. As a new student in the beit midrash, he was "dying" for the rosh yeshiva to talk to him, to acknowledge his presence. Eventually, he was invited by the rosh yeshiva to step into his office. Here is how he described this first visit:

> I came into the rosh yeshiva's office and he signaled me to sit down. I sat for a while and the rosh yeshiva said nothing. After a long wait, he asked me to please push his desk a bit forward. I did, and again he said nothing. After a while, he asked me to pull his desk back to its original position. I did this too, mystified, but compliant. The rosh yeshiva still said nothing. Then he asked me to open the window a bit, eventually asking me to shut it again—still saying

---

35 *Ktuvot* 96a.

nothing else. Finally, he said, "Shalom" and signaled that I may leave.

Totally confused, I left, and my friends rushed to ask me what the rosh yeshiva had said during this long-awaited visit. I related the confusing story and was told, "Don't you understand? He was making you his talmid by asking you to attend him!" In fact, a few minutes later, the rosh yeshiva entered the beit midrash, approached me, held me around the shoulders and asked how I was getting along in the beit midrash!

After only a half year, I decided to drop out of the premed course I was taking and continue my college studies only during the evening hours. A few weeks into this new arrangement, the rosh yeshiva invited me into his office and suggested that he thought I should transfer out of daytime college courses so that I could be in the beit midrash until the evening hours. Of course, he knew that I had already done so; this was his way of signaling his approval for what I had done. He was most skilled at showing approval. At a later point in my studies, a few weeks after I had decided to take a complete break from college and devote my whole day to Torah studies, he called me into his office and said that he thought it was time for me to devote myself completely to learning. Of course, this too was said only to show approval for what I had already done.

Now, as a full-time beit midrash student, I had the option of moving into the dormitory though I lived only a few minutes' ride from Chaim Berlin. I did so, as it permitted me to remain long hours at the study table. More than that, it led to my being asked to assume the position of dormitory supervisor, with responsibility for the well-being of the students over the course of years. This responsibility included dealing with youngsters who were ill and needed hospitalization, those contentious with their parents about remaining in the yeshiva, and even some who were on the verge of emotional exhaustion. I brought all of these problems to the attention of the rosh yeshiva personally. On the several occasions when the rosh yeshiva called me at home, he always introduced himself by saying, "This is Hutner" or "Hutner speaking." The rosh yeshiva never used a title, just his name.

Some of the dormitory students were still in high school and quite young, with their families far away from New York. For those not used to being on their own, this could be quite a difficult experience. One such boy went through a very serious emotional crisis and almost had a nervous breakdown. The rosh yeshiva sent him back home.

Several years after my stint as dormitory supervisor, one of the students tragically fell to his death from a fifth-floor window, apparently deliberately. I was greatly troubled and went to consult the rosh yeshiva. He told me that in the yeshiva world it was not very unusual to find some troubled youngsters who couldn't stand up to the pressure of the intense study and the religious atmosphere where students are constantly challenging themselves, and being challenged by their friends, to strive for maximum excellence in their studies and moral behavior and not to waste a single minute of what could be used for Torah study. It was important, therefore, to deal with these youngsters cautiously and sensitively. For most students, however, the pressure was not excessive, as those of us who performed successfully in that environment can readily testify. It was in fact an extremely satisfying and meaningful experience for me.

In another incident, an older student was having difficulty keeping up with the regulatory rules, such as arriving on time for tfillot, shiurim, and the like. He was asked by the rosh yeshiva to leave the school. He and another student had come from a specific out-of-town community upon the urging and encouragement of the local rabbi. When that rabbi heard of the rosh yeshiva's decision about his student, he immediately wrote to him that "If to the yeshiva he is just one student of many, for his hometown, he is one of only two students who ever came to New York to learn in a yeshiva." He requested that the rosh yeshiva change his mind and keep the student. The rosh yeshiva responded positively and eventually asked that local rabbi—Rabbi Avigdor Miller—to accept the position of mashgiach ruchani,[36] with this letter to the rosh yeshiva being one of the reasons for the offer.

Once, one of the students showed serious emotional stress toward the eve of the Sabbath. I felt that there was a real possibility that he would have to be hospitalized, perhaps even that Sabbath. I didn't feel qualified to make the decision myself regarding possible Sabbath desecration, and so I prearranged that if the question arose, I would call the rosh yeshiva on the Sabbath so that he would make the decision. When I did, in fact, make the call, he had his daughter, Bruria, who was not yet twelve, answer the phone for him.[37]

---

36 *mashgiach ruchani* (a spiritual supervisor or guide)
37 Frankly, I was distressed that while I had been compelled to desecrate the Sabbath he avoided it. Nonetheless, he acted correctly as we can see (שלחן ערוך, או"ח, סימן שכ"ח י"ב) because for me there was no alternative, but for him, his underage daughter could just as well answer the phone without causing any delay in helping the ill student.

Eventually, I reached the point where I was asked to escort the rosh yeshiva to a wedding of one of the talmidim, and to continue as his escort for a year's time. This provided an invaluable opportunity to benefit from שיחת חולין של תלמידי חכמים (informal conversation with a Torah scholar), which also provides a Torah study opportunity.[38] At the end of the year, another talmid was offered this privilege. Each year another student was approved for this opportunity to develop a closer relationship with him.

A special part of the curriculum was the musar *shmus*,[39] on what the rosh yeshiva called "Laws of Torah Thought and Obligations of the Heart." He delivered these one-hour lectures in his office at regular intervals. They constitute the core of his unique teachings.

The atmosphere of the shmus was electrifying. We crowded round the room and listened intensely, trying to catch the nuances, of which there were many. Sometimes there were long pauses, with everyone swaying softly waiting for the rosh yeshiva to continue. When a friend asked once what we were supposed to be doing while he paused, he replied, quoting *Shir Hashirim* 4, 11: דבש וחלב תחת לשונך. As expounded by the Rabbis

---

38 *Avodah Zarah* 19b.
39 *shmus* (talk: colloquially used to denote a moralistic presentation and discussion)

דברים המתוקין מדבש וחלב יהו תחת לשונך :(Chagigah 13a)
(things that are sweeter than honey and milk should be
under your tongue, i.e., unspoken). We were to understand that during his pauses he was thinking things that
are not to be spoken aloud. As he put it: "There is more
to be learned from the Rebbi's pauses than from his
spoken word"—but these were things that only those
of us who had sufficient background information and
insight into the Rebbi's thinking would have been able
to infer from the unspoken. This reflects, of course, the
fact that the rosh yeshiva was living and experiencing
the Torah content that he was presently teaching, and
not just presenting what he had prepared in advance.
Most of us felt the message during these presentations,
and I assume that this was the reason that the original pamphlets were published with a footer on every
page that read, "Confidential, intended for those who
heard it [the lecture] live." His Pachad Yitzchak series
of books is based on these discourses on the holidays.
The books are studied diligently today in almost all the
yeshiva world. For me, personally, his discourses on
Chanukah, more than of any other holiday, changed
my perspective on the holiday.

The need to apply the lesson with personal refer-
ence was reflected by the fact that he generally ended
the *shmus* without a concrete conclusion that could be

easily translated into a guide for behavior. Each student individually, he felt, had to interpret it practically, with behavior that he understood from the *shmus* to be pertinent to the spiritual level at which he was currently standing. This level, of course, was different for each student, and different within the same student at different times. The study of Torah is dynamic. He taught that all newly acquired knowledge must be integrated, synthesized, and modified to be coherent with the new insights.

When I joined Chaim Berlin, the musar *shmus* was given in the rosh yeshiva's office. The office room was too small to accommodate all the talmidim, and so it was strictly by invitation. After a few months, I had not yet been invited to this inner sanctum and was extremely jealous of those who were. I finally called forth the required courage and confronted the rosh yeshiva as to why I had not been invited. He laughed and responded that he was anxiously awaiting this moment. "Of course, you are invited. I just wanted you to ask," he said. He knew how to motivate and lead us to appreciate the privilege of studying musar with him!

He rarely told me not to do something that I had planned to do, even if he disapproved of my choice. Many years after I left, settled in Israel, and took a position at a professed religious university, he hinted to me that he thought I should have preferred a position at a secular university. My appointment, he felt, might have been seen as a kashruth certificate for the institution. Eventually, when he did tell me his opinion, it was only after I had gleaned it from the hint and asked him directly if that was what he was suggesting.

In addition to the musar *shmus*, we were accustomed to having a daily musar seder of fifteen minutes. It was a time for emotional arousal. We were taught by example. Sitting near the rosh yeshiva's study table, one could hear him chanting over and over מה תקוות הנברא אם לא ישים עמל נפשו ועיקר עסקו בדברים שנברא בעבורם, "What hope is there for a creature if he doesn't set the toil of his soul and his prime activity with those things for which he was created" (*Shaarei T'shuvah* 3,17).

Eventually, my Rebbi added *Rosh Chodesh*[40] to his repertoire of learning opportunities. He invited a very small group of us to his home on the eve of each *Rosh Chodesh*. There, we shared a light meal and were free to ask whatever we liked. The atmosphere was relaxed yet intellectually charged.

---

40 *Rosh Chodesh* (first day of every Hebrew month)

On one occasion, after the yeshiva's all-night Shavuot study session, I chose to look after and accompany the rosh yeshiva on his way home. He was relaxed and we were alone when some automobile passed by. He noted, "I can't think of any transgression that the driver is committing except that he is producing electric sparks, which would be considered *nolad* (a creative act that is not permitted by the Rabbis even on Yom Tov), but it does not appear to be a transgression of a Torah injunction." The far-reaching implication of that statement is that under certain specified conditions, the Rabbis suspend such injunctions, such as in times of non-life-threatening illness, or in the course of performing a mitzvah for the community rather than for an individual.

The personal relationship that he had fostered made it possible to question him sharply if one didn't understand why he had acted in a certain way. During the years of World War II, there were many emergency communal demands presented to the school and its talmidim. The rosh yeshiva was steadfast and refused all requests that required taking us out of the beit midrash. As he stated it: "Unless it involves *chilul* Hashem [desecration of Hashem's, i.e., God's, name] [ZD's aside], don't involve yeshiva students." From his point of view, hardly anything should be allowed to interfere with the students' learning schedule.

On one occasion, many years after I had left, a protest poster was published with the names of many yeshiva heads objecting to something then going on in Israel. His name appeared among others. I thought that the matter at stake didn't involve *chilul Hashem* and was surprised that he had endorsed this public opinion. I called to ask why he had allowed his name to be published on the poster. He rejoined, "Isn't that poster signed by Rabbi so and so, and by rosh yeshiva so and so?" I said, "Yes, but why is your name there? To me, it doesn't seem to involve *chilul Hashem.*"

To my great satisfaction, the rosh yeshiva responded positively, and without consideration for obligations that he may have felt toward the other signees of the protest, he courageously had his name removed. Subsequent posters on the issue appeared without his name.

Once, when his daughter Bruria was a young child and attended a Chabad kindergarten, the rosh yeshiva told me that she had recounted something that the teacher had said. Upon hearing this, the rosh yeshiva said that the teacher had erred in this matter. Bruria, as any child would likely do, went back to the kindergarten and told the teacher that her father said she was wrong. The teacher was surprised and called the rosh yeshiva, justifying what she had said. The rosh yeshiva accepted the teacher's statement as correct and told her that he would never again question anything she taught in the kindergarten.

More unusual was an experience at one of his weekly *shiurim*. As usual, the *shiur* was stimulating and included innovative thought. It was probably impolite of me but, following the *Chazal's* advice ולא הביישן למד (And the shy one does not learn—*Avot* 2, 5), I often allowed myself to ask questions during the *shiur* in front of the whole beit midrash. On this occasion, when I questioned his conclusion, he thought for a moment, closed his Gemara, and left the beit midrash. I was mortified! A while later, I went to his office to apologize. He invited me to sit down and asserted, "You think the main benefit comes from listening to my *shiur*? It comes from your disproving it!" Thus, he allowed me to feel free to question anything he said or did.

He allowed himself, occasionally and in private, to speak sharply to his talmidim. I remember an occasion in his office when an opinion I had voiced stirred him to shout, "Zecharia is a *plut* (an idiot)!" I walked out of the office duly chastised. A friend who happened by heard the shout. Unable to imagine that the rosh yeshiva would say something like that about me behind my back, he was relieved to see me walk out of the office in person. He realized that the rosh yeshiva had chastised me, but only to my face. The rosh yeshiva was objecting to something praiseworthy I had said about a Lubavitcher publication. Though he had a close personal relationship with the Lubavitcher Rebbe, he felt that his educational goals for us were incongruous with those of the Lubavitcher movement, and he discouraged our leanings toward them. On one occasion, I understand, he even told one of the talmidim that he would have to choose between the two approaches because they were incompatible.

Camp Morris

During my early years at Chaim Berlin it was becoming the style for yeshivas to establish summer retreats in the pastoral setting of the Catskill Mountains in upstate New York. Our institution established Camp Morris in 1946 on Kiamesha Lake. Together with the campers, a large group of the beit midrash students were invited to spend several weeks there with the rosh yeshiva and his family. It was both an unsurpassed learning experience and an idyllic setting for us city dwellers, enabling us to maintain our growth in Torah as well as vacationing. For the first two years of the camp, the talmidim of Lakewood Yeshiva were also invited. Having both a Red Cross certificate as a Junior Lifeguard and one as a Swimming Instructor, I was assigned to be one of the life guards at the swimming pool. Among my trainees were the current rosh yeshiva of Chaim Berlin, Rabbi Aharon Schechter (see picture), and also Rabbi Shneur Kotler, who succeeded his father as head of Lakewood Yeshiva.

Photo courtesy of Zecharia Dor-Shav

We would spend the evening hours on the porch of the rosh yeshiva's apartment, sitting at his feet, listening to his discourses. Spending the summer in such close proximity to him had a tremendous impact on all of us. It also expressed itself at our camp Sabbath table, especially the *shalosh seudoth*[41] meal, when we would sing together in the growing darkness and listen to his words of Torah until much past the onset of night and the end of the Sabbath.

---

41 *shalosh seudoth* (third and last meal of the Sabbath)

Before the camp was established, the rosh yeshiva was accustomed to vacation at his summer apartment at Rockaway Beach. There, too, we could visit him privately. On late Sabbath afternoons, I often sat and visited with him on his porch. No subject was taboo, and this helped me establish my outlook on life.

The Hijacking of the Rosh Yeshiva's Flight

After Jordan lost control of the West Bank in 1967, Palestinian terrorists moved their bases into Jordan and stepped up their attacks on Israel and its West Bank. One Israeli retaliation on a Palestine Liberation Organization (PLO) camp developed into a full-scale battle that led to an upsurge in Arab support for the fedayeen (militants). The PLO's strength in Jordan grew, and by the beginning of 1970, groups within the PLO had started to call openly for the overthrow of the Hashemite monarchy.

The PLO was acting as a state within a state, leading to violent confrontations with the Jordanian Army in June 1970—which came to be known as the Jordanian Black September. King Hussein wanted to oust the Palestinians from the country but hesitated for fear that his enemies would use it against him, equating Palestinian terrorists with civilians. These actions culminated in the Dawson's Field incident of September

6 in which the Popular Front for the Liberation of Palestine (PFLP) hijacked three civilian aircraft[42] en route to the United States from European airports, to a desert strip in Jordon. A fourth jet was diverted to Cairo and blown up. Three days later, the PFLP seized a fifth jet and diverted it also to the desert strip, taking the foreign national passengers as hostages and later blowing up the planes in front of the international press.

Most of the 421 passengers and crew on board the five planes were freed on September 11, but the hijackers held on to fifty-six hostages, mostly Jewish and American men—including the rosh yeshiva, who was on TWA flight 741 together with his wife, daughter, and son-in-law—and forced their landing in Zarqa. King Hussein saw this as the last straw and ordered the army to act.

Seventeen-year-old David Raab[43] was also on the plane with his mother and four siblings. An unsuccessful attempt was made to get kosher food to the rosh

---

42 PFLP members had also boarded El Al flight 219 earlier that day, but after being made aware of the suspicious passengers, the captain of the flight forced the two would-be hijackers to deplane.

43 For more information, see: Raab, David, *Terror in Black September: The First Eyewitness Account of the Infamous 1970 Hijackings.* New York: Palgrave Macmillan, 2007.

yeshiva. See Appendix 7 for a description of the attempt. When they were finally released, Raab wrote:[44]

> As we walked through the city, we saw fires burning and were told that the bodies of the dead were being burned to halt the threat of disease. George Freda recorded shortly afterward: "We started walking down the hill. I borrowed Rabbi Hutner's cane and converted it into a white flag with a piece of underwear." Our captors marched us to a warehouse and departed. A couple of hours later, the Red Cross appeared.

The rosh yeshiva was being held alone in an isolated location, while Jews around the world prayed for his safe release. The terrorists had tried to cut off his beard but were stopped by their commanders. He was reunited with the rest of the hostages only on September 18 and was finally released on the 26th and flown with his family to Nicosia, Cyprus. Israeli Knesset Member Rabbi Menachem Porush, who had chartered a private plane to meet the Hutners in Nicosia, took with him, among others, Zev Frommer, a talmid of the rosh yeshiva. Zev

---

44 Ibid., page 215.

gave the rosh yeshiva his own shirt and tallit katan,[45] since the rav's tallit, tefillin, shirt, jacket, and hat had been confiscated early on during his three-week ordeal. Also confiscated were all the notes he had completed editing for the publication of *Shaar Yarcha Tlisai (Chag HaShavuot)*,[46] the first volume of his great literary work, *Pachad Yitzchak*. Zev also brought a *tichel* (hair covering) for the *Rebbetzin*, assuming correctly that hers would have been lost during the captivity. This *tichel*, in fact, is still being kept by her daughter, Bruria David, as a memorial of their ordeal. Rabbi Porush reported that my Rebbi had lost twenty kilograms during the ordeal. Two students who were with him on the plane appeared similarly emaciated. On September 28 the rosh yeshiva and his group were flown back to New York, just in time for the first night of Rosh Hashanah. Rabbi Hutner died on Kislev 20, 5741 (1980), a few days before Chanukah, and is buried on Har Hazeitim (Mount of Olives).

---

45 *tallit katan* (prayer shawl, a four cornered small garment with an opening for the head and special twined and knotted fringes on the corners, known as tzitzith)

46 The book was printed one year after his release from captivity, after a tremendous effort to recover notes written by students at the original lectures. These notes provided a basis for the rosh yeshiva's final editing of the book.

The Jewish Theological Seminary (JTS)

During my years at Chaim Berlin, there were several students from the Jewish Theological Seminary who were attracted to come and study there, even as they maintained their connection with JTS. The first such was the brother-in-law of a Chaim Berlin student, Rabbi Meilich Silver, Principal of the Yeshiva of Eastern Parkway. Chaim Feuerman, a Phi Beta Kappa, was one of three students of the seminary who, shortly, followed him. Chaim was assigned to my guidance by my Rebbi. Upon graduation from JTS, he was charged with teaching a class in Introductory Talmud in JTS. He had prepared a four-page introduction that had stressed the concept that the Oral Torah, like the written Torah, was revealed to the Jews at Sinai. One of the deans of the school summoned him and notified him that, as Chaim put it, "You know that we don't follow this tradition at JTS." Chaim eventually became very observant and served as principal of a Hebrew Day School and eventually as the Golda Koschitzky Professor of Jewish Education at Azrieli Graduate School of Jewish Education and Administration at Yeshiva University, where he served for more than twenty-eight years.

Rabbi Professor David (Weiss) Halivni was a child prodigy in Sighet, Romania. His parents separated when he was just four years old, and he was raised in the home of his grandfather. He was ordained as a rabbi at the almost unbelievable age of fifteen, When he came from the concentration camps to the United States at the age of eighteen, he was quickly recognized as a Torah scholar; shortly thereafter he enrolled in Chaim Berlin during the period that I was dormitory supervisor. As a result of his acknowledged scholarship, he was nurtured by the rosh yeshiva, who asked me to give up my private room and move into one of the four-bed rooms, so that David could have privacy.

Once, when asked by the rosh yeshiva whether he had had any opportunity to learn Torah during his time in the forced labor camps, he related a story that went something like this:

> One day during a meal break I saw one of the guards discarding some paper that he had used to wrap a pickled herring. From the distance, I saw that the paper had Hebrew letters on it. When the guard wasn't looking, I went to the garbage, took the paper out and saw that it was a page from the *Shulchan Aruch*.[47]

---

47 *Shulchan Aruch* (authorized Book of Jewish Law)

At that point, he took a folded piece of paper out of his pocket and said to the rosh yeshiva, "This is what I studied for two years."

David had a unique approach to Talmud and, after several years, was invited by Rabbi Professor Saul Lieberman of the JTS to study with him there. He explained that he was accepting the invitation so that he would have adequate livelihood to continue studying and writing his highly acknowledged Torah insights on the *stamim*.[48]

In 1953, Rabbi Professor Lieberman created a clause to be added to the ketubah (Jewish wedding document), declaring that if the marriage was dissolved by a civil court and the woman was refused a *get* (religious decree of divorce) from her husband, the husband and

---

48 Referring to questions interposed by an anonymous *amoraic* Talmudic editor (*stam ha-talmud*) between a direct *amoraic* statement and its *tannaitic* (earlier Talmudic period) source, to highlight a problem in the text of the *tannaitic* source that may have prompted the *amoraic* comment. These also turn a nondialectic structure (text plus comment) into an explicitly dialectical one (question plus answer). Sometimes they afford the *stam ha-talmud* an opportunity to redefine the issue at hand with an agenda that may not have been shared by the *amora* who authored the original. The *stam ha-talmud* also introduces editorial comments and technical terms that explicitly define the function of individual sources within the subject matter (e.g., as questions, objections, proofs, or additional support), thus creating a continuous line of discussion out of what were discrete and disconnected texts. (Adapted from Encyclopedia.com, "Talmud, Babylonian.")

wife were obligated to arbitrate before a rabbinic court authorized by the JTS and heed their directives. This could (and usually would) include ordering the man to give his wife the get.

The Conservative movement proposed a meeting between the leaders of the Rabbinical Assembly (RA), representing the Conservative movement, and the Rabbinical Council of America (RCA), representing the Orthodox rabbis, in an effort to come to an agreement that the clause was valid from the standpoint of Jewish law and would be included in both Orthodox and Conservative documents. When the clause was proposed, it had some support in the Modern Orthodox community. Rabbi Joseph Soloveitchik is reported to have given the proposal his initial approval.[49]

My Rebbi, however, ruled that while the clause was halakhically valid, he could not support it, because putting it into the hands of a rabbinic court authorized by the Conservative movement would inevitably lead to Conservative rabbis, some of whom themselves were not strictly Sabbath-observant, to become adjudicators of this procedure—and that was halakhically invalid.

---

49 Adapted from Wikipedia.

In the 1990s, a mechanism originally suggested by Rabbi J. David Bleich and developed by Rabbi Mordechai Willig gained overwhelming halakhic approval throughout the Orthodox rabbinate. They called this prenuptial agreement the Heskem L'Kavod Hadadi (the Agreement for Mutual Respect). Rabbinical organizations such as the RCA and Young Israel and lay organizations such as the Orthodox Caucus and the Wedding Resource Center began a continuing effort to make signing this agreement a universal practice.[50] This effort, today, is meeting with growing success. The number of couples signing the prenuptial agreement is growing dramatically, as is the number of rabbis strongly recommending it, or even refusing to officiate without it.[51]

Regarding the JTS, it is interesting to note an observation made by my late brother-in-law, Joe Fuchs, when he was principal of a Conservative Talmud Torah. He once took his students for a visit to JTS. When he showed them the synagogue, its gender curtain separation, and its Orthodox prayer books, the

---

50 Alan Dershowitz worked with Nathan Lewin, a top litigator for Jewish causes, on the constitutionality of these efforts to procure a *get* from a recalcitrant husband.
51 Adapted from Wikipedia.

visitors were shocked to learn that at the core of JTS, strict Orthodoxy was practiced.

Another friend and classmate of mine from Torah Vodaath, Professor Dov Zlotnik, was a teacher of Talmud at JTS. An article that he wrote on mikvah became an inspiration to many Conservative congregations to build one. Until then, he wrote, it was difficult for members of Conservative congregations to go to an Orthodox communal mikvah, because they did not feel comfortable there. Dov's daughter, Karen Kirshenbaum, is a very well-respected teacher of Jewish subjects and lectures frequently in Israel. She is loved by her listeners, who often include my wife, Lee.

Professor Hayim Z. Dimitrovsky, who lived in Jerusalem, was also a professor of Talmud at JTS. His wife was a professor of psychology at Bar-Ilan, and one of their children is married to a child of Rabbi Professor Shmuel Sprecher, who had been the rector of Bar-Ilan University. Professor Halivni eventually resigned his membership in the international association of Conservative rabbis, the Rabbinical Assembly (RA), over the issue of ordaining women. He had showed me his letter of resignation in which he stressed that he never supported actions that were contrary to halakhah[52], and when the RA chose to ordain women he resigned, because this was contrary to his view of proper religious practice.[53] I believe that I heard that Professor Dimitrovsky also resigned over the same issue.

Early Professional Career

As suggested above, the rosh yeshiva had a controlling hand in almost everything that took place in Chaim Berlin. When I was approaching marriageable age and would soon be applying for semikah, I wanted to return to college and finish my degree. I still had fifty credits to complete and planned to do it all in one year. The rosh yeshiva gave the required permission, as did the college. I managed to continue attending the beit midrash during free time. When the year was over, the rosh yeshiva called for me and

Photo courtesy of Zecharia Dor-Shav

---

52 *halakhah* (authorized Orthodox Jewish Law)
53 See Kopelowitz, E. (1998). "Three Subcultures of Conservative Judaism and the Issue of Ordaining Women." *Nashim: A Journal of Jewish Women's Studies & Gender Issues* (1):136–153. Retrieved November 5, 2020, from jstor.org/stable/40326480.

asked what I thought to do when I left the Yeshiva. "I know you would like to be a rosh yeshiva," he said, "But what is your second choice?" He was realistic and knew that I had my eyes on a professional career in education, but it was de rigueur that every talmid must, first, want to be a rosh yeshiva. He asked that I agree to have him submit my name to the board of directors as a candidate for the position of assistant principal of the Mesivta High School. Furthermore, he requested that I meet with these *baalei batim* and make sure to impress upon them that I was also a "man of the world." They would have to give their approval, and I was asked not to act like a naive yeshiva *bochur*.

He understood me and supported a role in life for me that would combine Torah studies and secular education. The assistant principal's position involved only afternoon hours. During the morning, I would be free to continue my beit midrash studies. With his guidance, that position became the beginning of a career that kept me in two worlds at the same time.

After marriage, I left to become rabbi of the Young Israel of Malden, Massachusetts, and principal of its day school. The primary job was the school. It is interesting to speculate how a young, just-married man, could be considered sufficiently qualified to be appointed to this position. In my case at least, I did have some minimal experience in the Mesivta High School. In that capacity, I had also taught a class in biology—my childhood interest—in which I included some sessions on how to recognize kosher and non-kosher birds. The head of the board of the Malden Hebrew Day School at the time was Jimmy Cohen, a son-in-law of the very philanthropic Feuerstein family of the Malden Knitting Mills. It was well known in the Boston area, during the years before and after World War II, that any refugee who settled in the Boston area could always get a job in the knitting mills of Samuel Feuerstein and earn at least a minimal salary. (See Appendix 8 for an appreciation of the extent of the family's care for the needs of others.)

When I accepted this first rabbinical position, my Rebbi offered me, as was his custom, two bits of advice. Firstly, he suggested that a rabbi's community should never see him appear in public doing anything other than תורה, עבודה או גמילות חסדים—learning Torah, praying, or performing kind deeds. Secondly, he cautioned that since rabbis are often called upon to commit an עבירה לשמה (a transgression for the sake of Heaven), it is urgent that he never receive personal pleasure or benefit from the transgression (see Nazir 23b).

As with all his talmidim, he agreed to be sandek[54] at my oldest son's berith mila. The air shuttle from New York to Boston was not available during those years, and the rosh yeshiva traveled to my home, unaccompanied, on the overnight coach. Distance and personal discomfort were not obstacles. His devotion to us was no less than our devotion to him. The only thing he requested was that a mikvah be available before the berith mila, and that a contribution of eighteen dollars be made toward the publication of one of the pamphlets of his musar discussions. Of course, the sum was symbolic, but it made the talmid feel like a partner in the dissemination of these magnificent works. These pamphlets eventually became the Pachad Yitzchak series of books. In recognition of such contributions, our names were inscribed on one of the pamphlets.

Upon returning to New York City several years later, I found that the talmidim were no longer being invited to Rosh Chodesh meals with the rosh yeshiva. I suggested that those of us who had previously enjoyed these unique Rosh Chodesh experiences in his home, though older and now married, miss them and would like to have them reinstated so that when we were

_____

54 *sandek* (an honorific: assigned to hold the baby on his lap during his circumcision)

available, we could continue to benefit from them. He gave his approval and the seudoth were reinstituted, but now in the Kollel Gur Aryeh rather than at his home. I don't remember, however, ever having been able to participate personally during that period.

It is interesting to note how very highly the rosh yeshiva thought of Rabbi Kook. As Rabbi Eliezer Waldman, rosh yeshiva of Kiryat Arba, recalled, my Rebbi had frequently stated that "Rav Kook was 20 times as great as those who opposed him."[55] Similarly, Rabbi Moshe Zvi Neria heard him say that "If I would not have met Rabbi Kook, I would be lacking 50 percent of myself."[56] My Rebbi had a picture of him hanging in his sukkah. In later years, because of social pressures, I assume, he had the picture removed.

He is also reported as having notified Rabbi Professor Dovid Halivni, after he took a position in the Jewish Theological Seminary, not to visit him at the mesivta anymore. Finally, I note that he stopped referring to Rabbi Shlomo Carlebach by name after Reb Shlomo showed some behaviors of which the rosh yeshiva highly disapproved. He then began to refer to him as "the talented one."

---

55 As interviewed by Ari Shvat, March 29, 2016, 19 Adar II 5776.
56 *Chayei HaReiya*, Tel Aviv 1983/5743, p. 258. (Hebrew)

Hopefully, I have not embarrassed the rosh yeshiva's memory with my choice of direction in life. I have maintained a tremendous respect for his thoughts about the "obligations of the Jewish heart" and especially his teachings about the holidays. His initiative in publishing my name on one of the early pamphlets certainly contributed to this feeling. In my professional life, I have published articles that combine my interests in "the worlds of Torah and general wisdom." Today after retirement, I spend a substantial portion of my time studying in a beit midrash with a *chavrutah.* The rosh yeshiva's attention to what might be important to me, and what might match my personal inclinations, aided me in reaching many of my life's goals.

The First Bais Yaakov School in America

Vichna Kaplan was the founder of the first Bais Yaakov school in America. She started the school in 1938, with seven students around her dining room table. Two of her first students were the daughters of Rabbi Shraga Feivel Mendlowitz, principal of Torah Vodaath, who told her, "Take my daughters and build a seminary around them."[57] It started as an after-school program

---

57 Devora Kitevits, "An Appreciation of Rebbetzin Kaplan," in *The Torah Profile: A Treasury of Biographical Sketches*, 1988: Mesorah Publications, Ltd., pp. 306–328.

and in 1944 became a full-scale high school. She had been brought up in Baranowitz by her uncle, Rabbi Yisrael Yaakov Lubchansky (*mashgiach* of Rabbi Elchonon Wasserman's yeshiva), and her aunt, Faiga Malka Lubchansky (daughter of Rabbi Yossel Horowitz, the Alter of Novardok).

Vishna married Boruch Kaplan, an American studying in the Brisker Yeshiva, located in what is now Belarus. He eventually became my teacher at Torah Vodaath. Many of the first Soloveitchik rabbis were the official rabbis of Brisk, and each in turn was known as "the Brisker Rav." Rabbi Yaakov Yosef Herman,[58] Rabbi of the prominent Clymer Street Synagogue in Williamsburg, had a great influence on Boruch and had sent him to study in Rabbi Yehudah Heschel Levenberg's yeshiva, the Beis Medrash LeRabbonim in New Haven, Connecticut. This yeshiva, established in 1923, was probably the first yeshiva in America. Later he influenced him to continue his studies at the Slabodka Yeshiva in Hebron, in Eretz Yisrael. He was there during the 1929 massacre and was saved by an Arab who hid him.

---

58 The subject of the biography by Ruchoma Shain *All for the Boss*, New York: Feldheim Publishers, 1984.

After the massacre, Boruch went to the great European yeshivas, Mir and Brisk, where his *shidduch*[59] was made. Vichna's uncle opposed her moving to America, since it was a "*treifa medinah*," but the Brisker Rav told her, "For a boy like Boruch Kaplan, you have my permission to go anywhere in the world." She came to America in 1937, on the same boat as Rabbi Yaakov Kamenetsky. They were married in Torah Vodaath. The wedding meal consisted of salami sandwiches.

After completing my bachelor's degree, I applied to this former teacher of mine, Rabbi Kaplan, for the position of principal of secular studies at the Bais Yaakov. He refused to consider me because, as he put it more or less, "You are too pious to be the principal of a secular studies department. You would be providing the girls with a model of a pious person proficient in secular studies, and that is undesirable."

Needless to say, this is quite contrary to my own worldview about the use of secular studies for better understanding of religious values. As mentioned above, my Rebbi made a similar suggestion when he told me that he would rather have seen me teach in a nonreligious university than in Bar-Ilan University. With due

---

59 *shidduch* (a system of matchmaking in which Jewish singles are introduced to one another, primarily, in Orthodox Jewish communities)

respect to both of these Torah giants, I think that our current generation needs just such a testament from its religious leaders. General studies are extremely important for a Torah scholar in today's world, so that he can extract benefit from all true knowledge—and put it to good use in educating youngsters—provided he remembers what is to be primary in life and why we have been put into this world to begin with. We must know, as is quoted by a student of the *Gaon*[60] of Vilna in the Gaon's name, that "In proportion with how much one is lacking in [secular] wisdoms, so is he lacking one hundred-fold in Torah wisdom."[61]

---

60 *Gaon* (Torah genius)
61 From the introduction to the Gaon's book on mathematics, *Ayil Meshulash*, originally published in 1833. See *Encyclopedia Talmudit*, Vol 15, col. 55b.

Chapter Four
Coming to Israel

WE HAD ALWAYS thought of coming to live in Israel, but it was never at the level of "Let's go." My first wife, Netta, and I had been working on our PhD degrees. In the final stages of my degree, we began to think more seriously that perhaps the time had come. My thought was, "Why should I expend effort in preparing American teachers to teach non-Jewish children, when I could be preparing students to be teachers of Jewish children in Israel?" In fact, when we moved from our rented apartment on 53rd Street in Borough Park to our 54th Street private home, we had been very uncertain about buying since we thought that the purchase might make it harder for us to leave the country. In the end we realized that the acquisition could be an investment until our aliyah, and so we bought the home.

Opportunity presented itself in 1965, when Rabbi Kalman Kahana of Kibbutz Chofetz Chaim visited America in his capacity as deputy minister of education in Israel. I had just completed my dissertation and arranged for an appointment with him, asking if he might help us find proper positions in Israel. I gave him my CV and a list of people who might be consulted as endorsements. After several months, I began to hear that inquiries had been made of me.

Subsequently, I received a call from the Jewish Agency that Professor Moshe Smilansky, director of the Henrietta Szold Institute for Child and Youth Welfare in Israel, was arriving in New York City and wanted to meet with me. I had never heard of Professor Smilansky but, obviously, was excited about the anticipated meeting. After speaking to him for a while, it dawned upon me that he was offering me a post to do research on the study of Talmud at his institute. I told him I would consider it and walked out of the meeting "floating on cloud nine."

A very short while later, I received a letter from Professor Eliezer Stern, chairman of the School of Education of Bar-Ilan University, whom I also did not know. He wrote that, in his opinion, the suggested

Talmud research must be done only at Bar-Ilan University, and he would want me to join the staff of his school of education to work on this investigation there.

Before I was ready to respond to this latest communication, the Israeli Six-Day War broke out on Monday, June 5, 1967. While listening to the morning news, the correspondent quoted BBC to the effect that Israel had destroyed Egypt's air force during the first three hours of the war. This, of course, predicted the outcome of the war, as the Egyptian army now had no air cover. There was, however, much ground fighting still to be done.

Two days later, after nineteen years of Jordanian occupation, Jerusalem was recaptured. When we heard the broadcast of the sound of the shofar[1] blown by Rabbi Shlomo Goren at the Western Wall, I shouted to the family the verse in Isaiah 27, 13:

וְהָיָה בַּיּוֹם הַהוּא, יִתָּקַע בְּשׁוֹפָר גָּדוֹל, וּבָאוּ הָאֹבְדִים בְּאֶרֶץ אַשּׁוּר, וְהַנִּדָּחִים בְּאֶרֶץ מִצְרָיִם; וְהִשְׁתַּחֲווּ לַה' בְּהַר הַקֹּדֶשׁ, בִּירוּשָׁלָ͏ִם.

---

1   *shofar* (Ram's horn blown on Rosh Hashanah and in times of anguish and joy)

And on that day a great shofar will be blown, and the lost ones in Assyria and Egypt will come and bow to Hashem on the holy mountain in Jerusalem.

Someone in the room then exclaimed, "But that shofar will be heard from one end of the world to the other?" To which I replied with exaltation, "Well, here we are in Brooklyn and hearing the shofar blown in Jerusalem!" Rabbi Goren himself, in an interview with *Arutz Sheva* in 1994, reminiscing about that event, said:

Since the destruction of the Second Temple there was never such joy for the Nation of Israel as there was on that day of the redemption of the Temple Mount, Jerusalem and the Western Wall. Blowing the shofar for me was a prelude to the sound of the shofar of the Messiah.[2]

Commenting on the events, the Jewish Agency wrote:

With tensions mounting, the Straits of Tiran blocked, and Arab armies poised to strike,

---

2   Chagai Segal, Makor Rishon, *Yoman Supplement*, May 22, 2020, page 3. (Hebrew)

Israel decided . . . to launch a pre-emptive attack on the massive Egyptian forces aimed at her. Within 190 minutes the backbone of the Egyptian air force was broken, and by the end of the first day of war, 298 Egyptian airplanes were destroyed. Backed by complete air superiority, Israeli army divisions then thrust into the Sinai Desert approaching the bank of the Suez Canal. At the same time, Israel issued an appeal to Jordan to stay out of the war. Jordan refused and opened a heavy artillery barrage on both West Jerusalem and the Tel Aviv area, which forced Israel to counterattack. By June 8th the Israel Defense Forces . . . had defeated the Jordanian forces and captured the whole of Judea and Samaria. On the morning of June 9th, Israel attacked the Syrians and captured the Golan Heights. From these heights, Syria had shelled and destroyed 205 houses, 175 acres of orchards and 75 acres of grain.[3]

A Washington Demonstration

A huge pro-Israel rally took place in Washington. The demonstration's high point was ignited by the

---

3 Six-Day War June 1967, The Jewish Agency, April 16, 2015.

announcement that Egypt had agreed to the U.N. ceasefire resolution. The cheering could be heard inside the White House, but President Lyndon Johnson chose not to address the rally, nor did he welcome a delegation that had requested an audience with him. Under-Secretary of State Nicholas Katzenbach and Bromley Smith, secretary of the National Security Council, however, did accept a petition that called for peace along Israel's newly won borders, and unrestricted transit through Akaba Gulf and the Suez Canal.

While the Jewish young people sang and danced, a group of about one hundred Arabs and other Moslems chanted anti-Israel slogans in front of the White House. A heavy police cordon screened the Arab demonstrators from the pro-Israel demonstration and the general public.

A JTA press release describes the event:[4]

More than 50,000 Jews from all sections of the country jammed Lafayette Park opposite the White House here today to voice support for Israel and vow "that the victories won on the field of battle shall not be lost at the tables of diplomacy." The rally climaxed a two-day

---

4   *JTA Daily News Bulletin*, June 9, 1967. The picture on page 198 shows Israeli paratroopers standing in front of the Western Wall. Copyright: David Rubinger, GPO.

National Emergency Leadership Conference for Israel sponsored by the Conference of Presidents of Major American Jewish Organizations.

Speakers at the rally—Senators, Black-American rights leaders, labor officials and Jewish spokesmen—called on the Johnson Administration to put its weight behind direct Arab-Israel talks leading toward a permanent peace in the Middle East. An enthusiastic and orderly crowd cheered speeches that emphasized the U.S. and Israel shared the goals of freedom of the seas and an end to belligerency in the Middle East.

Dr. Joachim Prinz, chairman of the Conference of Presidents of Major American Jewish Organizations, opened the rally with a call for strong U.S. backing of a settlement based on Arab recognition of Israel's "permanent presence" in the Middle East. Rabbi Israel Miller, chairman of the American Zionists Council issued a direct call to President Johnson to, "Help once and for all end Arab belligerence against Israel."

Morris B. Abram, president of the American Jewish Committee and U.S. representative to the United Nations Human Rights

Commission, told the rally, "The peace of the Middle East must rest on non-belligerence, free navigation and the justice achieved through negotiations." These, he said, could best be secured by "ironclad non-aggression guarantees. Neither Israel nor America can be satisfied with another jerry-built, paper-clipped, glued-together peace." Mr. Abram declared.

At the announcement, our cousin, Baruch Chait, took out his guitar and started to strum, ה' מלך ה' מלך ה' ימלוך לעולם ועד (Hashem is king. Hashem was king. Hashem will be king forever after.)

On our way home from the demonstration, we stopped to buy some drinks. I paid the storekeeper and held out my hand for change. The storekeeper, however, held the change in his closed hand and exclaimed, "How much I respect Israel and the Jewish People!" Only then did he give me the change.

The six-days of fierce fighting ended with Israel's occupation of the Sinai Desert, the Gaza Strip, the Golan Heights, and the West Bank of the Jordan River, providing Israel's cities with a much-needed buffer zone and dramatically reducing the danger of extinction by a surprise Arab attack. Furthermore, the victory had a special religious meaning because of the resultant unification of Jerusalem and return of Jews to Judea and Samaria, part of biblical Israel. The war ended on June 10, when Syria agreed to observe a UN-mediated ceasefire.

Six-Day War, Photo by David Rubinger

Shortly after consultation with my family, I went to the Jewish Agency to volunteer my services. During the interview, all the skills that I thought might be useful were rejected. They didn't need a rabbi; they didn't need a psychologist; they didn't need a school principal; and they didn't need a first-aid instructor. I finally came up with a skill that they felt could be useful. I told them that one day when I was principal of the Malden Hebrew Day School, the bus driver of the school mini-bus had taken ill and I drove the bus to pick up the children. Their response: "You know how to drive a bus? [Not that I had a license to drive a bus.] Get your passport, we can use you!"

About then, we received a letter from our friend Tova Friedman,[5] a Holocaust survivor who as a child

---

5   See: ESN-TV. A conversation with Tova Friedman, Holocaust Survivor. At: youtube.com/watch?v=w-Ji1e2NVQA.

was already in the gas chambers with a group of other female children, when the concentration camp murderers decided that they didn't want to exterminate the girls on that day. She and her family had made aliyah shortly before the war. She poignantly remembered how her father had been forced to dig mass graves for the killing and burying of Jews in the concentration camps, and now—two weeks before the outbreak of the war—she was being asked to dig trenches and prepare graves for the expected many thousands projected to be killed by the war. She wrote, "We are digging our own graves!"

By the time our passports were issued on June 30, thank Hashem, the war was long over. We decided to travel to Israel in any event. We arrived on July 25, which corresponded with the Fast of the 17th of Tammuz. We did not include our son, Simcha Hillel, in the trip because he was in camp and said that he didn't wish to go. (We made the mistake of taking his objection seriously. I regret it to this day.)

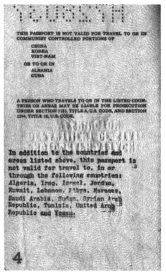

Photo courtesy of Zecharia Dor-Shav

As can be seen from the accompanying picture, our passports were stamped "not valid for travel to Israel," among other countries. That didn't deter us, and it was a special pleasure to use just these exact passports two years later when we arrived, finally, as new immigrants.

We weren't needed anymore for volunteer war duty, and so we rented a fiberglass Susita and during our six-day sojourn traversed some two thousand kilometers of the length and breadth of the land. We felt safe enough to travel to Nablus, Gaza, and even the Golan Heights. It was thrilling to see the white surrender flags hanging all over Gaza. The country was really ours, and we felt that we could travel safely anywhere we wished in the newly liberated areas.

We had much good fortune during the trip. Even things that at the time seemed very problematic turned out to be blessings. One week, we decided to spend the Sabbath in Safed and drove up on Friday afternoon. We had assumed that the drive would be uneventful and that we would arrive in good time. Unfortunately, we found ourselves on a one-lane highway behind a horse-drawn wagon and were much delayed. We arrived very close to candle-lighting time and found that no hotel rooms were available. With no other alternative, we rented a *tzimmer* (bed and breakfast) with a private family.

How lucky we were! The host was a representative of the Jewish Agency with the assigned task of exploring the newly captured Golan Heights to search out possible locations for Jewish settlement. Travel on the Heights was restricted, and all private vehicles were forbidden. Our host, however, gave us a letter identifying us as representatives of the Jewish Agency assigned the task of finding such potential locations. We flashed the letter to the soldiers at the various checkpoints and were permitted passage. The Heights was strewn with destroyed military vehicles, as well as abandoned villages and animals. The roads were filled with potholes. We traveled so closely to the Tapline Road[6] that we saw the UN flags on the other side. A bit farther on, on the road near Kuneitra, we also saw Syrian soldiers and a Syrian flag.

Later, on a trip somewhere in Central Israel, a tire on our car deflated, and we had to change it. A signpost on the side of the road there declared: "This is the Valley of Elah. This is where David killed Goliath. The Philistines were on that hill and the Israelites were . . ." What could have been a more inspiring place to change a tire?

---

6 A thirty-mile-long north–south road in the Golan, adjacent to the route of the now-defunct oil pipeline of the Trans-Arabian Pipeline Company.

During the weeks of this trip to Israel, I visited Bar-Ilan University to inquire about the letter I had received from Professor Stern. To my surprise, he immediately pulled the letter out from under other papers on his desk and offered me a job, pending permission from the various departments and agencies who had to give their approval. I told him that I would have to receive a firm letter of commitment before the end of March, so that I could give Long Island University proper advance notice that I was planning to leave. The letter did come eventually, in July, and I had to delay our departure for a year.

Meeting with the "Father of the Prisoners"

I had heard of Rabbi Aryeh Levin from my friend Dr. Pincus (Pinky) Rosenfeld, who had been a volunteer with some of the resistance groups before the establishment of the State of Israel. *Reb* Aryeh, as he was generally known, was the *mashgiach ruchani* of Etz Chaim Yeshiva in Jerusalem and was known for his compassion for the sick and the prisoners of the Jewish underground. In 1931, at the request of the British authorities, the Chief Ashkenazi

Rabbi of British Mandatory Palestine, Rabbi Avraham Yitzchak HaCohen Kook, had appointed *Reb* Aryeh as the official Jewish chaplain of the prison in the Russian compound where prisoners of the underground were incarcerated—a service he had already been rendering voluntarily since 1927. He visited them regularly to bolster their spirit and to write letters and appeals for them, as also to accompany and assist those sentenced to the gallows during their last hours. On the Sabbath and Yom Tov, he would regularly pay a visit to the prison to offer comfort and read the Torah for the inmates.

He was also the only rabbi who didn't hesitate to visit Hansen's Hospital for Lepers in Jerusalem and extend all necessary assistance to those suffering from this terrible disease. The inmates were captivated by *Reb* Aryeh's warmth and sincerity, his trademark two-handed caressing handshake, and the honor and respect with which he treated them. Mattityahu Shmuelevitz, whose death sentence was commuted to life imprisonment, wrote to a friend about *Reb* Aryeh, "There is one person in particular to whom I remain grateful first and foremost—a dear, precious Jew . . . who stormed Heaven and Earth for me, and more important, it was he who brought me closer to my Maker in those fateful days. . . . He left, and we remained in the prison. He couldn't take us with him out into the free world, but he always brought the outside world in to us."[7] Because of his outstanding love and compassion for the resistance fighters, he was called "Father of the Prisoners." He projected friendliness and love to everyone. The postage stamp pictured was issued in his honor.

One day, Pinky received a handwritten letter from *Reb* Aryeh that looked as if it had come off a printing press. Pinky, who was studying then for his PhD in psychology, was tremendously impressed by the unusual graphics of the letter. Since one of his teachers was a renowned graphologist, he decided to show her the letter. The letter, written in Hebrew, could not be read or understood by this non-Jewish professor, but she exclaimed immediately, "This man is in total conscious control of his behavior!" She then asked for the translation of one line in the letter that was just slightly larger than the other lines. It was: ותחזנה עיננו בשובך לציון ברחמים (May our eyes see Your return to Zion with mercy). She said, "That is the second theme in this person's personality." Pinky carried a copy of that letter in his wallet until his death.

I made it a priority to visit *Reb* Aryeh in his apartment in the Mishkenot Yisrael neighborhood of

---

7 Wikipedia: Aryeh Levin.

Jerusalem. He lived with great modesty and simplicity. His apartment was tiny and had few furnishings. Regarding his modest apartment he once said, "Many times they tried to tell me that I should move . . . to a more spacious place and I refused, [for we know] that after a long life, a man is taken from his apartment to [his grave]. So, for me, the adjustment will be easier, since my room isn't much bigger."[8]

I had come with my infant son, Etan. *Reb* Aryeh held out his hands, and Etan immediately came for a hug and a piece of candy—behavior that is not typical of a two-year-old. During our visit, I asked him if the underground fighters were religious. He responded with the following amazing story, which I paraphrase:

> One Sabbath when I was in the Russian Compound, reading the Torah for the inmates, a messenger arrived to tell me that my daughter had contracted a very serious stroke, may Hashem spare us, and that her life was in danger. Of course, I left immediately to tend to her. Several weeks later, my daughter was well enough for me to return to the prison to read

---

8   *13 Amazing Facts About Rabbi Aryeh Levin, on His Yohrzeit*, Hidabroot: The World's Largest Jewish Network, November 15, 2019.

the Torah. When the Cohen was called for the first section of the reading, he asked me to say a prayer for my daughter. As is customary when called to a reading of the Torah, the prayer is accompanied by a benevolent pledge, usually a donation to some worthy cause. When I asked him if he wished to make such a pledge, the inmate said, "Yes! I wish to pledge three years of my life for your daughter!"

Even though this was a most unusual vow, I didn't question him about it. The next person called to the Torah was a Levite, and he made the same request for a prayer, but he pledged a larger number of years. And so, it went from one to another, with each one adding more years. Finally, when it came to the final honor, maftir, the oleh said that he wished to pledge all of his life for my daughter. At that point, I could no longer remain quiet.

"All of your life? Why are you saying that?" I asked. He answered, "I have lived enough, let the rest of my years be given to your daughter!"

And though the doctors were very skeptical about my daughter's surviving the stroke—adding that even if she did, she would surely remain with serious impediments—in fact, she recovered completely, and no serious impediments remained.

That was *Reb* Aryeh's response to my question about these underground fighters and their religiosity. Draw your own conclusion as to whether or not he considered them to be religious Jews!

My Rebbi's Response to the Capture of Jerusalem

A few days after the war, as my Rebbi was about to give his usual lecture about the Yom Tov of Shavuot, he noted, "I was taught by my teachers that when the

Six-Day War

Torah returns to its rightful place, we are in the time when we can already hear the footsteps of the Messiah. And it has now been returned!" He was apparently referring to the fact that Rabbi Goren, together with several other very prominent rabbis, had accompanied the troops occupying the Temple Mount, while carrying his small Torah scroll with him!

In recently released IDF protocols, Rabbi Goren wrote about that day:

Miniret over the Gate of the Tribes

> When I reached [the Old City's] Lion's Gate, I began to blow the shofar, as per the mitzvah of the Torah to blow the trumpet or shofar when at war[9] . . . I entered the Temple Mount by way of the Gate of the Tribes. I found [General] Mota Gur and other officers on the mount . . . all the way I was blowing the shofar . . . reciting psalms . . . I prostrated myself on the ground.

---

9 וְכִי־תָבֹאוּ מִלְחָמָה בְּאַרְצְכֶם עַל־הַצַּר הַצֹּרֵר אֶתְכֶם וַהֲרֵעֹתֶם בַּחֲצֹצְרֹת וְנִזְכַּרְתֶּם לִפְנֵי ה' אֱלֹ־הֵיכֶם וְנוֹשַׁעְתֶּם מֵאֹיְבֵיכֶם: When war comes to your country, you shall blow the trumpet and will be remembered by the Lord, your God and will be helped against your enemies. (*Numbers* 10, 9)

After descending and praying at the Western Wall, he returned to the Mount, when General Moti Gur asked him if he would like to enter the Dome of the Rock. He noted:

> During conquest of the Mount this is permissible. . . . I took my Torah scroll with me, and the shofar, and entered. I think that this was the first and only time in history, since the destruction of the Temple, that a sefer Torah and shofar were in this location.[10]

A Unique Experience in the Old City

On one of our first visits to the Old City, amid the ruins and destruction around us, a stranger approached, all excited. This was Rabbi Moshe Zvi Segal, who said that he just had to talk to someone/anyone and share his latest escapade. He had just reoccupied the Chabad Center that had been in the Old City before 1948! I was there at just that propitious moment, and he

Photo processed by Zecharia Dor-Shav

---

10 Makor Rishon, Nov. 15, 2019, *Shabbat Supplement* (Hebrew). In the northeast corner of the Temple Mount, the Minaret pictured above is near the Gate of the Tribes. Picture from Wikipedia.

shared his excitement with me! Subsequently, I found confirmation that he was the first Jew to return to the Old City, on just that day that we met![11]

Only later did I discover what a very special person he really was. In 1929, he had organized a protest march to the Kotel on Tishah B'Av. During the Arab riots and pogroms of that year, he had defended Tel Aviv as a member of the Haganah and subsequently helped negotiate the formation of the Irgun Zvai Leumi (Irgun). Eventually he joined the Irgun High Command (with Yaakov Meridor as Commander in Chief) and still later changed his affiliation and joined the Lechi (Stern Group). He was also national commander of the religious semi-underground, called Brit Hashmonaim.

Earlier, the Mufti of Jerusalem (a good friend of Adolph Hitler), an uncle of Yasser Arafat, had come up with many humiliating anti-Semitic laws for those who wished to pray at Judaism's holiest site:

> In those years, the area in front of the Kotel did not look as it does today. Only a narrow alley separated the Kotel and the Arab houses on the other side. The British Mandatory government

---

11 Chagai Segal, *Zichronot V'Shofarot*, Makor Rishon, Pesach 5777. (Hebrew)

prohibited placing a Torah ark, tables, or benches in the alley in front of the Kotel. Even a small stool could not be brought there.[12]

From a different source:

It is forbidden to pray out loud, lest one disturb the Arab residents; it is forbidden to read from the Torah (those praying at the Kotel had to go to one of the synagogues in the Jewish quarter to conduct the Torah reading); it is forbidden to sound the shofar on Rosh Hashanah and Yom Kippur. The British placed policemen at the Kotel to enforce these rules.[13]

Defying the British Ban on Shofar Blowing at the Kotel

What gained Rav Segal notoriety among the British and fame among Israel's early underground was a seemingly small incident. During the years of the British mandate, in 1930, Rav Segal surreptitiously blew the shofar at the

---

12 Arutz Sheva: "Yom Kippur: The Shofar and the Wall," adapted from the Hebrew by Yanki Tauber and posted on Chabad.org, with some additional notes from "An Angel Among Men," pp. 220–221, and "The Man Who Sounded the Shofar," in *Jerusalem Weekly*, October 5, 2007.

13 Memoirs of Rabbi Moshe Tsvi Segal, at: saveisrael.com/segal/segalwall. htm. (An excerpt, translated from the Hebrew)

close of the Yom Kippur Day—and trained others to do so as well. As he recounts in his memoirs:

> On Yom Kippur of that year, I was praying at the Kotel. During the brief intermission between the musaf[14] and minhah prayers, I overheard people whispering to each other: "Where will we go to hear the shofar? It'll be impossible to blow here. There are as many policemen as people praying" . . . The Police Commander himself was there, to make sure that the Jews would not, God forbid, sound the single blast that closes the fast. I listened to these whisperings, and thought to myself, "Can we possibly forgo the sounding of the shofar that accompanies our proclamation of the sovereignty of God? Can we possibly forgo the sounding of the shofar, which symbolizes the redemption of Israel? True, the sounding of the shofar at the close of Yom Kippur is only a custom, but 'A Jewish custom is Torah!'" I approached Rabbi Yitzchak Orenstein,[15] who served as the Rabbi of our "congregation," and said to him:

---

14 *musaf* (special additional holiday service)
15 Rabbi of the Western Wall, who had been appointed by the Haganah to head the civilian sector of the Old City.

"Give me a shofar."

"What for?"

"I'll blow."

"What are you talking about? Don't you see the police?"

"I'll blow."

The Rabbi abruptly turned away from me, but not before he cast a glance at the prayer-stand at the left end of the alley. I understood; the shofar was in the stand. When the hour of the blowing approached, I walked over to the stand and leaned against it. I opened the drawer and slipped the shofar into my shirt.

I had the shofar, but what if they saw me before I had a chance to blow it? I was still unmarried at the time, and following the Ashkenazic custom, did not wear a tallit. I turned to a person praying at my side, and asked him for his tallit. My request must have seemed strange to him, but the Jews are a kind people, especially at the holiest moments of the holiest day, and he handed me his tallit without a word.

I wrapped myself in the tallit. At that moment, I felt that I had created my own private domain. All around me, a foreign government prevails, ruling over the people of Israel even on their holiest day and at their holiest place, and we are not free to serve our God; but under this tallit is another domain. Here I am under no dominion save that of my Father in Heaven; here I shall do as He commands me, and no force on earth will stop me.

When the closing verses of the ne'ilah (closing Yom Kippur prayer service) prayer—"Hear O Israel," "Blessed be the name" and "The Lord is God"—were proclaimed, I took the shofar and blew a long, resounding blast. Everything happened very quickly. Many hands grabbed me. I removed the tallit from over my head, and before me stood the Police Commander, who ordered my arrest.

I was taken to the kishla—the prison in the Old City—and an Arab policeman was appointed to watch over me. Many hours passed; I was given no food or water to break my fast. At midnight, the policeman received an order to release me, and he let me out without a word. I then learned that when the Chief Rabbi of the Holy Land, Rabbi Avraham Yitzchak Kook, heard of my arrest, he immediately contacted the secretary of the High Commissioner of Palestine, and asked that I be released. When his request was refused, he stated that he would not break his fast until I was freed. The High Commissioner resisted for many hours, but finally, out of respect for the Rabbi, he had no choice but to set me free.

For the next 18 years, until the Arab conquest of the Old City in 1948, the shofar was sounded at the Kotel every Yom Kippur. The British well understood the significance of this blast; they knew that it would ultimately demolish their reign over our land just as the walls of Jericho crumbled before the shofar of Joshua, and they did everything in their power to prevent it. But every Yom Kippur, the shofar was sounded by men who know they would be arrested for their part in staking our claim to the holiest of our possessions.[16]

Greer Fay Cashman, in the *Jerusalem Post* of May 10, 2007, describes the follow-up:

Each year, he [Rabbi Segal] trained two young men to blow the shofar. Because they were

---

16 An excerpt (translated from the Hebrew) from the memoirs of Rabbi Moshe Tsvi Segal, op. cit.

different young men each year, the British did not know their identities, and therefore did not apprehend them in advance. Segal was arrested and detained in unpleasant conditions several times in the course of his anti-Mandate activities, but he remained adamant in his commitment to continue the struggle for Jewish statehood in the Land of Israel. After the creation of the state, he and his wife Rachel settled in Kfar Chabad where they raised three sons and three daughters. One of the daughters, Aligal Kaploun, who now lives in Ramot Eshkol [my neighborhood in Jerusalem - ZD] and is in her 60s, still remembers her father taking her to the Western Wall when she was about five years old. "It was very congested, and it took us a long time to make our way through the crowd, so that we could touch the stones." That was before the War of Independence, and nearly a quarter of a century passed before her father took her to the Wall again.

In June 1967, when her father set up house in the Jewish Quarter, Aligal and her husband, Uri, were living in Melbourne as Chabad emissaries. Immediately after the paratroopers had captured the Old City, her father entered, determined to take up residence. The soldiers on guard were reluctant to allow him in, telling him that they could not take responsibility for his safety. Segal replied that he relied on a higher power for his safety, aside from which he reminded them of the risks taken by so many Jews to bring about the reunification of Jerusalem. "We have received a gift from God," he said. "Do you really expect me to remain outside while the Arabs are still inside?" The upshot was that he was escorted through the streets by an armored jeep. It was inconceivable to him, said Kaploun, that Jerusalem should be reunited without a single Jew living in the Jewish Quarter of the Old City. . . . After going to the Wall in the company of 18 veterans of Brit Hashmonaim . . . blowing the shofar, praying and weeping tears of joy, Segal went to look at the Beit Menachem Synagogue, named after Menachem Mendel, the third Lubavitcher Rebbe and today known as the Tzemach Tzedek synagogue, the name by which this Rebbe is better known. The shell of the synagogue was intact, and Segal immediately decided to restore it to what it had once been.

Looking around, he discovered that adjacent to the synagogue was another three-story building that had been Chabad property up to May 1948. It had a basement, a ground floor on which there had been shops, and an upper floor in which there were two residential rooms. The building was in terrible condition with lots of rubble, garbage, shrapnel, broken glass and refuse. Segal decided to clean it up and to live there while engaging in his restoration project. In this way he became the first Jew to officially take up residence in the Old City. He wanted to be sure that if anyone came to take a population census, they would be able to say that at least one Jew lived there. His wife, who supported him in all his endeavors, could not initially bring herself to join him. A survivor of the Hebron massacre of 1929, she was still traumatized by the thought of being surrounded by Arabs, said Kaploun. Although Rachel Segal visited her husband from time to time, she allowed more than a year to pass before actually deciding to live in the Old City, preferring to wait until more Jews had moved in.

In June 1967, after learning about what her father was doing, Aligal Kaploun ached to go to Jerusalem. She wrote a letter to the Lubavitcher Rebbe explaining how she felt and asked permission to return home. She had hoped that the Rebbe would release her from her work in Australia, but the response was negative. He did however allow her to visit with her youngest child who was then eight months old. She could hardly wait to get to Israel. "I thought [the] Messiah was coming, and that it was the time of redemption. I felt so distant in Australia, standing beyond the centrality of what was happening. It was all so far away." After Kaploun arrived in Israel, she and one of her sisters decided to spend a Sabbath with their father. It was already winter, and although he had spent much time and effort cleaning and fixing, he had given more attention to the synagogue than to the living area. The windows in the room in which the two sisters stayed were cracked, and it was bitterly cold. They went to bed in their clothes (including their coats) and literally froze all night. They were so cold that they were unable to sleep. Segal took his daughters on a tour of the Old City, and they noticed that none of the Jews were afraid of the Arabs, even though they were considerably outnumbered. "It was the Arabs who were afraid of the Jews," she recalled. Segal, who had once worked for an architect, had worked with amazing speed on the restoration of the synagogue, so much so that by Rosh Hashanah of that first year in the Jewish Quarter, he was able to open it up to worshipers, including then President, Zalman Shazar, who came from a Chabad background and remained close to the Rebbe and to Chabad Hasidim . . .

After his wife joined him in the Jewish Quarter, the couple lived for a while on Rehov Chabad and then moved to other premises in the quarter. Rachel Segal lived there for 10 years before she died, and Moshe Segal lived there for a total of 16 years.

A fascinating sequel to all of this is also reported:[17]

Abraham Elkayam was one of the last three shofar-blowers before the Old City and the

---

17 Israel National News, Western Wall Shofar-Blowers, Hillel Fendel, Six men who, as teenagers, braved the British to blow the shofar at the Western Wall on Yom Kippur decades ago, gather for a remarkable reunion. Sept. 14, 2010.

Western Wall fell into Jordanian hands during the War of Independence. After the liberation of Jerusalem in the Six-Day War in 1967, he visited the Western Wall. He saw a man with a shofar. "Can I blow it please?" he asked and blew it with all his soul.

Suddenly, another man came over to him and asked, "What's your connection to the shofar?" Abraham answered, "I was the last one to blow it in 1948." To which the man responded, "And I was the first in 1931." It was Rabbi Moshe Segal.

Significantly, Rabbi Segal died on Yom Kippur day and was buried on the Mount of Olives.

Our Tishah B'Av Visit to the Kotel Ha'Ma'aravi

During our visit, Tishah B'Av fell on the evening of August 8. We were staying with Tova Friedman in Ramat Motza,[18]

---

18. סוכה דף מה עמוד א—מצות ערבה כיצד? מקום היה למטה מירושלים ונקרא מוצא. יורדין לשם ומלקטין משם מורביות של ערבה...תנא: מקום קלניא הוה.

How was the mitzvah of willow branches performed? There was a place below Jerusalem called "Motza." They would go there and gather [long and] thin willow branches. . . . We were taught: the place was called "Colonia." (Succah 45a)

near Colonia[19] (where we saw our first free-crawling scorpion[20]), which is mentioned in the Talmud as the place from which willow branches were brought to the Temple Mount for the Succot celebrations. We went to the Kotel and its newly cleared square to commemorate the day of national mourning Tishah B'Av. It was thronged with people, all of whom were experiencing mixed emotions. On the one hand, it was the eve of Tishah

A view of the stone in the Dome of the Rock upon which the Aron Kodesh may have rested in the temple, Photo processed by Zecharia Dor-Shav

---

19 When the Yellin and Yehuda families of the Old City were establishing agricultural colonies in modern Israel (before Petach Tikva and Rishon LeZion), they chose Colonia, an area that the Romans had set up as a community for retired soldiers. The Arabs living in Colonia had fallen upon hard times and were delighted to sell some of their land to the Jews. The new settlers called the area by its Biblical/Talmudic name, Motza.

20 In the month of *Tishrei*, man is judged by the scale in Heaven, which weighs his deeds. If man is found to be guilty . . . he is subject to punishment in *Gehinnom* (hell). The lowest place in *Gehinnom* is described by our Sages as a place that is full of scorpions. If *chas v'shalom* (colloquial: Heaven forbid) the person was found guilty in the judgment of the month of *Tishrei*, he will be subject to the *Gehinnom* that is contained in the month of *Cheshvan*—the month of the "scorpion." (Rabbi Itamar Schwartz, Rosh Chodesh Mazal—011 Cheshvan | The Scorpion, bilvavi.net)

B'Av and we felt the loss of the Beit Hamikdash[21] some 1900 years earlier. On the other hand, we were thrilled to be part of this first generation in nearly two millennia to be able to pray under Jewish rule, so close to the holy Temple Mount.

I was part of a minyan that was listening to the reading of Lamentations on the stone floor near the Kotel—in fact, I was the reader—and I was being recorded. When replaying the tape, one can hear background sounds. Besides my voice, one can hear people reciting the Shehechyanu[22] blessing at having returned to this holy spot after nineteen years of Jordanian occupation. For us, of course, this was the first time in our lives.

The next morning, we returned to the Kotel and stayed only until about noon. To my everlasting sorrow, I was a bit overcome by the heat of the day and missed the opportunity to go up to the Temple Mount itself. Shortly after I left, Rabbi Goren came around to gather a minyan to go up to the Mount with him for the minhah prayer. Had I been there, I would have had the problem that I had not gone to the mikvah to purify myself, as is common and is halakhically mandated. If, however,

---

21 *Beit Hamikdash* (Holy Temple in Jerusalem)
22 ". . . He who has provided us with life, and sustained us, and brought us to this moment."

he had allowed it—since it could be considered an act of conquering or securing the Mount for Jewish use—I believe that I would have gone up with him.

Though I missed that opportunity, in later years, I was able to go up to the Mount more than once and pray silently. The first such occasion was on a Yom Kippur, when I was praying at the Kotel and decided to go up the Mount by way of the Moghrabi Gate—which was open then to visitors without restriction. Since I had gone to the mikvah the day before, and was wearing non-leather shoes (as also my Yom Kippur *kitel*—white cloak), of course, I went up. No one bothered me or even approached me as I prayed silently.

During the course of another private visit to the Temple Mount in May 1995, I was arrested! By that time, visits by Jews were becoming more prominent and the Waqf was very active. I went up with my friend Rabbi Professor Aharon Shapiro, who was visiting from America. He looked like a tourist, and no one was bothering him. I looked more like an Israeli and the Waqf agents were following me everywhere I went. Aharon was standing on the side as I started to walk around the high enclosure upon which the Temple stood, which now holds the Dome of the Rock. Tourists and Arabs were all around, some playing soccer, some eating on the grass, and others sitting on chairs or on the short stone walls. There was a plethora of garbage strewn around. I decided to sit down on a ledge facing the Dome—and this got me arrested and physically removed from the Mount. After being held in the Kishle Police Station and questioned for well over an hour, I was released categorically, but ordered to be available for appearance in court if the government should choose to recognize the arrest as legitimate and decide to prosecute.

Author being carried off Temple Mount

In later years, on another occasion that I went up, by chance I met Rabbi Benny Elon, who was then a Member of the Knesset. We were accosted by Waqf agents who were watching our lips "to see if they were moving in prayer." A policeman approached and, recognizing Rabbi Elon, chased the Waqf away. Clearly a sympathizer with our cause, he told us privately, "If you guys would come up with a very large group of several thousand people, we wouldn't be able to stop you."

Negotiating with the Jewish Agency

Shortly after my deadline for giving Long Island University proper notice had passed, we received the proffered offer for employment at Bar-Ilan University. The final approval arrived in June 1968, but we still had to sell our home in Borough Park. I had to delay my departure for a year.

In 1969, we were finally able to make the sale and move to Israel. We contacted the Jewish Agency and arranged to travel by ship, as this gave us twice as much storage space for luggage as by plane. We also discussed living in an Absorption Center until the promised apartment in the university faculty housing would be available. It is interesting to note how the agenda of the agency representative was so different from our own agenda. His first suggestion was that we go to an Absorption Center in the new city of Carmiel in the Galilee. We pointed out that since both I and my wife had arranged to work at Bar-Ilan University, it would be foolish to live in the Galilee, which, at that time, would have necessitated at least two hours of travel each way.

Their second suggestion was hardly better. They suggested Upper Nazareth (now called Nof HaGalil), which meant perhaps 10 minutes less travel time. Finally, they suggested the Absorption Center in

Yivneh (as the city of Yavneh was then called), just west of Rehovot. We said fine but listed four needs that had to be met so that we could live there and work at Bar-Ilan: easy travel; the possibility of buying prepared food; an available washing machine—because our youngest child was only four years old at the time—and finally, separate aliyah benefits for Nachum, who was seventeen and entitled to benefits, if he would have immigrated alone.

They immediately informed us that Nachum would not get the benefits, since he was immigrating together with us. We argued about this, but to no avail. Frustrated but undaunted, we notified them that we would send him to Israel alone, by plane, before our arrival so that he could be registered as a lone immigrant. They threatened to cable ahead to prevent this. Nonetheless, we sent Nachum off by plane, and, fortunately, they had not cabled to prevent this. They did restrict the apartment they were giving us at the Absorption Center to one usually assigned to a family with only two children. We put our three children in these limited accommodations.

The Effect of Visiting Israel

It is interesting to realize how powerful our visit to Israel had been, even after returning to my work. At that time, in addition to my regular assignment at Long Island University, I was teaching a course on cultural effects, to a group of retired high-ranking naval officers at the Brooklyn Navy Yard. One late afternoon, after I had finished teaching my regular classes, I went to the university parking lot, to get my car. There was always a guard in the station at the entrance. As I was about to enter the car, someone jumped out of the bushes at the side and threatened me. "Get into the car!" he shouted. His intention, apparently, was to steal the car and rob me. I responded immediately, "I will not!" and shouted for help. I then began struggling with him, and he knocked off my glasses but ran away. Quite shaken, I got into the car and found that the guard was not at his station. I drove on to the Navy Yard and realized that my glasses were crooked, and I was a bit disheveled. I found it necessary to explain to the class what had just happened, and how I had chased off the potential assailant.

A few weeks later, I gave the class a test in which one of the questions was about defense squads in Eastern European Jewish communities. It is well known that these Jewish communities had extensive social support systems (helping the sick, clothing the indigent, housing the travelers, etc.), but the one thing they did not have was a defense squad to protect themselves from malevolent neighbors.

One of the naval officers who had answered my question incorrectly explained, when we discussed the exam, that he knew very little about these Jewish communities but surmised from my story of chasing off the thief that I must have had that nerve because of my Eastern European origin. It was then that I realized that the only reason I had acted so bravely (even rashly) in the parking lot was because I had just returned from Israel, where the Israelis had just won the spectacular Six-Day War. Our people were no longer acting passively in the face of their enemies, and I too had the courage to act!

Chapter Five
Some Early Experiences in Israel

WE SAILED FOR Israel in August 1969 on the Greek ship *Queen Anna Maria*, with about two hundred other new *olim*.[1] Our spirits were very high. When the ship motors developed a malfunction and the boat had to slow its pace, turning a fourteen-day trip into an eighteen-day passage, we and many of our shipmates were most pleased to have the extra four days at sea. We had

---

1 *olim* (immigrants)

a kosher dining room on the boat, and we held many discussions about where to settle and how to adjust to the new country. We even had a daf yomi (page-a-day Talmud) study group on the ship. The Jewish Agency representatives gave us all the necessary papers and certificates that we would need and gave us instructions about the many new problems that we would face.

We disembarked at Haifa seaport on the day that Rabbi Yosef Kahaneman, the Ponevezher rosh yeshiva, had passed away. He had conducted *sheva brachot* for us in Florida, in 1951, during our first week of marriage, and we had tithed our wedding gift monies for the construction of houses for the aged in Bnei Brak.

We arrived with a Torah Scroll that had been saved from Austria after Hitler entered Vienna[2] and gave it to Simcha Hillel to carry down the gangplank. He led our family procession with the Torah wrapped in a tallit. As soon as his feet touched dry land, a policeman

---

2 This Sepher, as mentioned in Chapter Three, was rescued from under the nose of the Nazi army when it entered Austria during the Anschluss (March 12, 1938). When they entered Vienna, my former in-laws, Rabbi Elisha and Rivka Kohn, realized that not only must they find a way to leave Austria, but they must also rescue the Torah Scroll that the family had in their family synagogue. They packaged the Sepher for mailing to America and carried it to the post office in a basket of dirty clothes. They succeeded in sending it off while working at getting themselves to America, after an unsuccessful attempt to be smuggled into Switzerland.

approached and asked if that was a Sepher Torah. When he answered in the affirmative, the policeman immediately gave the Torah a kiss. That was how we arrived on Israeli soil!

Nachum met us and related that he had already learned two important things about the Hebrew language, as spoken in Israel:

1. Orange juice is called *mitz tapuzim* (lit.: juice of oranges), but the *mitz tapuzim* served to you in Israel can hardly be what we called orange juice in America. Rather, it tasted like some nasty and bitter orange-colored water.

2. Words in a newspaper or on a signpost that you can't understand are, likely, English words transliterated with Hebrew letters. For instance, ניאגרה, pronounced "neagara" (as in "Niagara Falls"), is a water-closet, and פנש'ר, pronounced "poncher," is a puncture, or a flat tire.

We were sent to a Haifa hotel for the night and then on to the Absorption Center in Yibna/Yavne, as we had agreed. We were, however, misinformed as to how the center would meet our specified housing needs. "Easy" travel to the university required walking twenty minutes on a dirt road to the main highway, where we could get a bus to the university; "prepared food" required selecting a live chicken from the shohet[3], having him slaughter and pluck it, and then preparing it at home; and the available washing machine, which was in the basement of the Absorption Center, didn't work.[4]

Some of the additional problems included: walkways that were bounded by low barbed wire, clearly dangerous for our four-year-old child. Hot water for washing dishes was available only in the shower room, where we could pile the dishes on the closed toilet seat and direct the shower head to spray on them. The only door in the apartment, aside from the entrance door, was for the shower room. Since these problems were substantial, we requested a transfer and were eventually relocated to the Absorption Center in Lod, which was very much better. Eventually we moved into faculty housing at the university, until we were able to find an apartment nearby.

This provided a wonderful experience that enabled us to know the eleven other professors and senior staff workers and families who were living there. These

---

3 *shohet* (ritual slaughterer)
4 Several years later, the author was interviewed by Maariv newspaper about this aliyah ordeal, but the interview was never published because the editors felt that it was too negative for public dissemination.

included Professor Shlomo Eckstein—who headed a project for the economic feasibility of the "Med-to-Dead Canal"[5]—and Professor Baruch Kurzweil, who "discovered" Shmuel Yosef (Shai) Agnon, which led to Agnon's receiving the 1966 Nobel Prize for Literature. He believed that Agnon and Uri Zvi Grinberg were the greatest modern Hebrew writers, while disagreeing strongly with Ahad Haam and Gershom Scholem, whom he saw as attempting to establish secularism as the foundation of Jewish life in Israel. Additionally, Professor Yehuda Friedlander, eventually the rector of the university, lived

---

5 Proposed canal linking the Mediterranean and Dead Seas. See Darvish-Lecker, Tikva; Eckstein, Shlomo, Journal of Policy Modeling 8,3 (1986). *Evaluation of an energy project under uncertainty: the case of the Mediterranean-Dead Sea Project.* pp. 391-413.

At a later point in time, I directed Professor Eckstein's attention to the prophecy of Zecharia (14:7–9) that at the "end of time," a stream of water will emerge from under the Temple Mount and become a raging river: "And there shall be one day which shall be known as the Lord's, not day, and not night; but it shall come to pass, that at evening time there shall be light. And it shall come to pass in that day, that living waters shall go out from Jerusalem: half of them toward the eastern sea, and half of them toward the western sea; in summer and in winter shall it be. And the Lord shall be King over all the earth; on that day shall the Lord be One, and His name one."

ז) וְהָיָה יוֹם-אֶחָד, הוּא יִוָּדַע לה' לֹא - יוֹם וְלֹא-לָיְלָה; וְהָיָה לְעֵת-עֶרֶב, יִהְיֶה-אוֹר. ח) וְהָיָה בַּיּוֹם הַהוּא, יֵצְאוּ מַיִם-חַיִּים מִירוּשָׁלַ‍ִם, חֶצְיָם אֶל-הַיָּם הַקַּדְמוֹנִי, וְחֶצְיָם אֶל-הַיָּם הָאַחֲרוֹן: בַּקַּיִץ וּבָחֹרֶף, יִהְיֶה. ט) וְהָיָה ה' לְמֶלֶךְ, עַל-כָּל-הָאָרֶץ; בַּיּוֹם הַהוּא, יִהְיֶה ה' אֶחָד, וּשְׁמוֹ אֶחָד.

He enjoyed the thought that perhaps this canal would be the fulfillment of that prophecy.

there. He had been a student of Professor Kurzweil. It fell to the two of us to sit with the latter's body in the morgue after his tragic suicide at the age of sixty-five. He was depressed over several matters at the time including the fact that he thought the university was not planning to do anything to recognize his approaching sixty-fifth birthday. In fact, they were secretly preparing to issue a commemorative book in his honor, but, sadly, it was being kept as a secret and surprise.

During our time in the faculty housing, we sought property near the sea and were successful in buying a plot of land on the sands of Herzliya. The location was magnificent. The only thing between us and the sea was the Dan Accadia Herzliya Hotel. In fact, when we moved in, our home was still unfinished, and we had to use the hotel's bathrooms for our needs. We also ran an electric wire from a neighbor's house. We had a good relationship with the hotel, and in later years, when we planned Etan's bar mitzvah on our lawn, we borrowed tables from the hotel for our reception. We also hired one of the cooks of the Tadmor Hotel to prepare the food.

We were the second house from the sands separating us from Tel Aviv, and this led to several unusual experiences. The first was on the night of our first Rosh Hashanah there. A very strong wind blew a yellow (poisonous) scorpion into our dining room, and it started to run toward our still-unemptied moving crates. We killed the dangerous creature. The second was when a poisonous snake tried to crawl into the house under a lawn door. I killed the snake and brought it to the biology department of the university. We were told that it was quite unusual for that specific snake species to be so far north. The third incident was on a Sabbath when the Coastal Road massacre of March 11, 1978, took place—the most lethal terror attack ever on Israeli soil. Fatah terrorists had landed on a beach near Kibbutz Ma'agan Michael, thirty kilometers south of Haifa. Two of the terrorists drowned when one of their landing boats capsized in the rough weather. Eleven terrorists continued their murderous mission and, upon landing, tragically met an American photographer, Gail Rubin, who was taking nature photographs. They asked her where they were, and after she told them, they killed her.

They then hijacked a chartered bus on the Coastal Highway carrying Egged bus drivers and their families on a day outing. The bus was finally stopped by a large police roadblock set up near our home. A firefight erupted, and police broke the windows of the bus and yelled to the passengers to jump out. The battle reached its climax when the bus exploded and burst into flames.

The explosion may have been set off by a burning fuel tank, or by grenades. A total of thirty-eight civilians were killed in the attack, including thirteen children. Seventy-one others were wounded. Nine of the eleven terrorists were killed.

The attack took place at minhah time, and I was in synagogue when we began to hear the drone of helicopters. Police cars with loudspeakers instructed all residents to go immediately into their homes and remain there until notified that it was safe to leave. Of course, we didn't sleep at all that night as soldiers combed the entire area for fear that perhaps one or more of the terrorists had escaped the bus and was at large. We went up to the roof of our house and saw squads of soldiers searching all around the nearby homes.

In the morning, a stranger saw us on the roof and asked if we had a television set and if so, might he come in to watch the special Israel Television program on the waylaying of the bus and its aftermath, which was about to be shown. It turned out that he was the TV correspondent who had filmed and recorded the story that we were watching.

Some Ultra-Orthodox spokesmen—described by scholars as Jewish-Fundamentalists—declared that the attack had occurred because the Egged tour took place on a Sabbath. This was a desecration of the Sabbath, they declared, and that's why the bus was consumed in fire.[6] Of course to the terrorists that was of no significance as they declared their original plan to seize a luxury hotel in Tel Aviv and take tourists and foreign ambassadors hostage in order to exchange them for Palestinian prisoners held by Israel.

According to a commander who had helped plan the attack, the timing was aimed at wrecking the Israeli-Egyptian peace talks between Prime Minister Menachem Begin and Anwar Sadat, and damaging tourism in Israel. Due to a navigation error, the attackers ended up forty miles north of their target and were forced to find alternative transportation to their destination.

Recognizing this mistaken "holier than thou" attitude, I allow myself a bit of introspection at this point. I regret a letter that I had written to the editor of the *Jerusalem Post*—published just one day before the Yom Kippur war. A few days earlier, someone had written a letter very critical of Orthodox Jewry as compared with other streams. He went on to praise the Conservative and Reform synagogues. Unfortunately, I too, responded in kind, and pointed out the faults of Conservative and Reform Judaism. I have pangs of

---

6   Based upon an *aggadic* statement in the Talmud *Shabbat* 119b.

conscience realizing that just one day before this terrible war broke out, I and the other writer were involved in divisive statements about fellow Jews.

The day after my letter was published, the Egyptians and Syrians demonstrated that to them all Jews deserve hate and destruction, regardless of their affinity to one or another stream of Judaism. In our correspondence with the newspaper, we had acted like the Jews at the time of the destruction of the second Beit Hamikdash—i.e., with שנאת חינם (unwarranted hate of a fellow Jew). I pray that my letter did not add to the calumny of Our People and contribute to the outbreak of the war.

Volunteering in a Rehabilitation Ward

During the 1973 Yom Kippur War, studies had been suspended because so many of the students and faculty were called up for army service. Being free from teaching, I made it my business to visit the Rehabilitation Ward of Tel Hashomer Hospital in Ramat Gan every day. The wounded soldiers, who had lost a limb, or more than one, were in the rehabilitation ward awaiting replacement limbs and physiotherapy to learn how to use them satisfactorily. Most of my time was spent talking and helping them with their needs and also assisting them in putting on their tefillin. The bravery of the men on the battlefield and their struggle with recovery left lasting impressions on me. Here are some of the highlights that I would like to preserve:

- One man, who had lost both legs on the Bar-Lev Line in Sinai, experienced a severe trauma when he looked at himself in the mirror for the first time wearing his temporary prostheses. To make learning to walk again easier, his temporary legs were fashioned ten centimeters shorter than his former height. The trauma of this tall, handsome officer seeing himself so short was extremely shocking. After a while, he was given permanent prostheses that restored him to his normal height.

- Two other men who had also each lost both legs were progressing fairly well. One of them decided that he was going to make a supreme effort to learn how to walk on his prosthesis. He did extremely well, even walking one hundred meters without help, but then—realizing that the effort had sapped him of all of his strength and he couldn't go any farther without resting—he suffered a deep disappointment and sense of hopelessness. The second soldier recovered much more slowly—he had suffered additional injuries—but eventually made a much better adjustment to his situation. The secret was that the first soldier was the main support of his widowed mother and got but little emotional support from her, while the second soldier had a large supportive family that helped him readjust to his new condition and maintain his self-confidence.

- A soldier who had lost an arm in battle had picked up the severed limb and, dazed, walked with it toward the Egyptian lines. The Egyptians panicked at the sight of a man carrying a severed arm, and they bolted. Their flight enabled the medical corps to rescue him. Unfortunately, he contracted tetanus on the remaining stump. The surgeons had to remove more and then more again of his arm—until there wasn't enough left for putting on tefillin.[7]

- Another soldier who had lost two hands while dismantling a bomb was struggling with how

---

7 There is a halakhic opinion that when the left arm is unavailable anymore, one puts the tefillin on the right arm without a blessing (see Magen Avraham 27:3 and Pri Megadim, EA 27:11). The consensus, however, is that the right arm is not an option for a right-handed person (see *Aruch HaShulchan* 27:7), and he is only obligated to wear the head part of the set of tefillin.

he would face his very young children with claws in place of hands, and pockmarks all over his face. He later recounted to me that when his one-year-old did not react in any way differently toward him, the three-year-old followed suit—after initial fear and reticence—and allowed herself to be embraced by him. Interestingly, forty years after his release from the hospital, he sought me out to thank me for helping him adjust to his new and sad situation. I had seen his wife assisting him with the tefillin, but struggling with the length of the strap on the severed arm. I went to the nurses' station, took a pair of scissors, and cut the strap to size. He felt the need to tell me that my action helped him greatly in accepting the fact that his hand was no longer there. It was important enough for him to have searched for me for forty years to express his gratitude for that act. A schoolteacher, he related how he got his students to accept the fact that he was still boss in the classroom. On the first day after he returned to the classroom, the children defiantly ignored him and continued their chattering. He picked up a piece of chalk with his claw and tossed it accurately at one of the children. That solved the discipline problems for the whole year.

- One soldier, who was a recent immigrant from the United States, had lost an arm and had additional injuries. On the field of battle a medic ran over to him to help and spoke to him in English—thinking that it would be comforting to the injured soldier speaking to him in his native tongue. The injured man pleaded with the medic to speak to him in Hebrew. He said, "I gave enough to my country for you to speak to me in Hebrew!"[8]

A final incident of our early years in Israel led to our son Nachum's marrying Schulamith. Shortly after our arrival, we purchased our first car in Israel and

---

8 This is reminiscent of an interview of my wife's grandson, Elisha Rosenzweig, who was injured in a suicide attack on a Jerusalem Street on January 27, 2002, by a twenty-eight-year-old Palestinian suicide bomber, Wafa Idris, who worked for the Palestinian Red Crescent in Ramallah. She managed to pass through the Qalandiya checkpoint while she was driving a Red Crescent ambulance and dressed in the organization's uniform. The explosive device was hidden in the ambulance. Elisha had been hospitalized for burns on his hands and shrapnel in his foot. A television team from Savannah, Georgia, had come to our home for a program on emigrants from Savannah and wanted to know if Elisha regretted his parents' having brought him to Israel. Elisha responded, "The fact that I was injured here only makes me identify even more with Israel."

decided to take a trip to the north. The only one who was free to travel with me at that time was Nachum. While driving along the Sea of Galilee in the vicinity of Tiberias we saw a small winding road that climbed a cliff overlooking the lake and decided to drive up and see the view. We were captivated by the beauty of the scene and stopped to enjoy it. After a while, we continued on to the top, which was the site of Poria Illit. This small settlement, 140 meters above the lake, was settled in 1912 and operated as a farm run by Jewish immigrants from the Second Aliya. Abandoned during World War II, it was reestablished in 1955 as a Yemenite farming community. All it contained now was two rows of private homes and an abandoned collapsed large building that had once been used as a vacation home for the Ponevezh Yeshiva in Bnei Brak. To our surprise, we passed two children wearing kippot in one of the front yards but disregarded them and continued on our way.

Several months later at a psychological conference in the university, I found myself sitting next to a religious pediatrician, Dr. Uri Levy. We chatted and he mentioned that he lived in Poria Illit. I asked if the children we had seen there were perhaps his children? He affirmed it and said that they were the only children in the settlement who might have been wearing kippot.

He then invited us to visit him in his home. Several weeks later we accepted the invitation—and eventually, Nachum married his daughter, Schulamith. She was born in 1955, exactly on the day that my father had passed away. Thus, the continuation of my father's family through me, by way of my oldest son, was set on his yahrzeit, as a result of these strange coincidences.

We enrolled our second son, Simcha Hillel, in the Kfar Haroeh yeshiva high school, which was headed by Rabbi Moshe Zvi Neria, the founder of the Bnei Akiva yeshiva movement and one of Rabbi Abraham Isaac Kook's most influential students. Shortly after Simcha's arrival in the yeshiva, Rabbi Neria was elected as a member of the Knesset for the National Religious Party. He served simultaneously in both positions from 1969 to 1974. Interestingly, on his first day in this yeshiva, when the teacher did a roll call of the students, and called out the name Dershowitz, two students stood up. One was Simcha Hillel and the other was the child of Yehudah Dershowitz, then of Bnei Brak, who albeit came from Pilzno but was not known to be related to us—obviously, he was from that "other" Dershowitz family in Pilzno, mentioned above.

After completing high school, Simcha was drafted and served as a tank commander during the Yom Kippur War. During the disengagement period after the war, his tank was among the frontline tanks on guard and assigned to reenter the Mitla Pass in case war was restarted. He and his crew slept under the tank during this tense period. He ended his army career as an officer in the air force, serving as a psychologist at one of its air bases.

My youngest son, Etan, had served in the intelligence corps on Mount Hermon, overlooking and observing the Syrian countryside leading to Damascus. Later, he worked in political advertising. In 2003, then-Prime Minister Arik Sharon proposed a unilateral disengagement from Gush Katif, i.e., the Jewish communities in Gaza. Under pressure from the general membership of the Likud, he committed himself in advance of a vote by the government Cabinet to abide by a general Likud party

Israel

referendum on the plan. Etan ran the campaign against relinquishing the Gush Katif settlements. The referendum was held on May 2, 2004, and ended with 65 percent of the voters voting against the disengagement plan. The prime minister, however, backtracked on his commitment, ignored the vote, and approved the disengagement. The accompanying picture is of our niece, Dvira Kvadrat, beseeching the soldiers not to evacuate them from the Gush.

Torat Eretz Yisrael, and Gush Emunim

One of the remarkable things that happened to us when we came on aliyah was having the writings of Rabbi Avraham Isaac HaCohen Kook, the first Ashkenazi Chief Rabbi of Palestine under the British Mandate, come to life. His influence was not very great in the yeshivas of America at that

Photo courtesy of
Ravkooktorah.org

time, and we really didn't identify with his teachings. We knew a bit of them, and we also knew that he had had a great influence on my Rebbi—and his picture hung in my Rebbi's sukkah on the roof of the yeshiva building.

When we came on aliyah, I began to study his works more carefully and began to identify with them, heart and soul. In 1913, while serving as Chief Rabbi of Yafo/Jaffa, Rabbi Kook visited Ein Harod and other settlements around the country. Samuel Thrope wrote about that trip:

The rabbi's goal was to teach and preach to the young socialists who had founded these small communities, part of a wave of Jewish immigration in the years leading up to the first World War that came to be known as the Second Aliyah. Between 1904 and 1914 some 20,000 Jews arrived in Palestine, mostly from the Russian empire.

These pioneers—as they were known—were fiery idealists, hoping to remake themselves, the land, and Jewish history through communal labor and cultural revolution. They were also vociferously anti-religious, having abandoned traditional, commandment-bound observance for the Zionist promise of a new Hebrew life, a fact that Rav Kook knew well. On kibbutz settlements like Degania, Kinneret, and Ein Harod, kosher food was not to be found. Even and perhaps, especially, Yom Kippur went uncelebrated.[9]

My Rebbi told me that despite the criticism of Rabbi Kook by many of the rabbis in Israel at that time, Rabbi

---

9   See Mirsky, Yehudah. *Rav Kook: Mystic in a Time of Revolution. Jewish Lives*. New Haven, CT: Yale University Press, 2014.

Kook had explained his reason for optimism regarding the antireligious settlers. He said, "While it is certainly true that they are currently non-believers, I am encouraged by the fact that they are asking the 'proper' religious questions. . . . At the 'end of days,' we will see a generation that knows (דור דעה). One cannot 'know' if he never asked the right questions and received the right answers. These pioneers are already asking the right questions."

Thrope, inter alia, quotes Yehudah Mirsky's noting that Rabbi Kook "could not talk the young revolutionaries into embracing precisely what they had come to Palestine to reject."

Thrope continues:

From the perspective of contemporary Israeli society, there is no small irony in Rav Kook's failure in this and other attempts to turn his messianic and mystical notions into political reality. Israel today is, in many ways, a country that Rav Kook made. Since the 1967 Six-Day War, the political power and cultural influence of those who look to the rabbi's work for guidance and inspiration has continued to grow. While a large part of Israeli society still sees itself as the inheritors of the pioneers' anti-religious socialism, messianic Jewish nationalists [e.g., Gush Emunim] influence the political agenda, and fealty to blood and soil is seen more and more as having the preeminent imperative of divine command.[10]

Notably, Rabbi Kook participated in the formal inauguration of the Hebrew University on April 1, 1925. My Rebbi told me that in exchange for gracing the event with his presence, he had extracted a pledge from Dr. Chaim Weizmann that purveyors of Higher Criticism[11] would not be invited to lecture at the new university. Seven years later (1932), he was deeply saddened to hear that elements of Higher Criticism were, indeed, being studied. The University had relaxed its commitment (apparently, by hiring Professor Naftali Herz Tur-Sinai [Torczyner], who belonged to that group of scholars)—notwithstanding that they had hired him under a different title, that of professor

---

10 Samuel Thrope, Many Admirers, Few Disciples: The Life and Legacy of Rav Kook," *Marginalia: Los Angeles Review of Books*, October 14, 2014.

11 "Higher" criticism, sought to investigate and interpret biblical documents like any other document of antiquity. Primarily, assuming a secular perspective of Scripture. Higher critics were interested not only in the Bible's primal literary sources, but also in the operative and undisclosed assumptions of the biblical writers themselves.

of Hebrew Language Studies. My Rebbi recounted that Rabbi Kook cried when he was informed of the appointment.

The appreciation of Torat Eretz Yisrael was exemplified and most fully developed by Rabbi Kook in his work *Orot HaTorah*, Chapter 13, "*Torat Chutz LaAretz V'Torat Eretz Yisrael* (The Torah of the Diaspora and the Torah of the Biblical Land of Israel)." There he elucidates a theory that is consistent with his wider mystical-nationalist philosophy. For Rabbi Kook, the Jewish nation is only fully in tune with its own spirit when living in Israel, its organic source. Only with the return to Zion, he wrote, can the Jewish people recapture their essence and reconnect with God, whose presence is manifest fully only in the Jewish homeland. The Midrash[12] teaches that the Torah of the Land of Israel is likened to the best-quality gold, in contrast with the Torah of the rest of the world, as its wisdom is unlike that of the rest of the world. Only through Torah study, mitzvah performance, Zionism, and cultural activity can the Jewish People achieve its national destiny.[13]

---

12 ויקרא רבה (וילנא) פרשת שמיני פרשה יג – "אשר שם הזהב" (בראשית ב, יב)
אלו דברי תורה שנאמר (תהלים יט, יא) הנחמדים מזהב ומפז רב: וזהב הארץ
ההיא טוב, מלמד שאין תורה כתורת ארץ ישראל ואין חכמה כחכמת ארץ ישראל.

13 Paraphrased from Shiur #18 by Rav Tzvi Sinensky: The Israel Koshinsky Virtual Beit Midrash (VBM) of Herzog College in Kfar Etzion.

On the occasion of Rabbi Kook's eighty-fourth yahrzeit in 5779, an article about him and his teachings appeared in the Besheva newspaper. Rabbi Yisrael Porat is quoted as saying:

> He was a spring that steadily increases its flow. He used to speak for several hours straight, spawning gems embedded with ornaments on the topics of halakhah, aggadah, kabbalah, and religious philosophy. His words were pure and refined, to the letter of the Talmud and Midrashim, Zohar and Moreh Nevuchim, and in all books of Judaism in all fields. When he sat down at the table to write, he wrote endlessly, page after page, as long as he wasn't interrupted.

In the same article, Rabbi Reuven Margaliot is quoted as having said, "1 asked Rabbi Aryeh Levin zt"l: 'What made Rabbi Kook so great?' Rabbi Aryeh replied, 'I am not the one who knows how to estimate his greatness, but I can only say this: I have never seen any *katnut*[14] in him.'"[15]

---

14 Lit.: small-headed. A Hebrew slang expression that negatively describes someone who doesn't like to make much of an effort and won't initiate anything on his own.

15 Quoted from *Likutei HaRaya*, Vol. 1, pp. 17–24, as edited and translated by Rabbi Eliezer Melamed.

Rabbi Shlomo Yosef Zevin, one of the great teachers of the previous generation, went even further, when he wrote in Ishim ve'Shitot:

> It would not be an exaggeration to say that Maran, the Gaon Rabbi Avraham Yitzchak HaKohen Kook zt"l, was the only one of the Torah giants in our generation who had a command of both halachah and aggadah. Rabbi Kook was without equal in nigleh (the revealed side of Torah) and nistar (the hidden side of Torah). . . . in fact, in a sense, he personified halachah and aggadah (p. 210).[16]

Following in his footsteps, his only son, Rabbi Tzvi Yehuda Kook, was appointed as head of the yeshiva upon his father's death in 1935. He dedicated himself to his father's vision of Torah and the Nation of Israel and spent the next fifty years teaching, expanding, interpreting, and publishing his father's practical-messianic ideas. Eventually, the elder Rabbi Kook's belief that settling and building the Land of Israel would bring the Messiah would be interpreted by his son to apply especially to lands captured in the 1967 Six-Day War.

---

16 Rabbi Shlomo Yosef Zevin: *Kol Mevaser.* Volume 1. (Hebrew)

Three weeks before that War, on Israel Independence Day, Rabbi Tzvi Yehudah had given a deeply emotional speech that set the agenda for the National Religious Party (Mafdal). After the trauma of the Yom Kippur War, this led, in 1974, to a meeting in Kibbutz Kfar Etzion in which he charged his students to "Establish a new bloc to include the entire settlement population, yeshiva heads, scientists and educators, rabbis, settlers and youths, that will act to ensure Israeli sovereignty over all of the Land of Israel and develop settlements in it."[17] The outcome of this meeting was the founding of Gush Emunim.[18] Here is part of his 1967 discourse:

> Nineteen years ago, on the night when news of the United Nations decision in favor of the re-establishment of the State of Israel reached us, when the people streamed into the streets to celebrate and rejoice, I could not go out and join in the jubilation. I sat alone and silent; a

---

17 Yehuda Litani in *Haaretz*, January 1974.

18 Gush Emunim (Lit.: "Bloc of the Faithful") was an extra-parliamentary national-religious movement advocating Israeli sovereignty in the Golan Heights, Gaza Strip, Judea, and Samaria by a massive civilian presence in these territories. Gush Emunim called for coexistence with the Arab population. (https://www.globalsecurity.org/military /world/israel/political-parties-gush-emunim.htm)

burden lay upon me. During those first hours I could not resign myself to what had been done. I could not accept the fact that indeed 'they have . . . divided My land' (*Joel 4:2*)! Yes [and now after 19 years], where is our Hebron—have we forgotten her?! Where is our Shechem?! Our Jericho—where? Have we forgotten them!?

And all that lies beyond the Jordan—each and every clod of earth, every region, hill, valley, every plot of land, that is part of Eretz Yisrael—have we the right to give up even one grain of the Land of God? On that night, nineteen years ago, during those hours, as I sat trembling in every limb of my body, wounded, cut, torn to pieces—I could not then rejoice.[19]

And then, just three weeks after his motivating lecture, Hebron, Shechem, Jericho, and more came under Israeli control!

My wife and I participated in a covert activity of Gush Emunim on October 8, 1974. It was the evening after Simchat Torah, and it was planned as the "Hakafot Shniyot Night Action." Thousands of

---

19 Micheline R. Ishay *The Levant Express, The Arab Uprisings, Human Rights, and the Future of the Middle East. New Haven, CT: [as elsewhere]* Yale University Press, 2019, p. 96.

followers and backers drove and trekked with their camping equipment through the mountains and wadis to help a unit of settlers make a third attempt to settle Elon Moreh overlooking the city of Shechem (Nablus) which (according to tradition) encompasses the Tomb of Joseph and his sons, Menashe and Efraim. In anticipation of this settlement attempt, the army and police had set up numerous roadblocks to block us from aiding the prospective settlers.

As a result of this police and army effort, the groups of sympathizers of which we were part divided up into sixteen groups. We were instructed to go to Yeshivat Nahal Yitzchak in Moshav Nehalim near Petach Tikvah, as if to participate in Hakafot Shniyot (post-Simchat Torah dancing). As we neared the moshav, we were stopped by a police roadblock and asked where we were going. As coached, we claimed that we were going to participate in the yeshiva's Hakafot Shniyot. When we got there, we saw that there were dozens of additional cars, all gathered for the same purpose. We were told to follow the lead car. We drove down the highway for a while and then turned off onto a side road that put us in the middle of Wadi Ayalon. At this point, we were instructed to turn off our headlights and use only moonlight and the car in front of us for guidance. We drove a long while and then reentered a paved highway. It was almost dawn as we approached our destination, the town of Sebastia, the ancient hilltop capital of biblical kings, later ruled by Roman conquerors, Crusaders, and Ottomans. We then encountered another roadblock and were stopped in our tracks. Fortunately, we were following the car driven by Meir Har-

Meir Har Zion, Israel

Zion, a highly praised captain of the Israel Defense Forces' Unit 101.[20] Chief of Staff Moshe Dayan described him as "The finest of our commando soldiers, the best soldier ever to emerge in the IDF." Ariel Sharon described him as "The elite of the elite." His

---

20 A special forces unit of the IDF, founded and commanded by Ariel Sharon on orders of Prime Minister David Ben-Gurion, in August 1953. It was armed with nonstandard weapons and tasked with carrying out retribution operations across the state's borders—in particular, establishing small-unit maneuvers, activation, and insertion tactics. Members of the unit were recruited only from kibbutzim and moshavim, by invitation only, and any new member had to be voted on by all existing members before they were accepted. The unit was merged into the 890th Paratroop Battalion during January, 1954, on orders of General Moshe Dayan, chief of staff. He wanted their experience and spirit to be spread among all infantry units of IDF starting with the paratroopers. They are considered to have had a significant influence on the development of subsequent Israeli infantry-oriented units. Wikipedia.

three-year military career was ended by injuries sustained in battle.

When the soldiers at the barrier saw him, no one had the audacity to stand in his way, and he drove through their line at about five kilometers an hour. I followed immediately after him. The rest of the convoy also continued right through. Very close to Sebastia, we were confronted again by a roadblock. This time we were effectively stopped! Some of the people began arguing with the soldiers but made no impact on them. Others got out of the cars and started walking in the hills around the roadblock to the destination. We asked for and received permission to organize a morning prayer service before we left, so as to at least show a minimal settlement action. This led, eventually, to the army allowing the establishment of Shiloh in an army base nearby and to the establishment of many subsequent settlements.

At a National Convention on the Oral Torah (הכינוס הארצי לתושב"ע) with the chief rabbi, Isser Yehuda Unterman, that we attended at Mossad Rabbi Kook, one of the attendees, Professor Jacob Levinger, asked about the obligation to bring a Pascal Offering now that the Temple Mount was in our hands. The question was a halakhic question based on the possible obligation to practice the sacrifice of the paschal lamb even if there is no Temple,[21] if the area of the Temple is available. Rabbi Unterman's response was simply an avoidance of discussion on the subject, "Yes! We all want the Temple. Now let's go on to the next question."[22]

---

21 רמב"ם הלכות בית הבחירה פרק ו הלכה טו - לפיכך מקריבין הקרבנות כולן אף
על פי שאין שם בית בנוי, ואוכלין קדשי קדשים בכל העזרה אף על פי שהיא
חריבה ואינה מוקפת במחיצה ואוכלין קדשים קלים ומעשר שני בכל ירושלים, אף
על פי שאין שם חומות, שהקדושה ראשונה קדשה לשעתה וקדשה לעתיד לבא.

22 The topic of offering the paschal lamb has been hotly debated over the centuries, with proponents including Rabbi Tzvi Hersh Kalisher, a nineteenth-century rabbi of Thorn, Germany, who published an entire work, Derishat Tzion, not only claiming that it is permissible to bring the offering nowadays at the location where the altar used to stand on the Temple Mount, but that there is an obligation to do so. Practically, however, this debate was not relevant for most of our long exile. This all changed with the retaking of Jerusalem by the Israeli army in 1967. Suddenly, this was a question with real-life implications. And the debate heated up.

The Lubavitcher Rebbe initially took a somewhat middle-of-the-road position. On the one hand, he agreed that it was highly doubtful that one would actually be required to bring a pascal lamb today. On the other hand, the verse states that if one is obligated and able to but fails to do so, he is liable for *karet* (spiritual excision). So, the Rebbe advocated, albeit never as a public campaign, that Jews leave Jerusalem on the 14th of Nissan (and again on the 14th of Iyar), since if one is at a distance from Jerusalem at the appointed time, he isn't halakhically required to bring a pascal lamb. Thus, they would be avoiding the issue. In 1975, the Rebbe wrote a letter explaining that due to the changed political and security situation, there was no longer a real possibility of building an altar on the Temple Mount. Therefore, he no longer saw the need to leave Jerusalem on Passover eve. (Extrapolated from Chabad.org, Can We Sacrifice a Paschal Lamb Nowadays? By Yehuda Shurpin.)

Rabbi Unterman's reticence in this matter is reminiscent of the time a group of modern-day zealots removed the sign that the chief rabbinate had hung near the Moghrabi Gate stating that it is forbidden to enter any area of the holy Temple Mount grounds. That statement is halakhically inaccurate, since in certain areas—with proper preparation—it is permissible, as most scholars will admit, but is marginalized by the chief rabbinate. After the sign was removed, the rabbinate rehung it but changed the language so that it doesn't present a blanket prohibition. At present, thousands of fully observant Jews visit the Mount regularly with proper preparation. On the Succot holiday, 5782 (2021), discreet prayers were also permitted by the police and hundreds of observant Jews took advantage of the opportunity.[23]

Rabbi Shlomo Goren

Rabbi Shlomo Goren founded the chief rabbinate of the Israel Defense Forces and served as the first IDF Chief Rabbi. After retirement from the army, he served from 1973 to 1983 as Ashkenazi Chief Rabbi of Israel. He had volunteered for the Haganah in 1936 and served

---

23 "In Shift, Israel Quietly Allows Jewish Prayer on Temple Mount." *New York Times*, Patrick Kingsley and Adam Rasgon, Aug. 24, 2021, Updated Aug. 25, 2021.

as a chaplain for the Jerusalem area during the War of Independence. To his credit, the army was made completely kosher and fully observant of the Sabbath (when emergencies didn't require its desecration). In this, he had the full support of Prime Minister David Ben-Gurion, who also wanted an army without sectarianism.

Wikipedia

He volunteered to qualify as a paratrooper after General Arik Sharon promised to make the Paratrooper Corps kosher if any soldier in his unit requested such food. After his enrollment he presented himself to General Sharon as a paratrooper requesting kosher food, and Sharon fulfilled his promise.

He won admiration for his dedication—often at great personal risk—in freeing *agunot*[24] by locating, collecting, and identifying bodies of soldiers whose remains had been left in the field. He retired with the rank of brigadier-general. Despite his efforts, a major task in which he did not succeed was keeping the Temple Mount in Jewish hands, in the face of fierce

---

24 *agunot* ("chained wives," as a result of husbands who had disappeared in war or in peace or who are refusing to grant their wives a religious divorce)

opposition by the defense minister, General Moshe Dayan, as recounted:[25]

> Lt. Gen. Mordechai "Motta" Gur's half-track led the attack [on the Temple Mount], crashing through the massive bronze doors onto the Via Delarosa. . . . He radioed headquarters: "The Temple Mount is in our hands."
>
> The brigade's chief communications officer, Ezra Orni, retrieved an Israeli flag from his pouch and asked Gur whether he should hang it over the Dome of the Rock. "Yalla [Sure!]," said Gur. Major Arik Achmon [chief intelligence officer for Brigade 55, who was celebrating his thirty-fourth birthday on that day] accompanied him into the Dome of the Rock. They climbed to the top of the building and victoriously fastened the Israeli flag onto a pole topped with an Islamic crescent.
>
> Except that then the flag was quickly and unceremoniously lowered. Defense Minister Moshe Dayan [only a few hours after Rabbi Goren had blown the shofar and blessed Shehecheyanu at the kotel] gave the order to

---

25 Makor Rishon, Cheshvan 17, 5780, Shabbat Supplement. (Hebrew)

immediately remove the Israeli flag that the paratroopers had raised. . . . [He] urgently radioed Gur and demanded: "Do you want to set the Middle East on fire?" Gur told Achmon to remove the flag. But Achmon couldn't bear the notion of lowering the Israeli flag, and so he instructed one of his men to do it instead.

It is, in retrospect, an astonishing moment of religious restraint. The Jewish People had just returned to its holiest site, from which it had been denied access for centuries, only to effectively yield sovereignty at its moment of triumph. Shortly after the war, Dayan met with officials of the Muslim Wakf, who governed the holy site, and formally returned the Mount to their control. While Israeli soldiers would determine security and stand at the gates, the Wakf would determine who prayed at the site, an arrangement that would effectively bar non-Muslim prayer. The Temple Mount was no longer in Gur's hands.

An unplanned victory ended in a spontaneous concession. No cabinet meeting authorized Dayan's move. The defense minister simply took advantage of his popularity within the Israeli public to manage Israel's most sensitive religious problem—an arrangement that has persisted ever since. In ceding the right of Jews to pray on the Mount, Dayan's intention was to minimize bloodshed and prevent the Palestinian-Israeli conflict from becoming a holy war.[26]

Personally, I never understood why Rabbi Goren left the Mount that fateful day to pray at the Western Wall. Had he stayed there and prayed publicly, perhaps Moshe Dayan would not have succeeded in relinquishing the Mount to the Waqf.

During the Yom Kippur War, when volunteering in Tel Hashomer Hospital, I turned to Rabbi Goren for his rulings on all of the religious questions that arose. The questions involved such things as how much of an amputated arm is necessary to be able to fulfill the mitzvah of tefillin? When may a soldier with a catheter in place pray or recite a blessing? And the like.

A thought-provoking and powerful experience with Rabbi Goren was when I was approached by an acquaintance for help in freeing his sister from her husband, who had been ordered by the rabbinical court to

---

26 Yossi Klein Halevi, "The Astonishing Israeli Concession of 1967," *The Atlantic*, June 7, 2017.

grant her a divorce but had fled and was hiding in the United States. I called Rabbi Goren and asked if he might be able to help. He heard the story and asked whether or not she was cohabiting with any man since her husband had fled. I told him that she was.

Since the woman herself was not acting like an *agunah* (lit.: chained woman), he responded that he would not publicly proclaim the annulment of the marriage, even though he could do so technically. Since the presiding *mesader kiddushin* (marriage official) who had served as one of the witnesses to the original marriage was known to be a desecrator of the Sabbath in public, the wedding was not religiously binding.

At that point, the brother asked if I would accompany him to the United States, where he was going to try to kidnap the recalcitrant husband and bring him back to Israel—where the rabbinate would try to convince him to grant the divorce they had originally ordered (They had no knowledge of the fact that the wedding was not religiously valid.) I declined but contacted Rabbi Moshe Feinstein and explained the situation to him. I inquired if the brother succeeded in compelling the man and bringing him to the *Rav*, would he be willing and able to force him to give the required *get* (Jewish divorce instrument)? The *Rav* said, "Get him to me and I will procure the required document."

The kidnapping attempt failed, because the husband saw the team that was trying to catch and anesthetize him and fled. Subsequently, I asked Rabbi Moshe how he had prepared for the attempt, and how would a forced divorce be valid? He told me that he was sure that he would have been able to convince the husband to grant the divorce. He had requested a *sofer* (scribe) to be in his house with all of the necessary materials and witnesses.

During an earlier time in Rabbi Goren's training, perhaps when he was at the Slabodka Yeshiva in Hevron, he was under the tutelage of my Rebbi, Rabbi Hutner. I once mentioned to my Rebbi what Rabbi Goren had ruled about zones on the Temple Mount—that if they are surely in areas in which halakhah permits a person who had properly immersed himself in a mikvah to enter, then he/she may enter those areas. My Rebbi exclaimed, "How could he take upon himself to rule on issues of the Temple Mount, when earlier great sages felt themselves unqualified to rule on such Klal Yisrael (Congregation of Israel) issues?" Of course, Rabbi Goren had ruled in his capacity as chief rabbi of the Israel Defense Forces and as such was required to rule on issues of the Mount that had only become relevant in 1967, after the site was conquered.

In 1972, he ruled on the well-documented case of the siblings Hanoch and Miriam Langer, who were born to a woman after she had left her first husband without a Jewish divorce, and remarried. This rendered them mamzerim (illegitimates: children of a union not sanctioned by biblical law) and thus forbidden to marry certain partners of their choice. Rabbi Goren set up a court of nine judges and ruled that the two were free from taint, because the first "husband," who was of non-Jewish Polish origin, had not truly accepted his own pledge to observe the laws of Judaism. This was evidenced by his continued attendance at his Polish church even after his "conversion," and other serious transgressions. This, despite the fact that the man, later in his home in Israel, lived according to halakhic requirements for a while.

Rabbi Goren set up his court after being asked by the then-minister of defense, Moshe Dayan, if he might be able to help these victims of their parents' conduct. He and the judges ruled as they did only after gathering much testimony, documents, and rabbinic opinions. I read the extensive responsa, as can anyone else, and understood their validity. Rabbi Goren, however, came under great criticism in many religious circles for the ruling and for the clandestine court.

He held a press conference and declared that the nine judges included heads of rabbinical courts, and even one who had been a member of a court that had previously ruled against the siblings. He said, however, that he would not publish the names of the nine for fear of reprisals against them by religious fanatics. After the decision, since he was also chief rabbi of Tel Aviv at the time, he ordered the local rabbinate to register Hanoch and Miriam Langer as marriageable according to Jewish law. Immediately after the ruling was announced, they married their chosen partners. Defense Minister Moshe Dayan was among the guests.

The Sephardi Chief Rabbi, Ovadiah Yosef, strongly disagreed with this ruling, bringing great dissension to the office of the chief rabbinate. Rabbi Goren later wrote that this matter was a source of great pain to him.[27] He called on his colleague Rabbi Yosef, and on all other rabbis and judges of religious courts in the country to make peace with him. Members of the Supreme Rabbinical Court said in reaction to the quickie court that they thought it undermined the judicial process. They wondered if the court appointed by Rabbi Goren had had time enough to examine the evidence carefully and hear all the witnesses.

A committee of top-level *poskim*[28] of the chief rabbinate of Israel affirmed Rav Goren's decision, but they

---

27 See Rabbi Goren's autobiography, *Rabbi Shlomo Goren—With Might and Strength*, edited by Avi Rath, Miskal/Yediot Ahronoth Books, 2013, Hebrew.

28 *poskim* (Orthodox Jewish adjudicators)

explicitly didn't publicize their names, so as to avoid the inevitable "shaming" that would have come from haredi circles. Rabbi Joseph B. Soloveitchik and Rabbi Yosef Eliyahu Henkin, who were undoubtedly leading poskim of the time in America, also agreed with Rabbi Goren's ruling and publicized their opinions.[29]

Despite his vindication, he ended his days in relative isolation. It was truly sad for me to meet him one Sabbath afternoon in a small synagogue near the King David Hotel, alone and apparently unrecognized by the regular congregants. At the conclusion of the Sabbath, as we left the synagogue, I accompanied him for some distance until he asked me if I lived in the direction that we were walking. When I replied in the negative and that I simply wanted to walk him home, he politely replied that he didn't want me to go out of my way for him. As per his obvious preference, I reluctantly left him to continue on his own way, alone.

Prime Minister David Ben-Gurion

One of our earliest trips around the country was in 1970 and included a visit to Sde Boker, the Negev desert kibbutz that served as the retirement home of

---

29 Ari Shvat, *Rabbi Goren and His Heter for Mamzerim in the Langer Case*, Yeshiva.org.il, Shevat 18, 5778.

Israel's first prime minister, David Ben-Gurion. Quite by chance when we arrived we found him sitting on the lawn, being interviewed by an American television team in honor of his forthcoming eighty-fifth birthday. When the interview was concluded, my wife and I approached him and introduced ourselves as new olim. He

Wikipedia

asked where we were settling, and we told him that we had made aliyah to teach at Bar-Ilan University, I in the education department and my wife in the psychology department. The American TV crew heard our statement and immediately reacted by saying that we were examples of reverse brain drain! Often, when possible, well-educated Israelis and other academics follow their career goals in the United States, because there are so many more professional opportunities there than in their native lands. Here we were, two well-educated academics leaving the United States and going to spend our careers in Israel. We, however, were well satisfied with our decision to "go home." This decision was quite in contrast to what an Irish colleague at Long Island University had said to me when told that we were leaving for Israel, "If I would think of leaving the United

States, I would never think of returning to Ireland. I might choose to go to New Zealand or somewhere else like that."

This reminded me of the joke that was current on the ship that carried us to Israel in 1969, about two ships that pass each other on the high seas, one going from Israel to America while the other was going from America to Israel. The passengers on the boat leaving Israel shouted, "*Meshuganas* (fools)*!* where are you going? Why are you leaving America, the land of opportunity?" In response the passengers on the boat headed for Israel shouted, "*Meshuganas!* Why are leaving the Jewish homeland?"

At that point, Ben-Gurion asked us our names, to which we replied, Dershowitz! He immediately responded, "You have to change your name and choose a Hebrew name!"[30] In fact, he was our inspiration, after my parents were no longer alive, to change our family name to Dor-Shav, maintaining the sound of

---

30 David Ben-Gurion himself was born David Green and had changed his name to Ben-Gurion, after one of the chief leaders of the First Jewish–Roman War of the year 66, Joseph ben Gurion. In June 1949, shortly after the War of Independence, he demanded that all names of places and geographical features in the Negev be changed to Hebrew. He also established the policy that government workers—especially those whose jobs require contact with the outside world—adopt Hebrew names.

the original name, but connoting "the returning generation."

The former prime minister was also involved in a five-letter exchange with Rabbi Simon Dolgin, rabbi of the synagogue in which we were praying in Jerusalem, Congregation Beth Jacob. The synagogue was founded by the rabbi with substantial funding from his for-

Photo courtesy of Congregation Beth Jacob

mer community in Beverly Hills and their Beth Jacob Synagogue. In 1952, as a young rabbi, he had sent a letter to David Ben-Gurion that resulted in an exchange that eventually was framed and hung in the rabbi's home. His primary inspiration for the letter is aptly portrayed by this excerpt:

> I take the liberty of writing to you concerning a problem which plagues me constantly since the State of Israel was established. . . . I live in the Diaspora, in America. . . . We anticipate the larger number of our children and grandchildren continuing as Americans. And that's the problem.
>
> Our grandfathers, yours and mine, had much in common with one another and with

Israel, the land. . . . We of this generation, too, have had much in common, although we reside in lands far apart . . . we have faced a common struggle and challenge. In our day Jewry has experienced its most devastating years. Long before Hitler, many of our people realized that Jews would be victims of their neighbors' treachery so long as Israel was homeless, and so long as a more progressive world order did not prevail. That is why you and many others ascended to Palestine, pioneered its neglected soil and made untold sacrifices to build the state. That is why you have espoused a socialist philosophy as embodied in Mapai and the Histadrut.

While the struggles and challenges which prompted you to build Israel did not motivate me in the same fashion—perhaps my experience was not so trying—I have, indeed, developed a tie with Israel. I had tried to give of my energy and finances to the building of the new state. It has meant much to me, not only because it has provided a haven for homeless brethren, but because it has proved to be a fulfilment of one of my dreams and labors of love. Indeed, I look forward to the day when I may visit, or perhaps settle, in Israel.

Hence, you in Israel and me—or we—in the dispersion have much in common. . . . What troubles me, however, is our grandchildren—yours in Israel and mine in America. What will they have in common as Jews? They will have no political, economic, or daily social identification with one another. They will be citizens of different lands and will be members of separate societies.[31]

The gist of Ben-Gurion's final response was that they shared two treasures that will help bind future generations:

I believe—that there is no complete, secure, and certain solution to this question, except for two things: a broadening and ever stronger bond with the State of Israel, and a Hebrew education at whose foundation lies the Bible.

The Bible is not only a religious book as is the Koran or the New Testament. Without doubt the Bible is the foundation of the Jewish

---

31 For the full text of the letters, see: "Can We Stay Jews Outside 'the Land'? An exchange of letters between Israel's Prime Minister, David Ben Gurion, and a Los Angeles rabbi, Simon Dolgin," *Commentary Magazine*, September, 1953.

faith,[32] but it is more than that: in it is found the source of the people, its supreme expression and its universal and Jewish vision of the future.

There may be various approaches to the Bible: the approach of the religious Jew who believes that this is a book given from Heaven, and all which a scholar has discovered or will discover is already indicated in this book. There is another approach to the Bible: in all its characteristics the Bible cannot be compared to the religious books of other peoples. In the Bible Jewish history lies treasured, the first appearance of our nation on the stage of history, and its development as a nation distinct in its type.

The Bible alone without the State of Israel will not suffice. Just as, according to my belief, Israel alone without the Bible cannot suffice. But this venerable creation—a religious, literary, poetic, and ethical creation—which is woven in the Bible [and] the historical regeneration of the people of Israel and of the spirit of Israel in the homeland of the Bible, are likely

---

32 David Ben-Gurion started the tradition of a weekly Bible study class at his official residence, a practice that was continued by Menachem Begin and Benjamin Netanyahu, when they served as prime minister.

to serve as a source of strength to the Jews who do not incorporate in their midst the State of Israel. But this cannot serve as a complete and full solution, because this can be realized only in Israel itself; it can serve but as a contributing cause for the existence of the Jews.[33]

Eventually, Rabbi Dolgin settled in Israel and became the director general of the Ministry of Religious Affairs—the first Western rabbi to hold that position—having been appointed by Minister Zerach Warhaftig of the National Religious Party. He related an incident regarding Ben-Gurion that had occurred shortly after his aliyah. At a commencement ceremony for Air Force pilots, he approached the prime minister and introduced himself. As soon as he said, "I am Simon Dolgin," Ben-Gurion excitedly exclaimed, "You must come to visit me in my office."

Rabbi Dolgin dutifully arranged for the meeting, and when he arrived, the prime minister instructed his secretary that he is not be disturbed even if a president or prime minister of a foreign land calls. At the

---

33 See: Itamar Warhaftig (ed.). *Mincha Le'ish*, Ariel: Jerusalem, 5751 (coauthored by Zecharia Dor-Shav).

meeting, among other things, he made two very profound statements:

1. When I have to make a crucial decision regarding the State of Israel, I sometimes feel as if the answer is rising up out of the ground and presenting itself.
2. If it weren't for the fact that religion in Israel is a political matter, I might even have decided to be religious.

Thus, we see that the leadership of the new State of Israel did not build the land from scratch only as a refuge from the oppression of the nations of the world. One might have thought that the inspiration of Zionism as presented by Theodor Herzl was the main drive. Zionism may have been instigated initially by the notorious antisemitic incident in which the Jewish French army captain Alfred Dreyfus was falsely convicted of spying for Germany. Herzl had been a witness to mass rallies in Paris following the Dreyfus trial and had stated that the Dreyfus case turned him into a Zionist. Also, that he was particularly affected by chants of "Death to the Jews" that he heard from the crowds.

Rather, the Zionist drive among the state leaders was rooted in the ancient prophetic literature of the

Torah, as Ben-Gurion stated in a major address to the members of the general staff of the nascent Israeli army, titled "Mission and Dedication,"[34] that he referenced to Rabbi Dolgin.

Buying into the "Jewish Head"

One of the impressive achievements of Bar-Ilan University School of Education was the work of Professor Reuven Feuerstein, assisted by his brother-in-law, Professor Yaakov Rand, with whom I shared my university office. Reuven's life-work was primarily the development of a theory of structural cognitive modifiability and mediated learning experience. It states:

> Individuals with brain impairment, because of congenital or acquired origin, may substantially and structurally improve their cognitive functioning, by a systematic intervention based on a specific, criteria-based type of interaction ("mediated learning"). Three application systems are based on it: a dynamic-interactive assessment of learning capacity and processes of learning, the LPAD (Learning Propensity Assessment

---

34 יחוד וייעוד (*Unique and Mission Oriented*) as published in the 1950 Yearbook of the State of Israel. (Hebrew)

Device); a cognitive intervention program called "Instrumental Enrichment Program," which trains cognitive, metacognitive and executive functions; and a program, which is oriented at working in context, Shaping Modifying Environments. These programs have been applied in widely different target groups: from children and young adults with learning and developmental disabilities, at risk of school failure, or having failed at school, because of socio-economic disadvantage or congenital neurological impairment.[35]

During the period of my service as chairman of the School of Education, the university was approached by Luis Alberto Machado, the minister for the development of intelligence in Venezuela, who was doing a worldwide search for methodologies that might be used to raise the general level of intelligence in his country.[36] Among the universities that he visited was Bar-Ilan University. Eventually, he invested in several programs, including Feuerstein's process of structured learning. In an informal moment of their negotiations with the

35 Jo Lebeer. "Significance of the Feuerstein approach in neurocognitive rehabilitation." *NeuroRehabilitation* 2016; 39(1):19–35.
36 See: Luis Alberto Machado, *Right to Be Intelligent*, First English Edition. Pergamon Press: 1980.

university, Machado's assistant in this search sat with me in my office and said to me in Yiddish, "He is looking to buy the Jewish Head."

Absorption of the Beta Israel Ethiopian Aliyah

The relationship between Jerusalem and Ethiopia began centuries before the birth of the State of Israel (see Appendix 9). The ruling imperial house claimed descent from King Solomon and the Queen of Sheba. Official titles of the emperors included "Lion of Judah."

Neither by appearance nor by dress were the Beta Yisrael distinguishable from other Ethiopians. Yet, they maintained their independence for over one thousand years despite continuous massacres, religious persecution, enslavement, and forced conversions.[37] Several theories have been proposed regarding the identity of their ancestors, suggesting their practices originated from one or more of the following:

1. Christians who converted to Judaism when they came in contact with Jews.
2. The Queen of Sheba by way of a child fathered by King Solomon.

---

37 Judith Antonelli, "The Plight of Ethiopian Jews," *Cultural Survival Quarterly* Magazine, September 1983.

3. Slaves of Solomon who were given to the Queen of Sheba as a gift.
4. The Agau, an ancient people from the northern and central Ethiopian Plateau.[38]
5. The Tribe of Dan, who fled Eretz Yisrael after the destruction of the First Temple.

The American Association for Ethiopian Jews (AAEJ) was established to help the Beta Yisrael rejoin the main body of Jewish people in Israel. They provided an assortment of student, tourist, and work papers allowing Ethiopian Jews to obtain passports, which made it possible for them to obtain visas for the United States. They then provided tickets routing the travelers to the United States—and on to Israel. They worked as quietly as possible to avoid interference from the Ethiopian government, although officials knew exactly what was going on. The process was full of obstacles, and the rescue of a single person often took as long as eighteen months.[39]

---

38 Ahmed Kradawi, "The Smuggling of the Ethiopian Falasha to Israel through Sudan," *African Affairs*, 90, 1991, pp. 23–49.
39 From records of the American Association for Ethiopian Jews (AAEJ), the American Jewish Historical Society of New York, and the Jewish Agency.

The world Jewish community had been mostly unaware of the existence of Jews in the Ethiopian province of Gondar and elsewhere. In the sixteenth century, the chief rabbi of Egypt, Rabbi David ben Solomon ibn Avi Zimra (Radbaz— רדב"ז) was asked to rule on a slave woman from al-Habash (Northern highlands of modern-day Ethiopia and the annexed Eritrea), who had been bought by a Jewish man and had a child with him. The slave mother claimed to be Jewish and said that prior to her capture into slavery, her Ethiopian husband was killed in a war, and their son wanted permission to marry a Jewish woman.

The Radbaz wrote a general halakhic ruling that "those who come from the land of Cush (southern Egypt and much of Sudan) are without a doubt of the Tribe of Dan." Throughout the nineteenth century, the majority of European Jewish authorities supported this assertion. The Radbaz added, however, that to marry out of their own community, they should undergo *giyur l'chumrah*.[40] Their eventual aliyah and absorption in Israel is a result of the ruling, in 1973, of Rabbi Ovadia Yosef, the Sephardi Chief Rabbi of Israel,[41] who accepted the Radbaz's ruling with his

---

40 *giyur l'chumrah* (conversion requiring only immersion in a ritual bath)
41 The Chief Rabbinate ruling is that *hatafat dam* and formal acceptance of the Laws of Israel are not required for *giyur l'chumrah* of the Ethiopian Jews.

qualification.[42] Rabbi Yosef added that giving them a proper Jewish education and the right to immigrate to Israel was a mitzvah. Rabbi Shlomo Goren, Ashkenazi chief rabbi at the time, agreed with Rabbi Yosef, based on a ruling by the previous Ashkenazi chief rabbi, Abraham Isaac HaCohen Kook. Rabbi Goren, however, did not issue an official statement to this effect, explaining that this was unnecessary in light of Rabbi Kook's 1921 letter calling for Jews across the world to "save their Falasha[43] brothers," and that this was still a relevant decree. Rabbi Yosef's ruling resulted in the Law of Return being applied to Ethiopian Jews.

---

42 יביע אומר, חלק ח' אבן העזר, סימן י"א - הרדב"ז בתשובה הנ"ל (דברי דוד, סוף סימן ה'), אחר שכתב שהפלשים האלו הם משבט דן בלי ספק, ומפני שלא היו ביניהם חכמים בעלי קבלה, תפסו להם פשטי הכתובים. ואילו היו מלמדים אותם לא היו כופרים בדברי רז"ל, והם כתינוק שנשבה לבין הגויים...ואפילו אם תמצא לומר שהדבר ספק (אם דינם כקראים או לא), מצוה לפדותם. וסיים, אבל לענין יוחסין אני חושש שמא קידושיהם קידושין, וגיטם אינו כתיקון חז"ל, שהרי אינם יודעים בטיב גיטין וקידושין.

(Free translation) "[According to the Radbaz] the Falasha are doubtless from the Tribe of Dan, but because they didn't have scholars of the Talmudic traditions, they assumed the literal meaning of the scriptural writings. If they had been taught our tradition, they would not have doubted its rabbinic interpretation. They are like children who have been abducted and raised among non-Jews. Even if we have some doubt about their Jewishness, it is our duty to redeem them." I conclude, "regarding marriage, I am fearful that their earlier method of marriage is religiously valid, while their divorce procedures are not [therefore they should undergo some type of minimal formal conversion]."

43 The name Falasha is a derogatory term meaning "landless, wanderers." It was given to the community by the Emperor Yeshaq I, in the fifteenth century.

When the chief rabbinate adopted this ruling[44] recognizing them as Jewish while requiring them to undergo this minimal conversion process, it was thereby providing the community with a tremendous accommodation! As Rabbi Yosef pointed out, the community's divorce procedures were not correct according to halakhah, hence raising the problem that some of their descendants might be mamzerim and forbidden to marry most normative Jews. The conjecture that some of them might not be of halakhic Jewish descent and need a formal conversion process guaranteed that they would now be able to marry any Jew, since converts cannot be ruled mamzerim! They were also required, at least while in the Absorption Centers, to send their children to the state public-religious school system.

In May 1991, after Ethiopian dictator Mengistu fled the country, the new regime consented to allow Israel to operate a continuous airlift, for a consideration of $40 million. This rescue was required as early as feasible. Thus, on the 24th and 25th of the month, which coincided with Sabbath, thirty-five Israeli flights transported 14,325 Ethiopian Jews to Israel in thirty-six hours of continuous nonstop flights. Seven babies were born during the flights. One of the Israeli pilots

---

44 The ruling was accepted by almost everyone. A notable exception was the Lubavitch community.

involved was a son of a childhood friend of our family, Bernard Reznikoff, of South 10th Street, Williamsburg.

Words cannot describe the excitement we felt upon turning on the television news that Saturday night and learning about the operation which was known as Mivtza Shlomo (Operation Solomon). It is unlikely that so many Jews had ever arrived in Eretz Yisrael over such a short period of time since the days of Ezra and Nehemiah when Cyrus permitted the return and construction of the second Beit Hamikdash.

It is noteworthy that once, while standing on the grand staircase leading to the Western Wall, I encountered a newly arrived Ethiopian Jew standing and gazing at the wall with great enchantment. When I engaged him in conversation, he said, "I have been waiting my whole life for this moment."

Personal Involvement in the Absorption of the Beta Yisrael

Six years earlier, after the first mass arrival of Ethiopian Jews in Mivtza Moshe,[45] the AAEJ wanted to arrange

---

45 Operation Moses. After it became clear that the immigrants who remained in the Sudanese camps were in danger, it was decided to pursue an operation of intense immigration, during which about eight thousand immigrants were brought to Israel using Israeli aircraft. Most of the immigrants in this operation originated from the Gondar area. Wikipedia.

a meeting of the rescuers and the rescued. One of the active workers of the organization was related to us by marriage, and we were asked to provide our home in Herzliya Pituach for this get-together. About a dozen rescuers came from the United States, and they invited and provided bus transportation for all the Ethiopians who were in the Absorption Centers to come for an afternoon Pesach outing.

Things in Israel regarding their religious absorption had not worked out as well as had been hoped. The Absorption Centers were under the direction of the Jewish Agency, and many of the directors of these centers were old-school left-leaning former Mapam and Labor Party members, who themselves were strongly opposed to their residents' interaction with rabbis and influential Orthodox leaders. Direct communication with the newcomers was difficult because the only language they spoke was Amharic, and interpreters had to be used. This posed a problem, because after the revolution and adoption of the constitution in Ethiopia in February 1987, the country was formalized as a Marxist-Leninist state. Consequently, the only highly educated Ethiopians were those who had studied in Addis Ababa University and had been indoctrinated with Marxism and antireligious sentiment. They were the only olim who knew both Amharic and English and were hired by the ministry of absorption to be official interpreters. There was a conflict between what the directors of the Absorption Centers wanted to see at the end of the acclimation period and what the Orthodox rabbinate wanted to see. The centers severely limited whom they permitted to enter and meet with the new olim, and the interpreters were helpful in censoring information that was intended to guide the assimilation of the olim toward a religious lifestyle.

So as to be in better control of their integration in Israeli society, a number of directors refused to let their residents come to our get-together. Of course, the residents were free to walk out of the Absorption Center whenever they pleased, but pressure was applied, and many did not board the buses that were sent for them. Nonetheless, over two hundred Ethiopians did come to spend the afternoon on the lawn of our home. It was moving to see so many people who had been rescued and to see their interaction with their rescuers. During the afternoon, the *kessim*[46] gathered the guests and offered prayers and blessings with all of the gathered affirming, "Amen." I understood the words "the God of Abraham, Isaac, and Jacob" and knew that our family was being blessed. In their homeland, the only

---

46 *Kes pl. kessim* (Ethiopian religious leader)

people who knew how to pray were the kessim, and the custom was for the community to listen to the prayers uttered by the kessim and answer Amen.

A most distressing sight at the get-together, however, was the several women with the tattoo of a cross on their foreheads. Some early Christians had taken the ancient practice of tattooing and infused it with Christian meaning. When some of these distressed women had come in contact with missionaries, seeking help, they were often enticed to be tattooed in exchange for financial assistance. Obviously, this practice is contrary to Jewish law, which forbids all tattooing—certainly tattoos with Christological significance. The Beta Yisrael, however, were not in touch with Rabbinic Judaism and may have interpreted the Torah injunction[47] as applying only to mourning practices. A typical

Photo by Donnie Adino Ababa, processed by Zecharia Dor-Shav

---

47 אנציקלופדיה תלמודית כרך א, אין מקרא מידי פשוטו—ושרט לנפש לא תתנו [וכתבת קעקע לא תתנו בכם], שאף על פי שדורשים ''לנפש'' לדרשה, מכל מקום אינו יוצא מידי פשוטו שאינו חייב אלא בשריטה על המת בלבד.

Talmudic Encyclopedia, Volume 1, *A Biblical Verse Never Loses its Literal Meaning* (Leviticus 19, 28). "You may not incise a skin scratch for a soul and a tattoo you may not place." Even though the Rabbis

reaction to their newly discovered normative Judaism is illustrated by the following:

> Hadas Nogah, an Ethiopian-Israeli who immigrated at the age of 9, remembers: "[Officials] told me that 'whoever has a tattoo on their body won't enter Jerusalem' When they told me that, I cried all day. I tried to quickly remove my tattoo, but a mark remained."[48] It is no wonder that many Ethiopians attempt to have their tattoos removed, if they can afford it.[49]

One year after Operation Moses, in my capacity as director of the Eliezer Stern Institute for Research and Advancement in Religious Education of Bar-Ilan University, we ran a conference of some four hundred professionals and Ethiopian leaders on the community's religious absorption. Among those invited was a group of about thirty kessim who were studying

---

interpret soul in other ways, one may not disregard the literal meaning of the verse, which refers to a departed soul.

48 Arnon-Ohanna, Yuval. *Jewish Exodus from Ethiopia: Children Describe their Journey from Ethiopia to Jerusalem Through Sudan*, Jerusalem: Misrad haBitahon, 2005, p. 163.

49 As quoted by Noam Sienna in *Eshkol Hakofer*, "Jews with Tattoos? Tattooing Traditions of the Beta Israel," February 24, 2019.

at a special *ulpan*[50] program of Machon Meir, under the direction of Rabbi Dov Bigon,[51] supported by the Ministry of Immigration. The ulpan was designed to enable the kessim to maintain their communal status—by teaching them normative Judaism. After two years in the ulpan, they were accepted by all religious councils in Israel as community leaders.

Kes Raphael Hadane.
Wikipedia

I used the occasion to honor the newly arrived *kes* Raphael Hadane,[52] who was chief kes of the Gondar section of Ethiopia. His son, Rabbi Yosef Hadane, had preceded him and had been taught and granted semikah by Rabbi Ovadia Yosef—becoming the first Ethiopian to receive that recognition. He eventually served a period

---

50 *ulpan* (adult education program)
51 Machon Meir was established by Rabbi Dov Bigon, a former commander in the Israeli Defense Forces, who took part in the liberation of Jerusalem and the Western Wall. Moved by the miracle of the Jewish nation's return, and driven to contemplate his personal attachment to Torah, he turned to study in the Mercaz Harav Yeshiva. Shortly after the Yom Kippur War in 1973, he founded Machon Meir to assist other Israelis in their first steps toward *teshuva* and began spreading the Torah of Love and Faith in the inclusive and passionate spirit of his teachers.
52 Recently deceased at the age of ninety-eight. For years, in Ethiopia, he had traveled from village to village to educate the Beta Yisrael in the Hebrew language and Torah. Sometimes he was away from home for months.

of time as Ethiopian Jewry's chief rabbi in Israel. To my surprise, when I introduced Kes Raphael as "chief kes of Ethiopia," an immediate objection was voiced by some of the kessim from the ulpan. One reason was the fact that many in the Ethiopian community were disappointed by the rabbinic ruling that they should undergo giyur l'chumrah since they felt that they should have been accepted as they are. Another reason was the disunity between the Jews of Gondar and Tigre. Eighty-five percent of the Beta Yisrael lived in Gondar Province, and the rest lived in the Tigre and Wollo Provinces. The lack of a unified leadership in the community was, I believe, part of the difficulty of their religious absorption.

Another difficulty was caused by Rabbi Yosef Hadane's apparent deception of some of the olim when he went beyond the ruling of the Chief Rabbinate requiring only immersion in a mikvah for giyur l'chumrah and performed hatafat dam[53] as well. Reportedly, he told the olim that this was being done for health reasons. When they found out that they had been deceived, they were very resentful.

A most serious point of contention with the Israeli religious establishment was experienced when, at a

---

53 *hatafat dam* (drawing some blood from the point of circumcision)

meeting of representatives of the community and the chief rabbinate, someone suggested, "All that we are asking of you is to immerse yourselves!" Some community representatives replied, "The missionaries, too, only requested that we immerse!" In response, the rabbis exclaimed, "Are you comparing us to missionaries?" At that point the meeting broke up.[54]

Photo processed by
Zecharia Dor-Shav

On the positive side, today, Beta Yisrael who came to Israel as children, or their descendants, are in the Knesset, the diplomatic service, the army, police, medical profession and in many other prestigious positions; Beta Yisrael crafts have become popular in Israel. The dream, however, that sustained them throughout the years of exile, i.e., their eventual return to the Land of Israel, has not been completely fulfilled, primarily because of problems in completing the reunification of families.

---

54 As reported to me personally by Dr. Shalva Weil, an expert in the subject of "lost" Jews, who was present at the meeting.

Most recently, the government has agreed to allow 5,000 of the Falash Mura[55] in, while many more remain in the camps.[56] President Yitzchak Herzog, formerly Jewish Agency chairman, called this a step in the right direction. Nonetheless, Herzog also insisted that the government quickly bring in all those still left behind. Approximately three-quarters of them have parents, children, or siblings in Israel, and all, according to activists, live today as Jews in Addis Ababa and Gondar and are ready to convert formally as soon as they reach Israel.

A ministry of education study of the religious absorption of the Ethiopian community, in which I participated as a professional consultant, was conducted by Dr. Shalva Weil, a senior researcher of the Hebrew University Research Institute for Innovation in Education. The study concluded that the olim generally devised one of four styles of adjustment:

---

55 Falash Mura is the name given to those of the Beta Israel community in Ethiopia and Eritrea who converted to Christianity as a consequence of the mission during the nineteenth and twentieth centuries. Wikipedia.

56 Read more at: al-monitor.com/originals/2021/11/israel-agrees-allow-entry-5000-ethiopians-links-judaism.

- Maintaining the practices that the community had developed over the centuries and continuing them in Israel.
- Synthesizing their previous practices with the new ones that are practiced in Israel.
- Conforming to the majority style of Judaism practiced in Israel, i.e., secular Judaism, and transferring out of the Religious School system as soon as possible.
- Adapting the Religious Zionist community's practices—especially the wearing of a knitted *kippah*—so as to be identified immediately as Beta Yisrael, rather than Negro.

In 2008, in recognition of the community's unique traditions, the Knesset legislated the Sigd Law, declaring the 29th of Cheshvan as a national holiday. Fifty days after Yom Kippur (similar to the holiday of Shavuot, celebrated fifty days after Pesach), the community marks the renewal of the covenant between the Jewish people, God, and His Torah. On Sigd, Ethiopian Jews pray and plead to return to Zion. The community also holds communal introspection, in addition to individual self-examination during Yom Kippur, because, according to their tradition, the whole populace must engage in communal introspection and repentance in order to be worthy of returning to Jerusalem from exile. Sins of the individual members of the community are forgiven during Yom Kippur and the following fifty days. On the fiftieth day, following communal intro-spection, the community returns to the Yom Kippur experience with prayers and abstention from food for the day.[57]

Despite the many efforts of all concerned, unfortu-nately, there is much evidence of poverty, discrimina-tion, unemployment, and suspicion of criminal activity in the community even today that does not exist with other, more established communities.

A Fortuitous Torah and Science Interface

An interesting interaction of Torah and science, in which I was tangentially involved, occurred as a result of my sharing an office in the university with Professor Moshe Arend. It led to a suggested proper understand-ing of the value of π (pi) as known by the Torah and as used by the Talmud.

The Dafyomi Advancement Forum (regarding the verse in Kings 1: 7, 23), among others, attributes the following to Rabbi Eliyahu ben Shlomo Zalman, known as the Vilna Gaon, and writes:

---

57 Sigd – Holiday of Ethiopian Jews – Knesset.

There is a superfluous letter 'Hei' in the word: v'Kav. . . . Alternatively, the ratio of the numerology of v'Kav with and without the Hei is 118/113=1.046 . . . extremely close to the correction factor (the circumference is really ?/3=1.04719 . . . times as big as the verse says it is. If we ignore a 'Vov' . . . and take this ratio, it is 111/106=1.04717, which is exceedingly close.[58]

My involvement was noted by Professor Isaac Elishakoff and Dr. Elliot M. Pines at the Fifth Miami International Conference on Torah and Science in 2003, during their lecture, "Do Scripture and Mathematics Agree on the Number π?" While referencing "On The Rabbinical Exegesis of an Enhanced Biblical Value of Pi" by Shlomo Edward G. Belaga of Strasbourg, France, the speaker stated:

A Hidden Value of π? Several authors comment upon a deep insight by Rabbi Max Munk, seemingly misattributed to the Vilna Gaon. The correct attribution is "Do Scripture

<hr/>

58 Dafyomi Advancement Forum, Point by Point Outline, comment on *Eruvin* 14a, point 7.

and Mathematics Agree on the Number Pi? B'Or Ha'Torah, 17 (5767/2007)," provided by Belaga, who associates it with correspondence with Rabbi Professor Zecharia Dor-Shav of Bar-Ilan University. . . . Rabbi Munk discovered a hidden second value of π through a comparative reading in depth of the relevant passages in I Kings and II Chronicles.

The two verses match when read out loud, but differ in their written versions. Rabbi Munk compared the gematria, or numerology, of the two different verses and found that the numerical value of the written form of the term "line measure" in I Kings equals 111, while in II Chronicles both its written and read-aloud form equals 106 and is read aloud as: וקו

וַיַּעַשׂ אֶת-הַיָּם, מוּצָק: עֶשֶׂר בָּאַמָּה מִשְּׂפָתוֹ עַד-שְׂפָתוֹ עָגֹל סָבִיב, וְחָמֵשׁ בָּאַמָּה קוֹמָתוֹ, וקוה (וְקָו) שְׁלֹשִׁים בָּאַמָּה, יָסֹב אֹתוֹ סָבִיב (Kings 1, 7:23)

(He made the "sea" of cast [metal] ten cubits from its one lip to its [other] lip, two circular all around, five cubits its height; a thirty-cubit line could encircle it all around.)

וַיַּעַשׂ אֶת-הַיָּם, מוּצָק: עֶשֶׂר בָּאַמָּה מִשְּׂפָתוֹ אֶל-שְׂפָתוֹ עָגוֹל סָבִיב, וְחָמֵשׁ בָּאַמָּה קוֹמָתוֹ, וְקָו שְׁלֹשִׁים בָּאַמָּה, יָסֹב אֹתוֹ סָבִיב. (Chronicles 2, 4:2)

(He made the "sea" of cast [metal], ten cubits from its one lip to its [other] lip, circular in shape, five cubits high; a thirty-cubit line could go around it.) Numerical values of the letters comprising the two written variations for "line," measure 116/111.

. . . The first draft of the paper appeared in October 1990, with a very gratifying response from both the Talmudic and scientific communities. . . Rabbi Dr. Nachum L. Rabinovich, of Maaleh Adumim, read the paper and suggested an important correction. . . Finally, and miraculously, Professor Edward Reingold, of Urbana, whose enthusiasm for the subject was most encouraging, introduced the author to Rabbi Dr. Zecharia Dor-Shav, of Bar-Ilan, who, by sheer coincidence, had just become aware of the existence of an exegesis and started to look for its source.

. . . In a week or so, the crucial references [Max Munk 1962, 1968] were found and transmitted to the author—all this has happened in the last week of April 1991, after eleven years of unsuccessful search for such a source! After hearing about the author's difficulties in locating the Hebrew references in Montréal, Professor Reingold found the articles in Urbana and sent the copies to the author. [slightly edited by ZD]

The fact is that as a result of a note to me from our son, Professor Nachum Dershowitz, friend and colleague of Professor Reingold at the Urbana campus of the University of Illinois, the question of the authorship of this analysis based on Chronicles came to my attention. My own colleague, Professor Moshe Arend, formerly of Frankfort, shared an office with me, and I asked him if he knew anything about this exegesis. His response was, "Yes, it comes from my former math teacher in Frankfort, Rabbi Max Munk, whose son lives in Bayit V'Gan in Jerusalem." I immediately called him and affirmed that his father had published this exegesis.[59]

A Terrorist Attack on Mercaz Harav Yeshiva

On March 6, 2008, Alaa Abu Dhein, age twenty-six, from the Arab neighborhood of Jabel Mukaber in East Jerusalem, shot numerous students who were in or near the library room of Mercaz Harav Yeshiva in Jerusalem. Eight students—including Yonadav Herschfeld, eighteen, a grandnephew of my wife by her first marriage—were killed. Eleven more were wounded.

The attack began at 8:30 p.m. local time and ended sixteen minutes later. Ten minutes after the shooting

---

59 Matityahu Hacohen Munk, *Three Geometric Problems in the Bible and the Talmud*, Sinai, 51 (1962), pp. 218–227. (Hebrew)

began, two police officers, one male and one female, arrived at the scene. The policewoman stopped a nearby passenger bus and prevented it from approaching, while the policeman entered the courtyard with a rifle. The terrorist noticed him through the glass door of the library and fired at him, but the officer, not knowing the precise source of the fire and afraid of harming innocents, did not return the fire and took cover.

The attacker was then stopped by a Mercaz Harav kollel student, Yitzchak Dadon. After hearing the shooting, he positioned himself on a small roof on top of the main entrance of the yeshiva that overlooks the courtyard in front of the library. Meanwhile, an off-duty IDF captain, David Shapira, a graduate of the yeshiva, heard the unusual noise in the street outside his apartment. He ran outside, grabbing his M-16 rifle, and tried to enter the compound. Police, who were already on the scene, stopped him as he approached the main entrance, instructing him to wait for the arrival of special forces.

He wasn't, however, prepared to wait and pushed the officer away, taking his police cap and putting it on his own head so that he shouldn't be mistaken for a terrorist. He entered the compound near the library door and positioned himself in a nearby corridor. Dadon, meanwhile, fired into the library, diverting the terrorist's attention. The terrorist stepped out of the library to see who was shooting. Dadon then shot and wounded him, stopping the terrorist in his tracks. Shapiro detected the terrorist and shot him dead. He received a citation for his bravery and responsibility in saving lives.

The murderous attack was praised by Hamas and, according to a subsequent poll, was supported by 84 percent of the Palestinian population. The terrorist worked as a driver for a private company that made deliveries to the yeshiva. He had entered the courtyard at its main entrance and continued into the entrance of the Yashlatz[60] high school building, which had a side door into the library. He was carrying a cardboard TV box concealing a Kalashnikov rifle with several magazines of shells. He took the weapon out of the box, firing first at some students who were standing in the courtyard, killing three of them. He then entered the library by way of the side door and opened fire, killing five students and wounding nine more. Seventeen managed to escape into an adjacent classroom and blocked the door with a heavy table. Altogether the terrorist fired as many as five hundred to six hundred rounds.

---

60 An acronym for Yeshiva LeTze'irim, the Mercaz Harav Yeshiva High School.

When the attack began, some of the high school students on the upper floors of the dormitory heard the shots and didn't know where the terrorist would be heading next. Many jumped out of the windows or from the porches. One of the rabbis was too scared to jump. The students pushed him over the wall. One of those who jumped injured his back and had to wear a brace for a period of time.[61]

Another survivor of the attack told me how *hashgacha pratit* (Divine Providence) had saved him from the massacre. He had arranged to meet one of the students who was selling *tchelet* (special, blue-dyed wool for tzitzith) just beneath the sign that had been posted at the high school entrance—the exact place where the murderer first took out his rifle. He wasn't quite feeling well and at the last moment called the student to tell him that he wouldn't be able to make their planned 8:40 p.m. meeting. Instead, he planned to leave for home immediately after the 8:30 p.m. evening minyan in the yeshiva shelter. That night, however, for the first time in memory, they couldn't get ten people together at prayer time. While they were waiting for a quorum, the attack took place, and they immediately locked

---

61 Information from personal knowledge as well as from Wikipedia and Jewish Action (Spring 2016).

their room. Had they prayed at the regular time, they would have left the shelter room just as the attack occurred. On that very same day, just two hours earlier, I had been studying in that library with my nephew and *chavrutah*, Gershon Bass. Several years later, the yeshiva put out a calendar in which they

Photo courtesy of Zecharia Dor-Shav

juxtaposed a picture of a bullet hole in the glass door of the library with a more current picture, which happened to show me in the same library studying with another one of my study partners, my cousin, Rabbi Meyer Fendel.

Chapter Six
Adventures on Sabbaticals

THE OPPORTUNITIES TO meet academics in other countries, as provided by the university once every seven years, gave us numerous opportunities to broaden our horizons. We made it our business to meet and study the Jewish communities in all of the many lands in which we had conferences or had made personal arrangements for meetings and observations. We visited Oslo, Stockholm, Miami, Savannah, New York City, Detroit, Toronto, São Paulo, Recife, Manaus, Sydney, Tokyo, Hong Kong, and many other venues. In 1993–1994 we took an assignment as visiting scholars at Melbourne University. Since the cost of a round-trip ticket to Melbourne was the same as a trip around the world, we availed ourselves the opportunity to circumnavigate the globe. Some of the more interesting, unusual experiences are recorded below.

The Downfall of Communism in the Soviet Union

Our adventure began with the Soviet Union. In 1989, in Moscow, Rabbi Adin Even-Israel Steinsaltz[1] had launched the first yeshiva in Soviet Russia since the communist revolution.[2] I was appointed to be scholar-

---

1   Rabbi Adin Steinsaltz (1937–2020) was born in Jerusalem to secular parents who had immigrated to Israel in 1924. His father, Avraham, was a devoted communist, a member of Lehi, who went to Spain in 1936 to fight with the International Brigades in the Spanish Civil War. Nonetheless, he sent his son, Meni, to a religious school. Meni quoted his grandfather as saying to his son, "being an *apikorus* (heretic) was better than being an *am ha'aretz*, (ignoramus)." Rabbi Steinsaltz became a *baal teshuva* and developed an attachment to Chabad and its variety of *hasidut*.

   In 1965, he founded the Israel Institute for Talmudic Publications and began his monumental work on the Talmud, including its translation into Hebrew, English, Russian, and various other languages. The Steinsaltz editions of the Talmud include a translation from the original Aramaic together with comprehensive commentary and notes. Based partially on Wikipedia.

2   He was recognized by the general public, no less than by the Torah community. As reported by Emily Langer in a *Washington Post* obituary on August 13, 2020, "Professor Walter Reich of George Washington University, a frequent commentator on Jewish thought and affairs,

in-residence for the Yamim Noraim season. The yeshiva was housed at the outskirts of Moscow; the former summer residence of the vice mayor of Moscow had been converted into a beit midrash and dormitory. The school itself had only seventeen students, of whom almost all had only one Jewish parent—and sometimes it was

Wikipedia

the father—thus making the child halakhically a non-Jew. Nonetheless, it had a significant influence upon hundreds of people throughout the Soviet Union. My assignment included lecturing in two Jewish universities that were also sponsored by Rabbi Steinsaltz, one in Moscow and the other in its affiliate in Leningrad. Generally, I lectured in Hebrew or English, and it was translated into Russian as needed.

---

wrote in an email, describing the rabbi as 'a genius . . . one of the greatest and most consequential scholars of the past thousand years of the Jewish people.'"

The only Israeli newspaper that didn't eulogize him was Yated Ne'eman, who had run articles condemning him and referring to strongly worded comments made by Rabbi Elazar Shach in 1989. It is clear that Rabbi Adin Steinsaltz's untraditional and "university oriented" approach is at odds with the *haredi* approach.

For the New Year, the yeshiva produced and distributed a Jewish calendar such as had not been available in the Soviet Union for decades. I know of at least one family in Leningrad who had celebrated Pesach a month too early because they didn't know that it was a leap year and that an extra month of Adar had been added to the calendar.

For Sukkoth, the yeshiva distributed seven hundred sets of lulab and ethrog. Every Sabbath, a number of local families came to join us for the Sabbath meals. On Rosh Hashanah and Yom Kippur, every available space on the floors of the halls of the building was covered with mattresses, as an overflow of guests arrived.

A particularly poignant but disappointing event for me was when one of the best students in the school decided to end his Jewish studies. Having a Jewish father and non-Jewish mother, rendering him non-Jewish, he decided to keep only the seven laws that obligate non-Jews and that are practiced by Noahides.[3] Among his reasons, he said, was a midrash (*Avodah Zarah* 3a) that he had heard from me. The midrash teaches that at the end of time, the non-Jews will complain that they,

---

3   These include prohibitions against worshipping idols, cursing God, murder, adultery and sexual immorality, theft, eating flesh torn from a living animal, as well as the obligation to establish courts of justice.

too, would have kept the laws of the Torah had it been given to them. In response, the midrash continues, they will be asked to observe the mitzvah of sukkah. They will immediately comply and built sukkoth, but when the day became uncomfortably hot, they will leave the sukkah and kick it down.

I had explained that in such a case, the halakhah does not require dwelling in the heat and one may move into more comfortable indoor quarters. Generally speaking, Jewish people would be disappointed but would not destroy the sukkah; they would rather wait and hope to be able to fulfill the mitzvah—whereas the non-Jews, generally, would fail the test by showing their disappointment and destroying what they had built, happy to have been relieved of the need to observe the mitzvah. The student said that he too is not anxious to do mitzvoth and would rather do only that which is required of him. Since he was a non-Jew, he said, "Why should I take upon myself additional obligations?"

Eventually he came to Israel and did seek to convert, but was deterred by the Rehovot rabbinical court judges, who said that they would like to wait and see whom he decides to marry before they convert him. Subsequently, he met a Russian Jewish girl who was happy to marry him even as a non-Jew, and he abandoned his quest to convert. In my opinion, had the rabbinical court acted more accommodatingly, he would not have married this girl unless and until she was willing to observe the laws.

I was in Russia when a momentous event took place during the "Ten Days of Repentance" between Rosh Hashanah and Yom Kippur in 1993. On September 21, Boris Yeltsin, president of the Soviet Union, in a televised address to the people, announced his decision to disband the Supreme Soviet and the Congress of People's Deputies. He declared his intent to rule by decree until the election of a new parliament and a referendum on a new constitution. This triggered a constitutional confrontation. Almost immediately, the Supreme Soviet declared Yeltsin removed from the presidency for breaching the constitution.

Since corruption in the country was rampant, violent crime was skyrocketing, medical services were collapsing, food and fuel were increasingly scarce, and life expectancy was falling, the coun-

Photo courtesy of Zecharia Dor-Shav

try was awash with popular unrest. By early October, Yeltsin, with the support of the Soviet army and the ministry of interior forces, established a massive show of force. Two days before Yom Kippur, he called up tanks to shell the parliament. The picture on the previous page is of the Duma (lit.: White House) with the top half blackened from the shelling, as I photographed it a few days later.

The television stations were closed with only CNN reporting from a hotel room overlooking the Duma. Since we had a TV set in our room, and were the only ones there who were fluent in English—the language in which CNN was broadcasting—our room became the central focus of everyone's attention. We informed the United States Embassy of our presence in Russia and were asked to give them the names of our next of kin in case something had to be reported to them. Telephone calls out of the country were not possible for us.

On October 4, the Soviet Union was at the brink of civil war, and communism lost final control of the country. Yeltsin's move toward constitutional democracy and capitalism succeeded. The Soviet Union was shattered, leading to self-governing independence for its fifteen republics. The streets were now full of people lining up to go to the churches. On the first Sunday after these events, we saw long lines of people, even stretching around the block, waiting to enter the churches.

The missionaries were out too. Jehovah's Witnesses were preaching to the Jews suggesting that this was the time for them to rekindle their connection to religion. In the yeshiva, teachers were warning the students about the inherent danger of these missionaries and suggesting that the students go out at this propitious moment and work toward connecting Jews to Judaism and Torah. In the words of one of the teachers,[4] "If you already know *aleph*, teach *aleph*. When you succeed in learning *bet*, then go out and teach that too."

During our stay, seventeen couples of young Torah scholars were also sent from Israel to different locations throughout the Soviet Union. They were under the responsibility of Rabbi Meir Schlesinger, who had served as rabbi of the Poalei Agudat Yisrael–affiliated Kibbutz Sha'alvim and in 1961 had founded its yeshiva. He and his wife were in the Soviet Union to help the young couples cope with their mission.

In anticipation of the holiday of Sukkoth, the yeshiva planned a meeting of leaders of many Jewish communities in what was now becoming the former Soviet Union, to discuss how they might celebrate the holiday—since religious practices had now become permissible. Among the novel situations that they faced

---

4 He himself was one of the fortunate ones, despite growing up under Communism. He had his circumcision as an adult, on the kitchen table of his home.

was one presented by the leader of one community who stated that his community plans to build a sukkah but would not have kosher food to serve. Would they be permitted, he asked, to say the blessing over the sukkah for a meal of non-kosher food?

A question that came to Rabbi Schlesinger from one of the couples in a far-out community in Siberia was how to deal with their custom of building the community sukkah inside the synagogue, as it was too cold to sit and eat out of doors.[5]

On the eve of Yom Kippur, the Kiev community called to ask four vital questions. These included whether or not an elderly man who wanted to attend a synagogue on the holiday, but lived twenty kilometers away, would be permitted to travel there on public transportation. As a retiree he was permitted to ride the train for free. Also, a young mother wanted to know if she could carry or wheel her infant to synagogue through the public areas, so that she too might be able to attend. This set of questions was turned over to me because, as it turned out, Rabbi Schlesinger was not

---

5   The congregants did not know that the law requires one to eat at least one bite of bread in a proper sukkah on the first night of the holiday. In fact, in Moscow it was generally too cold, and it was raining on that first night. We went into the wet sukkah for the sanctification meal and had that one required bite.

available at that moment and the yeshiva asked me to respond in his stead.[6]

Chabad had a significant presence in Moscow, where they had taken over a building that was originally a synagogue—but had been converted into a theater—as well as other buildings, including a former mikvah. Rabbi Cunin was the representative of Rabbi Menachem Mendel Schneersohn, the last Lubavitcher Rebbe.

During the Bolshevik revolution, the Russian government seized and nationalized a large Lubavitch library of about fifteen thousand books and manuscripts, which have been housed for the past century in the Moscow State Library. This has been the center of a decades-old property dispute between Russia and Chabad representatives based in the United States. Chabad had won the right to reclaim the texts from a Soviet court in 1991, but after the collapse of the USSR, the new Russian authorities threw out the judgment. In 1992 and 2005, all 100 US senators requested that the

---

6 Interestingly, Rabbi Schlesinger agreed with all of my rulings even though, initially, he thought that I might have erred on one of them. My assumption is that I had heavenly help, since when I gave the answer it was to a real question that was relevant just then. When he heard the question, it was no longer pertinent since it was already in the midst of Yom Kippur and too late for his opinion to have an effect on the questioner's behavior.

Russian government return the materials. Chabad sued the Russian government in an American court. In 2013, the American judge ruled in Chabad's favor and added that the Soviet Union should pay a fine of $50,000 per day for failing to release the library. The US Senate repeated its request in 2017.[7] In July of that year, however, the Russian State Library finished scanning and putting online the books in the collection, thus, at least making them accessible at the click of a mouse.

Rabbi Cunin had been told by the Rebbe not to leave the Soviet Union without the books. As the years moved on, he had to return to the United States to resume his responsibilities. In 1992, however, the Rebbe had suffered a massive stroke that left him unable to speak, and Rabbi Cunin could not ask to be released from the pledge. Consequently, when we were in Moscow, we found that Rabbi Cunin had left two sons as security until the library was released. The Soviet government did not return the books but did invite a Chabad librarian to pick out the books that had belonged personally to the Schneersohn family. He selected 4,651 books, which were then moved to a special Schneersohn Collection at the recently opened Jewish Museum and Tolerance Center in Moscow.

---

7   See: S1572, Congressional Record—Senate, March 2, 2017, for text of the letters.

After our stay in Russia, we continued our journey around the world. We had planned our six-week stayover in Melbourne to coincide with Pesach, where, among other things, we ran the seder for the motel/hotel owned by the well-known Chabadnik philanthropist Rabbi Joseph Gutnick. Alongside our seder, Chabad ran a separate seder for several hundred tourists, at a very nominal fee. This style of public service is part of the Chabad outreach program in over one hundred countries and in all of the fifty United States.[8] Unfortunately, some of the Israeli tourists drank too much wine and became raucously abusive. The police had to be called to quell the unrest.

A Miraculous Recovery in Hong Kong

At the end of our stay in Melbourne, we traveled up the coast of Australia to Cairns and farther north to the rain forest that borders the Great Barrier Reef. During the last day of our stay in the rain forest, I was bitten by some insect that I didn't see but whose bite I felt. As scheduled, we traveled on to Hong Kong for our next stop. On Thursday night, I began to feel unwell and developed a very severe case of diarrhea.

---

8   On many occasions during our world travels, we availed ourselves of kosher food at Chabad facilities.

This required a visit to a doctor on Friday morning, I took tests and was given medicine to tide me over until the results and diagnosis came in. Later that day, I understood that the medicine was not helping, and I was becoming completely dehydrated. Realizing the seriousness of the situation, I feared that I might need to be hospitalized on the Sabbath and prepared my passport and insurance papers to be available in case of need.

I went to bed and slept through the night, until about 11:00 a.m. on Sabbath morning. When I awoke I was drenched in sweat. My wife told me that upon awakening I told her of a dream I had dreamt, in which I saw my brother Yitzchak, who was no longer alive, stretch out his hands to me and say, "Come." In the dream, I rejected his hand and said, "I am not yet ready." That Sabbath afternoon, I was recovered sufficiently to go to synagogue for minhah.

From there, we moved on to Bangkok, Thailand, where I received a fax from the Hong Kong doctor in which she identified the cause of my illness and told me that the medicine she had given me was totally ineffective for that illness and that I would probably continue to have medical flare-ups from time to time. My kidneys were damaged, and ever since, I suffer significant partial kidney failure. I believe that I am alive, however, because I refused to take my dead brother's hand as offered (see note to Item 237[9] in Sefer Chasidim[10]).

A Visit to Shanghai

While traveling to a psychological conference in Beijing, we planned a stop in Shanghai to study the history of the Jewish community that had escaped World War II by fleeing there. In the summer of 1940, several students of Yeshivat Mir heard that the Dutch ambassador to Lithuania was willing to provide destination visas to the Caribbean island of Curaçao.

Chiune Sugihara. Wikipedia

In addition, Chiune Sugihara, the Japanese consul in Kovno (Kaunas), then the capital of Lithuania, provided the refugees with permits for legal passage via Japan. Sugihara, at great personal sacrifice, violated explicit Japanese policy and worked nonstop to issue

---

9 הרואה נכרי בחלום...שכבר מתו, ואומר לבוא אחריו, או אם יהודי בא...וישביענו ...ואינו רוצה לבא אחריו, וגם הוא לא יבא אלי...

"One who sees in a dream, a non-Jew who is dead, who says, 'follow me' . . . or a Jew . . . should respond, 'I don't want to follow him, or for him to come to me.'"

10 Authored by Judah ben Samuel of Regensburg, a leader of Hassidei Ashkenaz, a movement of Jewish mysticism in Germany.

some six thousand such visas.[11] This route necessitated transit visas to a Soviet port on the Pacific Ocean whence they could depart for Japan, and from there on to Hong Kong, where they remained until 1947. A Jewish delegation headed by Rabbi Zerach Warhaftig, head of the Israeli National Committee to Save Polish Jewry and eventually a signatory of Israel's Declaration of Independence, turned to the Soviet Union for permission for passage. In August 1940, he received a positive reply, providing they would not remain in the Soviet Union.

Before the visa holders could leave, however, Lithuania lost its independence and became a Soviet republic. The authorities closed all foreign missions. As a result of these earlier fortuitous events (seen by many to this day as acts of divine providence), thousands of Jews—including three hundred Mir Yeshiva students—succeeded in fleeing across the Soviet Union on the Trans-Siberian Railroad.[12]

---

11 Sugihara was dismissed from the Japanese Foreign Service for disobeying specific instructions not to issue the visas. On October 4, 1984, Yad Vashem recognized him as Righteous Among the Nations. The Lithuanian government declared 2020 "The Year of Chiune Sugihara," promising to erect a monument to him and issue postage stamps in his honor.

12 He went from yeshiva to yeshiva trying to influence them also to leave for Shanghai with such a transit visa but, sadly, was unsuccessful with a number of them.

They were initially accommodated in shabby apartments and in six camps belonging to a former school. The Japanese occupiers regarded them as "stateless persons" and in 1943 required them to move into what was called the "Jewish Ghetto." As World War II intensified, the Nazis stepped up their pressure on Japan to hand over the Shanghai Jews for extermination. The Nazis regarded their Japanese allies as "Honorary Aryans" and were determined that these allies help them apply the Final Solution to the Jewish Question also there.

As told to me by an Amshinover Hasid, the Japanese military governor of the city sent for the Jewish community leaders—who included the Amshinover Rebbe, Shimon Sholom Kalish—to try to understand why the Nazis wanted to exterminate the Jews. The governor asked, "Why do the Germans hate you so much?" Without hesitation, and knowing that the fate of his community hung on his answer, the Rebbe asked to be permitted to speak for the gathered group and told the translator (in Yiddish): "Tell him they hate us because we are Orientals." The governor broke into a smile and said that they need not worry because he would not accede to the German demand. The Shanghai Jews were never handed over.

Curiously, the Shanghai Academy of Social Sciences established a Center of Jewish Studies. We had arranged to meet with Professor Pan Guang, director of the Center. At that meeting, to which he had invited several other Chinese faculty members, we were given a lecture on the Jewish refugees—some eighteen thousand souls—who had found haven there from Nazi Europe. Professor Guang assigned a master's student to give us a guided tour of the Jewish ghetto, including the Beth Aharon Synagogue that had housed the Mir Yeshiva:

> Homeless. Stateless. Penniless. How would they survive? And what would become of the Torah scholarship? The "solution" had been orchestrated 10 years earlier, when a wealthy, assimilated Jew named Silas Hardoon had a dream one night about building a full synagogue complex in Shanghai—complete with seating for 250 people, a kitchen, dining room, and mikvah.
>
> Inexplicably, Hardoon built such a synagogue . . . which sat unused . . . until the Mir Yeshiva arrived to find the perfect, predestined home.[13]

---

13 Aish.com—Simmons, The Rabbi *from Shanghai*, Jan 3, 2015.

When I asked our Chinese student-guide what she had written about in her master's degree paper, she surprised me by saying, "The Second Aliyah."[14] I asked why she, a Chinese woman, was interested in the subject, and why she was interested in Jewish and Israeli history at all. She answered, "All Chinese are interested in the Jews." She and Professor Pan Guang gave me several important insights:

- The Jews had arrived in Shanghai just as poor as all the other refugees, and as most of the Chinese natives who had been living in the crowded sections of Shanghai. Nonetheless, they had lifted themselves up by their bootstraps and had become a self-supporting community. Furthermore, when they left, they continued to support the local Shanghai community by building health centers and other facilities.
- The Jews loved books and learning. While they were there, they published more than thirty newspapers and magazines.

---

14 The Second Aliyah was an important and highly influential [period of Jewish immigration] that took place between 1904 and 1914, during which approximately thirty-five thousand Jews immigrated into Ottoman-ruled Palestine, mostly from the Russian Empire, some from Yemen. Wikipedia.

- Finally, the Chinese were very impressed by the British-Jewish mercenary Morris (Moishe) Abraham Cohen, better known by his nickname "Two-Gun Cohen," who eventually became the personal bodyguard and

Wikipedia

aide-de-camp of Dr. Sun Yat-sen and a major-general in the Chinese National Revolutionary Army. Sun Yat-sen eventually became the provisional first president of the Republic of China and the first leader of the Kuomintang (Nationalist Party of China).[15]

A Side Trip After a Conference in Beijing

One of the scheduled side trips for conference participants was a bus trip to the world-renowned terra-cotta sculptures in Xi'an, China. Qin Shi Huang, the first

---

15 The *Jerusalem Post* ("Two-Gun Cohen: The Chinese General Who Swung the UN Vote," by Ruth Corman, Independence Day Supplement, 2021, pp. 14–15) reported that in 1947, Cohen heard that China intended to vote at the UN against the creation of the Jewish state and presented to the Chinese representative at the UN a letter that he had received twenty years earlier from Sun Yat-sen, expressing his sympathy for the Zionist movement. This led to the Chinese abstention on the vote.

emperor of China, had buried over eight thousand full-size terra-cotta warriors, each with the face of a real-life warrior, for the purpose of protecting him in his afterlife. As chance would have it, we were seated near a group of Mormon psychologists for the duration of the trip. For me, this afforded an opportunity to investigate the veracity of a long letter I had once received from a recanted Mormon, who had returned to her Jewish heritage. For them, when I introduced myself as from Jerusalem, it was an opportunity to proselytize a Jew from the Holy Land.

My informant had studied in a Mormon college in Utah and was very familiar with the theology and missionary goals of that church. She had said that the prime mission of the church is to convert the Jews. In the earliest days of Mormonism, Joseph Smith had taught that the indigenous peoples of the Americas were members of some of the Lost Tribes of Israel. Later, he taught that the Mormons themselves were Israelites. Furthermore, my informant related that the Mormons had dedicated a location on the Mount of Olives in Jerusalem to be a future Mormon temple:

> He [Orson Hyde, President of the Quorum of the Twelve Apostles] recorded that before dawn on October 24, 1841 he climbed up

the Mount of Olives . . . and recited a prayer, which read in part:

. . . safely arrived in this place to dedicate and consecrate this land unto Thee, for the gathering together of Judah's scattered remnants, according to the predictions of the holy Prophets—for the building up of Jerusalem again after it has been trodden down by the Gentiles so long, and for rearing a Temple in honor of Thy name.

He departed the mountain after building a small altar with stones.

The Brigham Young University Jerusalem Center for Near Eastern Studies was established on the Mount of Olives as a satellite campus of Brigham Young University, the largest religious university in the United States. The "religious right" in Israel were decidedly against the building of the center or any other similar Christian structure. Larger political parties also faced a loss of their political strength if they stood opposite on this issue. Many Israeli officials, however, such as Teddy Kollek, mayor of Jerusalem, along with others, supported the center because of what the church had done for the city. Kollek specifically stated that "the Mormon Church's presence in Jerusalem can do a great deal of work in providing the bridge of understanding between the Arab and Jews . . . because its members look with sympathy and understanding at both sides."

When I asked the Mormon psychologists if it was true that the purpose of the Mormon Temple in Jerusalem was to facilitate their mission to the Jews. After initial denial, one of them admitted that the mission was most surely their goal.

The temple and center is located at a spot that, when viewed from the grand staircase in the Old City descending to the Western Wall, is seen squarely above the wall. I once noticed that the building was illuminated at night in a manner that depicted a cross. The staircase of the Temple is exactly in the middle of the building, and they kept it illuminated. Additionally, the floor below the top was completely illuminated. Thus, when looking from the spot where I was standing, one saw a very large illuminated cross right above the wall. I contacted the Ministry of Religion and complained about the matter. After investigation, they came back to me and said that the cross has no significance to the Mormons. Nonetheless, from then on, the Mormons no longer illuminated the building in that manner.

I had once asked Minister Yosef Burg, who was either minister of internal affairs or minister of religious affairs at that time, why he had agreed to this construction. Sadly, his lame answer was, "they gave me a batch of papers to sign, and I didn't examine each one separately."

Meeting with the Anusim

An opportunity to hear firsthand the history of a family of Anusim[16] was provided when we were scheduled to visit São Paulo during July 2005, while in Brazil for a psychological conference in Iguassu Falls. Through a series of fortuitous events, a descendant of one such family (Tamar) had come to Israel and had undergone full conversion by Rabbi Simcha HaCohen Kook of Rehovot. She then moved to the Tiberias area and, needing the services of a physician, called upon the father of my daughter-in-law, Dr. Uri Levy. She mentioned her Brazilian background to the doctor, who then revealed it to my daughter-in-law, Schulamith,[17]

---

16 *Anusim* (the coerced)

The preferred halakhic term for Jews forced to abandon Judaism against their will. Typically, while forcibly being converted to Christianity. The pejorative, *Marranos* (pig eaters), is Spanish and of unknown origin, although various explanations have been suggested.

17 Her publications include "Descendants of the Anusim (Crypto-Jews) in Contemporary Mexico," by Schulamith Chava Halevy, published as a monograph based on her doctorate at the Hebrew University, 2009. She has lectured extensively on the subject and has been used by the Israeli Rabbinical Conversion Board to testify on behalf of tens of Anusim. She also currently advises the Anusim community in Mexico that she investigated for her doctorate, as also a community in Portugal, in their fragile return to their roots.

who has been very deeply involved with such families for many years and soon befriended her. Tamar told her that she was returning to São Paulo but was leaving a son in Israel in a yeshiva.

I invited her son to visit me on the Sabbath, and he brought along another Brazilian yeshiva student. During the course of the day, I mentioned that I was planning to spend some time in a resort in the Amazon region and would be flying to Manaus, far up the Amazon River, and from there we would cruise two hours by boat to the resort. To our complete surprise, the boy's friend said that he comes from that city and would love for us to meet his mother while there. Of course, we agreed to do so.

Our guest had also suggested that we might want to stay in an apartment in his parents' house in São Paulo, and be accommodated for meals with them while there. This was a fantastic coincidence and gave us an opportunity to meet with an authentic descendant of the Anusim and with the local Jewish community. We planned our arrangements accordingly.

Tamar had long known that she was a descendant of Anusim but had been raised as a Catholic. Nonetheless, because of many odd behaviors that her grandmother had revealed to her—such as washing the floors of the house on Fridays, burying the family dead with some soil from the Holy Land, burying the afterbirth of her children near the gate of the house, and frequently reading from the Book of Psalms—her grandmother eventually hinted that she was of Jewish descent.

As fate would have it, Tamar married an Ashkenazic Jew and started to raise a family. Her oldest child contracted a mysterious medical condition in his infancy that the doctors could not identify. Despairing of help, she went to a lecture by an itinerant spiritualist and brought her infant child with her. After the lecture she approached the spiritualist and asked for his help regarding the child's condition. Looking at the child, he declared him as having a case of rickets—which he recognized from frequently having traveled the villages of Brazil where the condition is not uncommon—and then declared, "You are Jewish, and so am I."

Shocked by the statement but impressed by the fact that he had correctly diagnosed the condition of her infant—which was promptly eradicated by proper treatment—she saw this as a heavenly sign to return to the religion of her ancestors and become observant. Her husband, who had come from a traditional Jewish background but was not observant, agreed—and suggested that since they were going to be living as observant Jews, they ought to move to Israel and start living their Orthodox Jewish life there. In Israel, she underwent a proper conversion and sent her oldest son to yeshiva in Jerusalem. Eventually, they sent their two sons to study at Yeshiva University (based in part, possibly, on the letter of recommendation that I wrote).

Our meeting with the other student's mother in Manaus took place in the local synagogue because we had indicated that we would like to learn something about the Manaus Jewish community. The community was established by immigrants from Morocco during the rubber boom of the late nineteenth and early twentieth centuries. In 1824, they organized the first synagogue, Eshel Avraham, in Belém, Brazil, at the mouth of the Amazon River. With the rubber boom, thousands more Moroccan Jews entered the Amazonian towns. The many merchants and other workers who had come during the height of Jewish immigration established new communities along the interior of the river, in Santarém and Manaus in Brazil, and as far as in Iquitos in Peru. In fact, the agent of the resort to which we were going, a descendant of that Peruvian community, had his office in Manaus. Many of these Jews married Native American women, and their children grew up in a culture of many influences: Jewish, Christian, Moroccan, and Amazonian. Since the late twentieth century, some of their descendants have studied Judaism and formally converted to allow their Jewishness to be accepted in Israel.

The Story of the Kahal Zur Israel Synagogue in Recife, Brazil

This next account was, doubtless, one of the most interesting "coincidences" that we experienced in Brazil. As indicated, one of my goals for the trip was to meet descendants of the Portuguese Anusim. Having been informed that there was a community of their descendants in the old port section of Recife in the District of Pernambuco, we arranged to spend a Sabbath with the Shavei Yisrael[18] rabbi in that area.

Wikipedia

18 Shavei Israel is a nonprofit organization founded by Michael Freund. In 1996, he was appointed deputy communications director to Prime Minister Benjamin Netanyahu. In the spring of 1997, a letter arrived at the Prime Minister's Office from the Bnei Menashe community of northeastern India, which claims descent from the lost tribe of Menashe, requesting to return to Zion. "I remember opening the battered letter . . . it was in a crumpled, orange envelope . . . and reading it with a mix of incredulity and surprise," Freund recounts. They had been writing to Israeli prime ministers since at least Golda Meir, and probably since Ben-Gurion and the founding of the State of Israel, but had never received an answer. Freund scheduled meetings with the community . . . and became convinced that they are, in fact, descendants of the Jewish People. . . . He established Shavei Israel. (From Shavei Israel Facebook)

To our astonishment, we found that the community was just then marking 350 years since the rebuilding of the Kahal Zur Israel Synagogue, which had been abandoned for centuries. After World War I, the Safra banking family had moved to Beirut and later to Brazil. During the 1960s, Joseph Safra and his father, Jacob, founded Banco Safra in South America. Quite by chance, they decided to open a small storefront branch in the old port of Recife. While building on location, they discovered that they were on top of the remains of the ancient synagogue. The original drawings of the synagogue were available, and Safra rebuilt it as a museum of its Jewish past. The rabbi in Recife decided to try to reestablish it as an active synagogue. Coincidentally, on the next Sabbath after our planned visit, and just two days after we were scheduled to leave, they were planning a landmark first Friday-night service for the descendants of the original Anusim.

Let's go back a bit in history. The Spanish Alhambra Decree (the Edict of Expulsion) was issued on March 31, 1492, by the joint Catholic monarchs (Isabella I of Castile and Ferdinand II of Aragon). It ordered the expulsion of Jews from the Kingdoms of Castile and Aragon and its territories and possessions by July 31 of that year (at sunset, that day became the 8th of

Av, 5252—the eve of our day of national mourning, Tishah B'Av).[19]

Among the most unfortunate refugees were those who fled to neighboring Portugal. In 1496, King Manuel of Portugal concluded an agreement to marry Isabella, the daughter of Spain's monarchs. As a condition of the marriage, the Spanish royal family insisted that Portugal expel its Jews. King Manuel I,[20] reluctant to lose his affluent and accomplished Jewish community—now New Christians (i.e., Jewish; their Jewish roots were an open secret)—he made sure to keep them under his thumb in the New World. Hired by the King in 1500, navigator Pedro Álvares Cabral and his team, including several New Christians, landed in what is now Brazil and laid claim to it in the name of King Manuel. To colonize the

---

19 Three days later, on August 3, 1492, Columbus sailed from the Spanish port of Palos, to find a western sea route to China, India, and the fabled gold and Spice Islands of Asia. He wrote in his journal, "*thus after having driven all the Jews out of your realms and dominions. Your Highnesses in the same month commanded me to set out with sufficient armada to the said countries.*" Thus, begins the account of his sea journey.

20 In the end, only eight Portuguese Jews were expelled; tens of thousands of others were forcibly converted to Christianity on pain of death. The Chief Rabbi, Simon Maimi, was one of those who refused to convert. He was kept buried in earth up to his neck for seven days until he died of starvation. In the final analysis, all of these events took place because of Tomas de Torquemada, first Grand Inquisitor in Spain's movement to homogenize religious practices with those of the Catholic Church, otherwise known as the Spanish Inquisition.

newfound land, Portugal encouraged settlers to populate the new colony. Many New Christians, seeking to distance themselves from the Inquisition, took advantage of the opportunity to flee. Eventually, they constituted possibly 15 percent of the European population in the area of Recife, capital of the State of Pernambuco. They introduced, by example, some sort of order and industry. In 1503, under the leadership of Fernando de Noronha, another New Christian, they taught the local people the culture of sugarcane, and Pernambuco became a prosperous center for its production. The Anusim also exported wood and prospered significantly. According to official records, during the fifteenth century they comprised two-thirds of the area's white residents. Unfortunately, in 1591, Portugal extended the Laws of the "Santo Ofício" to its newly discovered colony, sending the first Inquisitors to cities in Brazil.

In 1630, when the Dutch occupied Pernambuco, the Anusim of Recife began to experience some religious freedom. Pernambuco, unfortunately, remained under Dutch rule for only twenty-four years. Under that rule, Jews were practicing their religion openly and even established an organized community. Its members were mainly newcomers from Holland and earlier arrived Anusim. In 1636, they established what became the first synagogue of the Americas, Kahal Tzur Israel.

Conversely, most of the members of the Brazilian Jewish community were persecuted and arrested by the Inquisition. Hundreds were sent to Lisbon to die as "heretic New Christians." Whole families were arrested in the countryside of Brazil and executed in the squares of Portugal. One of the New Christians, Diego Fernandez, the greatest expert in sugar plantations, was accused of being a "Judaizer." The Inquisition dispatched an official inspector (*visitator*) to seize and confiscate his possessions. An inquisitional commission was established in 1593 in Olinda, the port of Recife. After the inspector left, surveillance of New Christians was continued by the bishop of Brazil, with the assistance of the local clergy and Jesuits.

In 1654, Portugal retook control of Recife, and the Jewish community disintegrated. Those who had only now openly professed their Judaism became victims of the Inquisition. After many difficulties and as the First Anglo-Dutch War ended, most of the 150 Jewish families received permission and left Brazil together with the Dutch. A Dutch state document dated November 14, 1654, reveals that four ships bound for the French island of Martinique were diverted because of strong winds and made land in Jamaica. One of these ships, carrying twenty-three Recife emigrants, eventually reached the city of "New Amsterdam"—later called New York. They were among the first Jewish people to arrive in North America in the seventeenth century and establish a community.[21]

Freedom of religion in America was tested when Peter Stuyvesant, Governor of New Amsterdam, refused to allow the Jewish passengers (who had no passports) to settle there and join the existing community of Jews with passports from Amsterdam. Stuyvesant attempted to have Jews "in a friendly way . . . depart" the colony. As he wrote to the Amsterdam Chamber of the Dutch West India Company in 1654, he hoped that "the deceitful race—such hateful enemies and blasphemers of the name of Christ—be not allowed to further infect and trouble this new colony." He referred to Jews as a "repugnant race" and "usurers" and was concerned that "Jewish settlers should not be granted the same liberties enjoyed by Jews in Holland, lest members of other

---

21 The first Jews arrived in New York City to escape the Inquisition. German immigration later brought large communities of Ashkenazi Jews. Starting then and continuing until 1820, the early Jewish immigration to America arrived but totaled fewer than fifteen thousand Jews. From 1820 to 1880 the second wave came, bringing a quarter million German Jews. A third major wave of Sephardi Jews came from the Balkans and the Middle East from 1880 through the 1920s and after the Turkish Revolution. The outbreak of World War II and the Holocaust led many German Jews to flee to the United States. During the period from 1881 to 1924, over 2 million Eastern European Jews arrived. From the 1980s to 2009, some 620,000 people arrived from the former Soviet Union, not all of them halakhically Jewish. Today, Jews comprise some 2 percent of the population of the United States.

persecuted minority groups, such as Roman Catholics, be attracted to the colony."

Stuyvesant's decision was rescinded only after pressure from the directors of the company. As a result, Jewish immigrants were permitted to stay in the colony as long as their community was self-supporting. An Ashkenazi Jew, Asser Levy, one of the twenty-three refugees, prospered and in 1661 became the first Jew to own a house in New Amsterdam,[22] which also made him the first Jew known to have owned a house anywhere in North America. Nonetheless, the company agreed that the Jews would not be allowed to build a synagogue, forcing them to worship in a private home. Within a decade, together with support from other religious groups, the first known civil rights case in the New World regarding religious civil rights ended with guaranteed religious freedom of worship.[23] Shortly

22 Hertzberg, Arthur (1997). *The Jews in America*. New York: Columbia University Press, p. 17.

23 Some of this material is based on "The Phenomenon of the Anusim in Brazil," by Matheus Zandona Guimaraes, an Italian/Portuguese Jew who immigrated to Brazil in the beginning of the twentieth century and studied at the Hebrew University.

Much of the balance of the material is from promotional literature of the synagogue, as also from The Museum of the Jewish People— Beit Hatfutsot, The Jewish Community of Recife, the Virtual Jewish World: Recife, Brazil, JStor, and impressions from my personal visit to Brazil.

thereafter, the Spanish and Portuguese Synagogue in New York was established. Fortuitously, we were present in Recife just then, at the reopening of the building as a synagogue, which took place simultaneously with the celebration of the 350th anniversary of the establishment of the Spanish and Portuguese Synagogue in New York (1654–2004). I was privileged to pray in Kahal Zur Israel, at least privately, just before its renewed use as a place of prayer.

Chapter Seven
Members of
the Greater
Dershowitz Clan

THE INFORMATION ON the Americanization and adjustment of my paternal uncles and aunts and their descendants is, unfortunately, less than complete. This is simply because I could access only a limited amount of information from some of the families. As with my siblings, so too with my father's siblings. Each family developed a personal style of life and contributed to society and Jewish life in the United States. Many of their descendants took the bold step of leaving the comfort of America and participating in the building of Jewish life in the Promised Land. As indicated previously, my father was the oldest of his siblings. The others are here reported upon in their birth order.

Sol Dershowitz

Sol went through two marriages but, sadly, was unable to father children. He sweetened the family choir with his high-pitched soprano voice. He became everybody's Uncle Sol. As indicated in the section about our lives in Williamsburg, Sol worked in the needle trades during the years when most everyone there felt compelled to work on the Sabbath.

Photo courtesy of
Zecharia Dor-Shav

Against the odds, and uniquely, he succeeded in observing the Sabbath. When he retired, he moved to Israel and lived for many years in a small boardinghouse in Netanya with several other retirees. He would often spend the Sabbath or Yom Tov at the home of one of the three relatives who lived in Israel at that time: Moshe Chait, my brother Yitzchak, or myself.

An interesting anecdote preserved in the family is that Chaim Shmiel (Samuel) and Shulem (Solie) switched their English names when they entered school for the first time. While waiting in line to identify themselves, the younger of the two didn't like his name, Solie. He ran ahead of his older brother and gave his name as Samuel—which was Chaim Shmiel's English name. There was nothing left for Chaim Shmiel to do but to call himself Solie—which was Shulem's English name, and so it remained for the rest of their days!

He loved the sea, and even after he turned ninety, he continued to take a dip in the sea almost every day. Much of the rest of the day was spent in the synagogue, praying, or participating in study groups. He died on Erev Tishah B'Av at the age of ninety-five and was buried that night in Jerusalem. He left his small inheritance to a charity, the Chofetz Chaim Yeshiva, which was headed by Rabbi Moshe Chait. My brother Yitzchak took it upon himself to urge an immediate burial, on the eve of Tishah B'Av—even though it meant that not many people could be notified about his death, and only a small group would be present at the funeral. I always felt that though he left no descendants to sit shiva for him, all of Israel sat shiva—because on Tishah B'Av,

Jerry Bass and others at Sol's gravesite. Photo courtesy of Zecharia Dor-Shav

most synagogue congregants sit on the floor until about noon. Every year since then, on the day of his yahrzeit, our nephew, Jerry Bass[1], has taken it upon himself to see to it that he is not forgotten and organizes a minyan of people to visit the grave on Har HaMenuchot.

Samuel Dershowitz

Sam was a charitable man, a great salesman, and a good father. He married Ida Mehr, and they had three daughters: Rivel Dyckman, Libby Mandel, and Miriam Altshuler. As the story goes, he was making an appeal in synagogue for Torah Vodaath—where he eventually served as vice president of the board of directors—

Photo courtesy of Zachary Dyckman

and to get things rolling announced a large donation at that time ($50, I was told)—which he did not have. He pawned his wife's engagement ring to make the payment. Ida did not appreciate this, and he eventually redeemed the ring. The family still treasures it.

---

1 Rabbi Dr. Jerry Bass, husband of Miriam, son-in-law of Sylvia Fuchs, served in various capacities in the Foreign Currency Department of the Bank of Israel for twenty-seven years.

For much of his life he worked as a salesman, selling corrugated boxes. He was very *ehrlich* (honest) and principled. He produced cheese from *cholov Yisrael* (Jewish milk) in his kitchen, using Breakstone's[2] supervised and certified kosher sour cream.

He may have been the brains behind the "Rabbi for a Week Club" in the family synagogue that enabled several European rabbis to arrive in the United States and be saved from the Holocaust (see: Williamsburg and the Family Synagogue, Chapter 1). On one occasion when he was hospitalized for a medical condition, his daughter came to visit and saw one of these rabbis at his bedside. Sam asked his daughter to give the rabbi some money. She exclaimed, "You mean he came to the hospital to ask you for money?" Sam responded, "Not at all. He came to visit, but I know that he needs money." In fact, Sam helped support several of these refugee rabbis, regularly, for an extended period of time. He also supported the Palestine Aid Society, among other charities.

Rivel (Ruth) worked as a bookkeeper after her children, Larry and Zachary, were of school age. Even as a young woman, she sacrificed to avoid working on Shabbat, being unemployed for almost a year until she

---

2   Founded in 1882, by two Jewish Lithuanian brothers, Joseph and Isaac Breakstone, who opened a small dairy on New York's Lower East Side.

found a bookkeeping job that did not require her to report on Shabbat. Libby worked as a school secretary in the public-school system. Miriam was sickly for many years and never worked. Rivel passed away at the age of ninety-nine, after several years in an assisted-living facility in Borough Park. Until the last two years of her life, she did volunteer work regularly in the Borough Park neighborhood YM-YWHA.

Sam and Sol often got into predicaments together. Once they went to look at a house that they thought was unoccupied. They broke a window to enter and were met with a gun. Being a salesman for men's underwear at the time, Sam bribed the homeowner to let them leave safely by promising him free underwear.

He venerated learning and imparted that respect to his children. Perhaps because he had only daughters, he helped found the first Bais Yaakov in Williamsburg (see Chapter 3). Some years later, Libby sought admittance for her younger daughter, Suzy, in the Yeshiva of Brooklyn Elementary School for Girls. The principal, Rabbi Mandel (no relation), was hesitant to admit her because the family was modern Orthodox. Libby told the rabbi, a graduate of Torah Vodaath, "My father gave you a shot [by devoting himself to the Yeshiva's success], so you should give my daughter one."

Libby often recounted how during a dispute with a tenant who started moving the family's Hebrew bookcase, she rebuked and warned him not to touch the holy books! She said this was because of her upbringing. Among Sam's books was a first edition of the *Mishna Brurah*.[3] When the family worked in the pocket purse business in the ladies' section of the family synagogue, Sam learned to repair sewing machines. Libby's daughter, Suzy (Flax), remembers Grandpa Sam giving her a toy sewing machine.

The family bought several small buildings during the Great Depression. Ida ran them as boardinghouses. She accommodated some of our refugee Czechoslovakian cousins in those apartments.

A gifted artist, she used her talent to paint the apartments in the buildings. She also volunteered to do taharah (washing the dead). From her young teen years, she helped her parents in their butcher shop. Her father, Yehuda Leib Mehr, was a learned man and completed the study of the entire Talmud seven times. Although he was a butcher by occupation, he studied Torah each day after he had butchered the meat for the day.

Sam bought a summer vacation home with his brother, Hymie, and two other people. Once, on the vacation farm, Libby, on a dare from her cousins, put

---

3 A book that in recent years has become a prime commentary on the shulchan aruch.

a match to the gas tank of her dad's model T Ford and blew it up. At twelve she also ventured to drive the replacement car and actually drove over someone, but there were no injuries to the person because the car was so high off the ground. Traumatized, she never drove again.

Rivel's children lived in Silver Spring, Maryland, while Larry worked as a CPA for the US Government Accountability Office (GAO). He and his wife, Sharon, have three children: Elisa, Steven, and Joseph. Zachary, an economist, also worked for the United States government in various agencies before becoming self-employed. He and his wife, Vivian, also have three children: Michael, Joshua, and David. David made aliyah and lives in Ramat Bet Shemesh, Israel. His wife, Deniela, worked as a nurse in Hadassah Hospital in Jerusalem.

Libby has two daughters, Batsheva Leinwand, a health/physical education teacher, and Suzy Flax, an attorney. Batsheva has three sons: Dr. Joshua, Dr. Gabriel, and Benjamin. One of Suzy's children, Rabbi Keith Flaks, is living in Nachlaot in Jerusalem.

Miriam married a Lubavitch Hasid and had two daughters: Sarah, and one whose name I don't recall. Unfortunately, her husband was not very stable, and the family objected to the marriage. Miriam disregarded the family's objection and eloped. Though the family tried to get to the Lubavitcher Rebbe to prevent the marriage, they never succeeded in contacting him before the marriage was a fait accompli.

Many of Sam's descendants studied in Israeli yeshivas, including Sam and Keith Flaks at Yeshivat Hakotel, and Gabriel Leinwand at Eretz Hatzvi. Keith served as a madrich at Reishit Yeshiva in Bet Shemesh, headed by Rabbi Ari Marcus—the husband of our cousin Mindy Fendel—and also taught at other yeshivas. He now runs the Simcha Center in Jerusalem Kollel, under the auspices of Shlomo's Tent, in memory of Rabbi Shlomo Carlebach.

Sadie Hochhauser

Sadie, as the fourth child and oldest daughter of Zecharja and Lea, was just three weeks old when her father left Pilzno for the American shores in 1888. She married Barney Hochhauser, who had come to America at about the age of fifteen with his parents and eleven older siblings. They had five children: Malkie, Leibi (Sydney), Shaindi (Selma), Chanie (Ruth), and Esther.

Photo courtesy of family

Sadie was a teenager when Zeide Zecharja and family

left the East Side and moved to 94 South 10th Street, in Williamsburg.

After a while, Barney generated excitement and became a novelty in the neighborhood by purchasing an automobile. He was the first of the family to have indulged in such luxury. When not using the car for work, he often took the family for an outing at the beaches of Far Rockaway.

Eventually, the Hochhausers moved into the family home on South 10th Street. When Zecharja died in 1920, it fell upon Sadie to assume many extended family responsibilities in addition to responsibilities for her immediate family. She took responsibility for her widowed mother—who lived on the floor below, with Rosie. She became the one upon whom everyone in the family relied. Her brother Sol, too, who was childless, lived with Sadie and Barney for a while, after his second wife died. Every Friday it was her responsibility to bake cakes for the kiddush[4] in the family synagogue.

After Bubba died in 1942, the Hochhausers moved to a house with a wide porch, in Borough Park, about a two-hour walk from Williamsburg. Some of us cousins often walked there on the Sabbath, to visit with Aunt Sadie and family, whose home was often bursting

---

4 *kiddush* (small sanctification repast)

with people—and cake—especially on the Sabbath and holidays.

Malkie had moved to Los Angeles with her husband, Max Gold, who became an undertaker; Selma married Buddy Schulman; and Ruth married Moish Kaufman—who had shed his Hasidic Satmar background and garb as soon as he got to America. The Kaufmans were pioneers in the exodus of New Yorkers to suburbia. They were the tenth member-family of the newly established Young Israel of West Hempstead, in what eventually became a very significant Orthodox Jewish suburb of New York City. Esther married Dan Overland.

Sydney opened a toy store with his father on the East Side, so that Barney would no longer need to be a customer peddler. Earlier he had worked for the wholesale dry goods firm of Fendel, Rubinson, and Dershowitz. At that time the company was involved in a drive for the unionization of small businesses in New York City. As mentioned above, one day, union hooligans entered the store and overturned several shelves of merchandise to force the firm to let their one worker (Sydney) join the union and be represented by it. One of his nieces, Toby, married the son of Captain Rabbi Samuel Zaitchik, his army chaplain during World War II.

Shaindi's daughter, Ronnie Lichter, remembers Bubba Lea buying fish and keeping them alive in the bathtub until they were needed to make gefilte fish for the Sabbath. Sadie died at age seventy-two on Purim, 1960, and though the family was very supportive of Barney, his love for her was so great—they always walked hand in hand—that he couldn't really live without her and died only eleven weeks later, on Shavuot. Ronnie remembers how forlorn he felt during those eleven weeks.

Ruth died in 2020. She had worked as a diamond cutter in a man's world, and when her youngest, Amy, was about two, she entered Adelphi College. It took her eight years to earn a social work degree, but she was proud of her thirty-year career with the Cerebral Palsy Association of Nassau County, where she helped many families and pioneered sibling and grandparent support groups.

After her husband had passed away, Ruth moved to a care center in Port Washington, Long Island, where she made a whole new set of friends, took classes, and found a talent for crafts—surprising herself, as her husband, Moish, had been the family artist. Years later, her good common sense and professional training helped guide her daughter, Sheila's, early intervention program with Sheila's son, Zachary—who suffers autism with behavioral and pervasive developmental disabilities. He lives in a group home for disabled persons. Her practical tips ranged from "Fold as you go" (laundry, etc.), "Never leave a sink full of dishes overnight," "Balance your checkbook," "Follow your instincts," "Steer clear of phonies," "Be honest," and "Always look your best (wear lipstick)," to name a few.

She died in the nursing care unit of the care center, the day before it was closed to private aides and restricted to all visitors because of the onset of COVID-19. Thus, she fortunately escaped a lonely death—as happened to so many of the COVID-19 victims. Her son was permitted to be at her side.

Gussie Mines

Gussie (Gela) was born in 1894, on the Lower East Side, first of the three siblings who were born in the United States. She remembered how her father Zecharja had so very strongly warned his children against work on the Sabbath. She described how, when my father was beginning to look for regular work, Zecharja said to him, "If you work on Shabbos, I will sit shiva over you!"

Photo courtesy of Naomi Chait

She married Boris Mines (Chaim Baruch, born in 1890) from Bialystok—then part of the Russian Empire, and later part of Poland—who had arrived alone in the United States a few years before the immigration of his parents, Moshe Tzvi and Chaya, and their six remaining children: Benny, Jack, Irving, Kaila, Henrietta, and Martha. According to the Russian census of 1897, the Jews were then over 60 percent of the Bialystok population.

Boris's arrival in the United States was enabled due to an unusual experience. When he was seventeen, he realized that he was subject to being drafted into the Russian army. He wanted to remain pious and knew that this would not be possible in the army. To avoid being conscripted, he hid on the floor of a truck, covered by a large haystack. When the truck reached the border, the border police, checking for possible draft dodgers, stuck a sharp pitchfork repeatedly into the hay. Blessed be Hashem, they missed him, and he crossed the border safely. Gussie always spoke about what an incredible miracle that was.

In the course of time, when the rest of his family made it to America, some of the women threw their wigs overboard, having heard that "you can't be pious in America." As opposed to his siblings,

Chaim Baruch wanted to become even more religious and was regularly invited to the Zecharja Dershowitz family home for Sabbath meals. That's where he met Gussie. When he proposed, he asked, "Gussie, you think it could work?" She replied simply, "I think it could be okay." It was! They married and established their home in Williamsburg. He, as so many others, started as a peddler, taking orders from door to door and, eventually, upgrading to owning a furniture store in Manhattan. He invited his brothers, Jack and Benny, to join him in the business, and also Kaila's son, David Butler. The store grew and became quite successful.

Gussie and Boris had five children: Chani (Ruth), who married Irving Selevan; Dovid; Esther Raizel, who married Rabbi Moshe Chait; Zecharia, who married Libby Balgley; and Chaya (Ila), who married Ruby Menzelefsky of Toronto. The two boys went to Torah Vodaath, and the girls were sent to the neighborhood Public School #16 on Wilson Street in Williamsburg.

In 1935, when Chani was only fifteen, their father, totally unexpectedly, had a stroke and passed away within a week's time. Aunt Gussie and her children moved into the family home on South 10th Street. They had only a minimal amount of savings. Boris's brother, Irving, provided the family with a weekly check from the furniture store earnings. Dovid, however, who was assigned the task of picking up the check, was traumatized by it! He was ashamed that they needed the money and that he had to go to pick it up. That may have been the beginning of his subsequent fits of depression.

As a young man, Dovid took upon himself the position of hazan at the prominent Clymer Street synagogue in Williamsburg while, simultaneously, studying under Rabbi Moshe Feinstein. Sadly, as time went on, he suffered occasional fits of depression and eventually simply disappeared! While he was on a bus trip to his sister in Toronto, we were informed that he had disembarked near Buffalo, New York, and never arrived in Toronto. The family made every possible effort to locate him but was unsuccessful. A mysterious postcard was received once that looked as if it might have come from him, but it was insufficiently conclusive. All trace of him was lost.

Chani left school and worked as a secretary at Golden Brothers to help cover the family's living expenses. In 1941 she married Irving Selevan, with whom she had five children: Leah, Reuven, Chaim, Zvi, and Rachelle. At a very young age, it was discovered that Rachelle was profoundly deaf.[5] Her compensation, perhaps, was her high intelligence, as she said about herself:

I thank God that I have a good brain and was somehow able to pick up language through reading. I was given a lot of speech training in school, but it was not real language. When one repeats a single word like "ball" again and over, this cannot be considered learning language. I was told by several people that I was a difficult child and had temper tantrums, but that

5 We use the lowercase "deaf" when referring to the audiological condition of not hearing, and the uppercase "Deaf" when referring to the unique group of deaf people who share American Sign Language (ASL)—as well as a unique culture. The members of this group use sign language as a primary means of communication among themselves and hold a set of beliefs about themselves and their connection to the larger society. They distinguish themselves from those who lost their hearing because of illness, trauma, or age, although they share the condition of not hearing. The latter group does not have access to the knowledge, beliefs, and practices that make up the culture of Deaf people who have found ways to define and express themselves through rituals, tales, performances, and everyday social encounters. The richness of their sign language affords them the possibilities of insight, invention, and irony. Furthermore, the mistaken belief that ASL is a set of simple gestures with no internal structure has led to the tragic misconception that the relationship of Deaf people to their sign language is a casual one that can be easily severed and replaced (Paraphrased from: Carol Padden and Tom Humphries, *Deaf in America: Voices from a Culture.* Cambridge, Mass.: Harvard University Press, 1988).

was because I could not communicate and was frustrated.[6]

It is interesting to read some of what she said at the *hesped shloshim*[7] of her mother. There, she described how the family and the world reacted to her limitations (somewhat edited by ZD):

I would like to honor my parents; may their memory be a blessing! They did not shelter me, but let me experience the good and bad during the years I lived with them.

Even though I have never attended shloshim[8] before and do not know what others have said, I would like to think that while we may talk about Mom's life, we should also talk about her effect on us, now. I know that you do not like to hear about this, and you think that these times are long over. Still, I think that we have all been told that many

---

6   She also said: "I am not in the hearing world or the Deaf world. I like both, so I live in my own world. I do not need labels such as disability, because our focus is on abilities. The Deaf Community is becoming stronger. Our language and culture is being recognized."

7   Eulogies offered at the end of the thirty-day period of mourning, during which the mourner is forbidden to marry, have a haircut, or attend a festive meal. Men also do not shave during this time.

8   *shloshim* (lit. 30, the 30-day mourning period following a burial)

children, after a parent passes away, feel that they had not done enough for their loved one. I remember that our grandmother told me that one mother can take care of ten children, but ten children cannot take care of one mother. I would like, however, to reflect on the fact that we made Mom happy, that we have families and that they follow the Torah path. Mom was very excited about the birth of the twins when we were together to share Chaim's and Renee's joy. Her eyes sparkled and she nodded her head to indicate happiness. It was to Renee's credit that we had that surprise anniversary party for Mom and Dad. How could we know that this would be the last time that, together, we would do something for her? Mom thought it was primarily a party for Clara who had just gotten engaged. She was very excited that Clara had come to visit with her future husband, Jeremiah Steinman.

By the last two weeks of Mom's life, I knew that she was unsure that she would still be here for the wedding. She said, with some uncertainty in her voice, "A wedding on Aug 15th?" I said to myself that it was up to Hashem. I am very sad, now that Mom will not be with us, but she would want us to be happy on that date. A friend who has gone through our experience told me that having a wedding can bring some comfort. I hope that you all are looking forward to the wedding, and that you will be ready with dancing feet.

Yes, it is true! I am uncomfortable because I cannot participate in conversations with all of you together, and at the end, I do not feel good. Although I keep in mind Mom's wish for the family to stay together, it was Mom who was the main person to keep me informed all these years. Mom was the only one to call me frequently using Teletype (TTY) communication, not Relay Service. Even in her last year she would still use TTY. She said that emailing sounds good and seems interesting but would be difficult for her to learn because it would require her walking to the library to get instructions on how to use the computer. Fortunately, much closer to home, she had wonderful programs in which she could participate without difficulty. She was able to develop her artistic talents while continuing with other learnings. A woman who came to the shiva informed me of this group attended its whose monthly meetings mom attended for thirty years, primarily to learn and to give charity. While reorganizing things in my home, I came across Mom's song written after the Six-Day War, if you remember it. I made copies of that for distribution here.

I do not know if you think that I was difficult to be raised. The fact is that this is not at all unusual for many of the deaf children whose parents are hearing and do not know how to communicate well with them. I feel that Mom gave all of us, her children, freedom to be ourselves. She never pushed us around.

Rachelle was extremely successful in the Lexington School for the Deaf and was chosen as the class valedictorian at graduation. Nonetheless, she continues:

After high school, even though I was a very proficient lip reader, other than Gallaudet (the first school for the deaf in the U.S.) in Washington, D.C., I was not accepted by any college to which I applied. Among the things that the colleges and universities felt would be problematic was that teachers would have to turn to face me whenever they were speaking, so that I could see their lips.

Thanks to Mom for contacting her first cousin, Zecharia Dor-Shav[9]—at that time, assistant professor of education at Long Island University in Brooklyn—I was accepted by that university. College was very difficult at the beginning, and I wanted to quit. Mom, however, made her point that either I would have to go to work in an office or work harder at college. Despite the difficulty at college in the beginning, by the third and fourth years, I had made the dean's list several times.

Rachelle changed her college major from math to economics but, after college, could not find a job for two years. She went, instead, to graduate school at New York University and married Samuel Landau, who is also deaf. When their oldest child, Clara, was growing up, she became the interpreter of the world for her parents.[10] This task was particularly challenging because Rachelle uses American Sign Language (ASL), while

---

9 The author of this book. She added, "What is more, he has been a true friend/relative of our family with whom I have maintained contact via email over the years. Our family also had the pleasure of having him and his wife at our daughter Clara's wedding, as well as at several later happy occasions."

10 I used to call Clara a princess, because of the wonderful role she played in helping her parents cope with the hearing world. Nevertheless, I recognize that it was extremely uncomfortable for them to rely upon their child for some of their communication with the hearing society. Parents like to be "givers" to their children, and not "receivers."

Samuel, who was raised in Israel by deaf parents, uses Israeli Sign Language.[11] Clara is proficient in both English and Hebrew and is relatively proficient in their respective sign languages.

Rachelle taught deaf children for six and a half years at the State School for the Deaf. She was, however, denied a license by the New York City Board of Education, without any opportunity to reopen the case. This was before the Americans with Disabilities Act[12] was passed.

---

11 Samuel was born to deaf parents who were Holocaust survivors. He has, for many years, read the Torah at the Deaf Service on Rosh Hashanah for the whole Deaf community. He is careful to enunciate every word correctly and is the only one in the community who knows how to do this. The members prefer Samuel, instead of a hearing person who does not really understand Deaf society and who is coming to the service just to read the Torah, which creates a less satisfactory atmosphere.

Samuel sometimes also helps with parts of the Yom Kippur service for their friend Rabbi Fred Friedman of Baltimore, who finds it very difficult to do the service alone for the entire day. Rabbi Friedman has semikah from the Yeshivas Ner Yisroel in Baltimore. Samuel had tried in the past to study for semikah in Yeshiva University but was not accepted—just as Rachelle was not accepted by Stern College for Women. This is very unfortunate, because the president of the Brooklyn High School for the Deaf, run by the Brooklyn Hebrew Society of the Deaf, suggested that it would be very valuable for Samuel to have semikah to be able to give the community more of what it needs. The members of the Society are not religious, for the most part, and really do not know prayers or even Hebrew language. Samuel, however, continues to study Gemara, Rambam, and other classic Jewish books.

12 The Americans with Disabilities Act of 1990 or ADA is a civil rights law that prohibits discrimination based on disability. Wikipedia.

After moving to New Jersey, she began to teach ASL to hearing high school students. Since she wanted to learn more, she found a new program at Teachers College and in 2000 continued in graduate school for a second master's degree. By that time, she already had four children. As of this writing, she still teaches high school students, as well as college-age students at Montclair State University in New Jersey

Esther Mines went to Seward Park Public High School on the Lower East Side, where she was very popular and became president of its student council. Simultaneously, she went to a Talmud Torah for Jewish youngsters, to learn Torah and other Jewish studies in the afternoon. When the first evening school for girls in Brooklyn (also called Bais Yaakov) opened in a storefront on Lee Avenue, Esther transferred there with a couple of other girls, to benefit from the additional Hebrew subjects that they could study. After she graduated from high school (with honors), she worked and at the same time attended Brooklyn College.

Her husband, Moshe Chait (born January 11, 1921), was friends with Dovid in the Chofetz Chaim Yeshiva. He used to come over on Friday nights with some other students for peanuts and chocolate cake. When Esther was dating, someone said, "Why don't you go out with Moshe Chait?" On May 30, 1945, when he was twenty-four, they married. Moshe got semikah and eventually became the founder and head of the Chofetz Chaim Yeshiva branch in Israel. At his death, the position of rosh yeshiva was taken over by their son Rabbi Dovid, who had been a protégé at the home of Rabbi Henoch Leibowitz, in the yeshiva's American branch.

Photo courtesy of Naomi Chait

The Chaits at first rented an apartment on South 9th Street in Williamsburg, and Gussie, together with her other then-unmarried, fatherless children (Dovid, Zecharia, and Chaya), eventually moved in with them. Moshe took care of the coal furnace in the building, removing the ashes and shoveling coals at night, so that they wouldn't have to pay someone to do it. Esther got a job polishing diamonds, and Moshe was learning in the kollel, getting paid $55 a month. Every month, he would send $5 from his paycheck to his mother to help out.

Esther is quoted as saying that her happiest days were when Moshe was learning in the kollel and they were living very very frugally. One year later, their first child was born, Chaim Baruch (Burry), who became a musician and composer. Among his songs are מי האיש

and כל העולם כולו, which he composed together with Shlomo Carlebach. The Chaits' other children are Dovid, Alter Reuvain Eliezer, Brenda, and Chaya Leah.

Gussie's youngest son, Zecharia, became an eternal student at Chofetz Chaim Yeshiva in Queens. After he heard just one *shiur* from the rosh yeshiva, Rabbi Henoch Leibowitz, he was convinced that he had found his place—and never left his learning. Many years later, when I told him that I was learning every morning with Meyer Fendel, he asked, "and what about the afternoon hours?"

Photo courtesy of Zecharia Dor-Shav

At a memorial tribute to him, at the seventy-eighth annual dinner of the yeshiva, he was described as a "Masmid, Rebbi, Baal Tefillah, Mashgiach, Rosh Yeshiva, Marbitz Torah, and Mekarev." One of his students was his nephew, Rabbi Baruch Chait, who described him at the dinner, as follows:

His patience was incredible; he always took things in stride and nothing ever ruffled him.

When the boys needed to be disciplined, he would stop and deal with the trouble, and then move on. He felt that if a boy did not learn so well today, it was okay; he will learn tomorrow. He had such a simple, dedicated, and special way in which he would deal with his talmidim.

He was well known for his very long *shmoneh esrai*[13] prayer, because, as he put it, he wanted to be sure that each word was said with proper concentration. When he was no longer receiving a salary, he supported himself by lending money, under proper strictly halakhic bounds.

The youngest sibling, Ila, experienced two striking accidents during her childhood. As a very young child, she fell off the third floor of an unfenced roof but was uninjured because she hit several clotheslines on the way down. Also, she swallowed a nickel, which had to be removed from her stomach; a picture of her appeared then in a local newspaper. She and her husband, Ruby, had four children—Burry, Bryna, Leah, and Duvie—and several grandchildren. They were among the founders of the Agudath Israel Branch in Toronto and very active in the Jewish community.

---

13 *shmoneh esrai* (standard 18 blessings recited 3 times a day by observant Jews)

Hymie Dershowitz

Hymie (Yechezkel), sixth child of Zecharja and Leah, married Anna Rubinson, who had also been born in New York City. Her father, Berish, had immigrated to America earlier. They had four children: Chaya, Esther, Zecharia, and Yussel. As noted above, during his younger years he was a partner with his brother-in-law, Joe Fendel, in the wholesale dry goods store that they

Photo courtesy of Zecharia Dor-Shav

opened on the Lower East Side of Manhattan.

His Connection with the "Malachim"

In 1937, Hymie gave his daughter, Esther—who was only fifteen years old at that time—in marriage, to a neighbor, Rabbi Yaakov (Yankel) Schorr, who was twenty. The wedding took place in North Carolina because underage marriage is forbidden in New York, while it is permitted in North Carolina, with parental permission. The story was written up in the *Brooklyn Daily Eagle* (February 16, 1937) as a "cult" marriage. It noted that the first place they went to, after the wedding, was the home of Rabbi Chaim Avraham Dov Ber Levine HaCohen, known as the Malach (The Angel).

Esther had married the leading scholar among his followers. Not long after giving her in marriage, he gave his older daughter, Chaya—who was seventeen at the time—in marriage to another member of Rabbi Levine's followers, Mendel Rosen.

The Malach arrived in the United States in 1923,[14] having received semikah from Rabbi Yitzchok Elchonon Spector at a young age. He was also esteemed as one of the closest followers of Sholom Dovber Schneersohn, the Mitteler Rebbe of Chabad, and tutor of his son, Yosef Yitzchok Schneersohn, who eventually became the sixth Chabad Rebbe.

Initially, he assumed the leadership of a small Bronx synagogue called Nusach Ari. His followers, ultimately, were called the Malachim. Eventually, he parted ways with Lubavitch. Perhaps conscious of the Malach's sense of rejection by Lubavitch, his followers organized themselves as a separate community. Shared responsibility for the group was assigned to Rabbi Yaakov Schorr and Rabbi Meir Weberman,[15] both former students of Torah

---

14 Other sources cite a later date, 1927.
15 A descendent of Moshe Weberman (see below). It is curious that currently I find myself often sitting and studying at the same table as a member of this family in a yeshiva kollel in Israel headed by my nephew, Rabbi Akiva Dershowitz.

Vodaath.[16] Two years before the Malach's death on Shavuot, 1938, they formed their own yeshiva—"Nesivos Olam" in Williamsburg—under the leadership of Rabbi Yaakov Schorr, who took over the helm of the community. They named their Williamsburg synagogue in acknowledgement of Rabbi Judah Loew ben Bezalel, known as the Maharal of Prague, who authored a book by that name.

The Story of the Malachim

Rabbi Levine combined the influence of very different mentors: the intensity and depth of Chabad fueled his davening, while the penetratingly analytical method of Rabbi Chaim (Halevi) Soloveitchik guided him in his study of Talmud. He presented a type of study that was mostly unknown then in America except, of course, by the Soloveitchik family.

Moshe Weberman—whose son, Ben Zion, was a prominent Williamsburg lawyer who was active in the very early years of Torah Vodaath—"discovered" the Malach while vacationing together in a hotel in Spring Valley, New York.[17] His son, Ben Zion, brought the Malach to the attention of Rabbi Shraga Feivel Mendlowitz, principal of Torah Vodaath, who was

---

16 Jerome R. Mintz, *Hassidic People: A Place in the New World*, Cambridge, MA: Harvard University Press, 1992.

17 *Mishpacha* Magazine, January 9, 2008.

always eager to expose his American-born students to the great men of Europe and took note of the Malach's arrival. He introduced a group of his chosen students to this holy Jew from Ilya (near Vilna). Many students of Torah Vodaath visited the Malach on different occasions. These sincere, wholesome young boys were captivated by his personality, holy intensity, and ideas. He endowed them with a very deep appreciation for their sacred Jewish legacy and imbued them with derision and contempt for the American street.

The parents of some of the youngsters became worried. As reported, "it had not occurred to Mr. Mendlowitz that the Malach would become a living icon" to some of them. As time went on, the Malach "began to exhort them concerning their personal beings, instructing them to allow their beards and *peyes* (sidelocks) to grow longer, to give up wearing ties and other frivolous and Gentile attire. He convinced them of the desirability of wearing distinct dress, such as black kapotes (coats) and hats, and to forgo secular learning completely." They were taught that they are not "Americans," rather, they are Yidden (Jews). Their unforeseen adherence to Hasidic ways was a revolutionary turn in belief and conduct.[18] It was reported that some of them adopted an extreme

18 Op. cit., *Hasidic People*, p. 24.

asceticism, which led to their sleeping on the floor while using a stone for a pillow.

Mr. Mendlowitz was dismayed when the boys announced that they would no longer attend secular classes. Suddenly, the term Malach was no longer just an admiring acknowledgment of the master's conduct; it was a scornful label for boys who appeared not to know how to behave like regular people—rather, they were Malachim, angels.

> This radical change [in his students] left Rabbi Mendlowitz in dismay. The student followers of the Malach stood in direct opposition to his philosophy and to the standards of the yeshiva. He worried about their possible effect on the other students in the yeshiva. The members of the yeshiva governing board and most of the parents seemed to agree that the ultra-pious students set a dangerous example. They undermined the balance of secular and religious studies, and they contradicted the modern perspective of the yeshiva. Parents feared that their sons too might be influenced to return to the European manners that they on their own had so willingly discarded.[19]

19 Yitzchok Levine, *The Malach,* The Jewish Press, 22 Av 5775—August 6, 2015.

At a meeting of the board of directors, "it was decided that those who insisted on continuing to go to the Malach weekly would not be permitted to attend classes. In 1933, the followers of the Malach were expelled from the Yeshivah."

According to Rabbi Nesanel Quinn, the then-director of the yeshiva, they left on their own. However, according to Rabbi Meir Weberman, of the Malachim, Quinn expelled them, for which he later apologized.[20]

Years before World War II, the Malach had told his Hasidim that the skies over Europe were red with blood and that soon, America would become the host country to the remnants of Jewry. It was up to them to prepare the ground for the expected arrivals. Their beards, he assured them, would cleanse the atmosphere, and their long coats and Yiddish speech would purify the streets. Eventually, many of the original Malachim were absorbed by reborn American Hasidic movements led by newly arrived Rebbes like Satmar and Chabad. Hymie and his son, Yussel, were attracted to Satmar—perhaps because Yussel was employed by the community. Others of the followers later founded small

---

20 Wikipedia: Malachim (Hasidic Group). The truth is probably somewhere between these two versions (ZD).

communities in Monsey and Williamsburg, where they transmitted the Malach's message of Torah to their own children.[21] The influence of the Malachim made that part of the Dershowitz clan—at least outwardly—more similar to the traditional Eastern European shtetl comportment than the rest of the clan.

Among the descendants of Esther and Yankel are the Lemmer brothers, Yaakov (Yankie) and Shulem, who are Belzer Hasidim and very prominent in the world of Hazanuth and Jewish music.

Photo courtesy of Yaakov Lemmer

Yankie currently serves as head cantor of Lincoln Square Synagogue in New York City, and as he puts it, "I've been blessed to perform in concerts and ceremonies all over the world, including Poland, England, Israel, Germany, Denmark, France, Belgium, and the United States. Additionally, I've performed at the lighting of the National Menorah in Washington, D.C. five times." At one Memorial Day ceremony,[22]

---

21 Yisroel Besser, Contributing Editor, *Mishpacha* Magazine, Article 8376.
22 This took place on Jewish Heritage Night, 6th Night of Chanukah, December 2014, as the only known Basketball menorah was lit at Brooklyn's Barclay Center, where the Brooklyn Nets played the Detroit Pistons.

during which he sang "The Star-Spangled Banner," he stated, "On this Memorial Day, I think back to the time I stood alongside service personnel and sang for this, our country." He continued, "remembering the fallen and also honoring my distant relative, Morris Dershowitz,[23] who served in World War II."

In 2017, Shulem signed a contract with the prestigious Universal Music Decca Gold Label Group. When he was invited to sing "God Bless America" on April 7, 2019, at the Mets/Nationals Game at Citifield, he was the first Hasidic singer ever to have been invited to sing there during the seventh-inning stretch. *Tablet* magazine, the daily online magazine of Jewish news, ideas, and culture, wrote about Shulem, "His music is able to reach across cultural divides and touch people of diverse faiths and backgrounds."

Back to Hymie's Family

One of Chaya Rosen's daughters, Rivki, married Rabbi Dovid Pinchos Rosenberg, who published a book

---

23 He discovered this relationship at a concert at which he met Professor Alan Dershowitz. He remarked that he knew that he has some connection with the Dershowitz family but didn't know exactly what. As a result of that statement, which was brought to my attention by my niece, Miriam Bass, I invited him and his brother, Shulem, to visit me in Jerusalem. We clarified that they are my first cousins twice removed, and Professor Avi's second cousins once removed.

about her.[24] She became a renowned teacher—originally, in several Hasidic girls' schools. Later, when the family relocated to the fledgling Torah community of Monsey, New York, she and her husband opened an educational institution that evolved from the playgroup she had opened in her home. The facility ran for close to forty years.

Hymie's son, Zecharia, had a troubled life. Hymie felt that he had to protect Zecharia from the world and put great effort into keeping him happy and out of trouble. Perhaps that was why he left the dry goods business and purchased a farm in partnership with his sons and sons-in-law. My sister-in-law, Claire, mother of Alan Dershowitz, was in frequent contact with the family and tried to help them through hard times. Alan was called upon to defend Zecharia in the courts—as also Mendel, for a different offense, a liquor still in Loch Sheldrake operating without a license. The farm gave Zecharia a safe place in which he could work and live.

Their youngest son, Yussel, was just a bit older than I, and we were good friends. He became a renowned artist whose many paintings give life to religious scenes

---

24 Rabbi Dovid Pinchos Rosenberg, *They Called Her Morah Rivka.* Feldheim Publishers, NY, 1918, 464 pages.

and personalities. Among these paintings is one of the family synagogue in Williamsburg that is reproduced as the cover of this book. The original hangs in Lakewood in the home of Rabbi Allen Dershowitz, son of my brother Menashe.

Photo courtesy of Leibe Storch

I love Yussel's artwork. In fact, I think that his first published work was in 1942 for the Torah Vodaath High School journal, *The Scroll*, of which I was coeditor. The offset printing press had just been invented (ca. 1940) and was becoming popular in the printing world,[25] making it possible to print illustrations without the tedious and expensive medium of engraving the pictures. The attached is one of his illustrations in that yearbook.

Photo courtesy of Zecharia Dor-Shav

As mentioned, Yussel eventually became a Satmar Hasid. He would sometimes

---

25 An American printer, Ira W. Rubel, accidentally discovered the process in 1904. In this process, the printing content and the non-printing content, i.e., pictures, are on one surface.

get up on a milk crate in Gramercy Park, or elsewhere, to talk about what was wrong with Israel. Tragedy took the life of one of his youngest daughters in a fire.

Rosie Fendel

Rosie, probably because she was the youngest child of the family, was apparently the only one of her siblings to graduate from high school. She married Joseph (Zalman Hillel) Fendel, the only Litvak (non-Hasidic Lithuanian origin) in the family, and they had two children, Meyer and Zechariah. Rosie, who was sickly, passed away at the age of fifty-two. She is remembered for her sweet personality and gentle demeanor.

Photo courtesy of Hillel
Fendel

During November 1918, a group of recruits were standing on a line ready to be inducted into the U.S army. Among them was her future husband, Joe. When it was just about his turn to be interviewed, the person in front of him said, "I guess we don't have to wait any longer. The war is over, and Germany is suing for peace." Joe and all the other inductees were "off the hook," and thus ended his army career that never really began.

In the beginning of his work career, Joe engaged in a wholesale dry goods enterprise at 496–500 Broadway, in Manhattan. The display window proclaimed, "Joseph Fendel and Co.," along with a dummy called "Big Yank" modeling the overalls and other clothes sold in the store. He was a customer peddler and would take samples of merchandise from one store to another, looking to make a living. To make the wares lighter, he wouldn't use a suitcase, but rather a cardboard box. Unfortunately, during the severe depression of the 1930s, many stores were forced out of business. Those were indeed difficult years, but nonetheless, Joe's business continued to thrive, albeit in a more limited manner.

He was a wonderful Torah Reader for the family synagogue; he never got up to read before the congregation unless he had reviewed the reading seven times. In his spare time, he always sat with an open Talmud book. This he did for thirty years, even though during the last twenty of them he had to wear an ileal pouch for a serious illness that he had contracted.

Meyer reports that he can still picture his father's partner retrieving items from high up on the shelves, skillfully toddling the ladder from place to place. Meyer also recalls

Photo courtesy of Zecharia Dor-Shav

spending Friday afternoons with his brother, helping (and mostly playing) in the store. The big cartons were great for their games. They often got into the cartons and were busy happily dividing up the goods among themselves.

Zechariah recalled that his father always had a tremendous desire to learn Torah, and that our grandfather Zecharja was "thrilled" when he met him: "Here was a Ben-Torah[26] for his youngest daughter, Chaya Raizel!" On his deathbed, he was in great pain, and his nephew, Moishe Chait, suggested, "Let's bring something that will bring him joy—a Gemara!" They did so, and, in fact, he became calm and felt better. In a similar vein Meyer recalls, "I can hardly picture him without a Gemara or other Sepher. After his very long day at work, I frequently fell asleep to the beautiful sound of his Gemara tune. I remember how excited he was when he first received an answer to a question he had on a Talmudic commentator—via a new gadget called a 'telephone.'"

Zecharia Fendel.
Photo courtesy of
Zecharia Dor-Shav

---

26 *Ben-Torah* (Torah scholar)

Both Meyer and Zechariah were visionaries of *chinuch* and *kiruv rechokim* (Jewish educational outreach). While working for Torah Umesorah, Meyer was sent to West Hempstead, Long Island, to help the developing Jewish community, which had just opened a synagogue and was planning a Hebrew Day School. After the first few meetings with the community, he was invited to become rabbi of the synagogue and principal of the developing school, the Hebrew Academy of Nassau County (HANC), with an initial enrollment of just thirty students. He retired after thirty-two years and moved to Israel with his wife, Goldie. Today the school encompasses four campuses and serves more than 1,200 students, from nursery through high school, who come from fifty communities throughout Long Island and Queens.

Meyer's son, Rabbi Dovid, established the Afikei Daat Hesder Yeshiva in Sderot, with hundreds of students, combining intense Torah study with Israeli army service. The students also volunteer in many *hesed* (nonprofit charitable) programs around the city helping the community and

Photo courtesy of Afikei Daat Hesder Yeshiva

spreading Torah. The Yeshiva has been a linchpin for the community's resilience under the face of frequent enemy fire from the Gaza Strip. The author is a member of the *amutah* (official nonprofit corporate body) of the yeshiva.

During their first trip to Israel in 1952, the two brothers met the Chazon Ish, Rabbi Avrohom Yeshaya Karelitz, who was the acknowledged *posek*[27] in Israel at that time. When Zechariah informed the Chazon Ish of his ambitious project to write English books that would imbue youth with a deep appreciation of Torah values and provide answers to questions of faith that were common among them and newly-observant Jews, the Chazon Ish blessed him and said, "You are engaged in the work of Mashiach (the Messiah)." He received semikah from the Chazon Ish in addition to his semikah from Yeshiva Chofetz Chaim. He published nearly twenty books on Jewish thought, which in aggregate sold over 100,000 copies. One of Zechariah's former high school principals, Rabbi Alexander Linchner, said that he generally kept a copy of one of Zechariah's books on his desk.

Interestingly, I also found one of his books in the small synagogue on Oahu Island in Hawaii, where I had spent Shavuot during a sabbatical leave from the

---

27 *posek* (halakhah decisor)

university. In fact, Meyer's *chinuch* work was also evident during that visit. Here is what happened:

There had been a large Conservative synagogue in Oahu, but no Orthodox synagogue. A private family had borrowed a Torah scroll from Chabad on the mainland and converted one of the rooms of their home into an Orthodox synagogue. I called and asked what hotel might be nearby so that I could stay there for Yom Tov and daven with them. They very graciously invited me not to rent a hotel room, but come and be their guest for the holiday. When I arrived on Erev Yom Tov, I saw a Polynesian woman mowing the lawn and assumed they had hired a local native to do the work. When I entered the home, however, I found that the story was quite different. The house was full of invited guests who were using the home as a kind of commune for the holiday. They included sailors from Pearl Harbor, converted Polynesian women who were married to newly observant mainland Jews, and everything in between. They were cooking and baking the food for the holiday (and mowing the lawn).

When evening fell, there were just ten men, including me—but eventually, a few more men and women arrived. After the maariv prayer service, we had a wonderful meal with singing and happy conversation. We later assembled to study Torah, and the guests were invited to present their own Torah thoughts to the group. Among those presenting was a daughter of the homeowner. She delivered a beautiful Torah thought. When asked where she had gotten her Jewish education, she said that she had studied in the Hebrew Academy of Nassau County, under Rabbi Meyer Fendel—and, in fact, was the salutatorian at her graduation. The family had moved from West Hempstead to Hawaii a few years earlier. And so, Meyer and Zechariah were both represented in that home and synagogue, in the middle of the Pacific Ocean.

When all those who wished to do so had presented their diverse Torah teachings, it was still early in the night, and I suggested that, if they wished, I could teach something too. Of course, they agreed, and I taught for several hours, until morning, when it was time for the Shacharit prayer. It was a magnificent Yom Tov for us. We prayed Shacharit facing one direction and musaf facing the opposite—since Hawaii is just about equidistant, both East and West, toward Israel.

It dawned upon me, "Look what my father brought about! He founded Torah Vodaath, where I and both Fendel boys had studied. The Chofetz Chaim Yeshiva, a break-off of that school, as reported above, was where the Fendels had received their semikah. Their educational work led to my having a proper synagogue in which to pray on that Shavuot, on the Island of Oahu."

Chapter Eight
Personal Experiences with Great Rabbis of My Generation

AS INDICATED IN the introduction to this book, the Dershowitz family is unusual in that "for the most part . . . [the] family has become more religious" with the passage of generations. The religious outlook, philosophy, and behavior of a large part of the family has become more knowledgeable, more advanced, and more sophisticated. Consequently, the family has produced far more Torah scholars and rabbis than were present in the early immigrant period. These scholars and their families were greatly influenced by the abundant yeshivas and rashei yeshiva who headed them. The author of this book was fortunate to have been acquainted with a large number of those located in the New York City area. Of course, each institution had its own style and raised thousands of students who followed its way. Many of the rashei yeshiva gave rulings and published books reflecting their unique approach and religious decisions on significant modern questions that were referred to them. Some of these rulings had a vast influence on Jewish national life in the United States and elsewhere.

In one of the important rulings cited below, I was privileged to have had a significant role in its promulgation. Others of the rulings that were made to me personally, and some of my personal observations of these outstanding leaders, are instructive and worth noting. The presentation of the rabbis is in alphabetical order, with no suggestion of ranking their relative importance.

Rabbi Moshe Feinstein

When "Reb Moshe" (1895–1986), as he was known in the yeshiva world, came to the United States from

Russia, he settled on the Lower East Side of Manhattan and served as rosh yeshiva of Mesivta Tifereth Jerusalem. He was world-renowned for his expertise in Jewish Law and his compassion toward all who approached him with halakhic questions. In his time, he was the acknowl-

Wikipedia

edged *posek* for the yeshiva world of North America and beyond. Everyone knew that he was readily available to all because he kept a phone on his desk in the beit midrash, so as to be instantly available to any questioner—except when he was giving a *shiur.* In our childhood home, whenever we were struggling with a halakhic question, my mother would say, "Why don't you just call Reb Moshe?"

It was most surprising, therefore, that when we called to ask if on Yom Tov, when one is permitted to cook and kindle a fire, may one lower the gas flame even when it is not for cooking purposes, he requested that we come to his home for a face-to-face answer. When we arrived, he immediately ruled on the question but carefully explained a similar case in which the ruling would not apply. In his published book of responsa, he chose not to reveal the ruling because of the possible misapplication. I too, therefore, will abstain from being more specific regarding the matter.[1] The lesson in caution when publishing books as compared to face-to-face discussion is compelling.

Another unusual and interesting ruling, regarding the conversion of children, was rendered to me regarding a brother and sister who were attending the Day School with which I was connected during one of my sabbatical leaves. A prominent member of the school community had married a woman whose conversion had some halakhic problems. The oldest of their children, a son, was approaching bar mitzvah age, and the school was not ready to let him continue unless his "Jewishness" was affirmed. Furthermore, they questioned the validity of his circumcision, because his mother might not have been Jewish at the time of the original circumcision. We decided to ask Reb Moshe for a ruling on this child and on his younger sister. During a three-way conference call (the local

---

1 שו"ת אגרות משה אורח חיים חלק א סימן צג—ובדבר להקטין אש הגעז ביום טוב אם עדיף ממכבה לגמרי, איני רואה בזה טעם שיהיה עדיף, דבהקטנה הוא גם כן מכבה כמו מכבה לגמרי. ויש אצלי חידוש גדול ואיני רוצה לכתוב זה בכתב.

(Igrot Moshe, Orach Chaim I 93) With regard to lowering a gas flame on *Yom Tov* [when not needed for the cooking process], is it preferable to shutting the gas completely? I don't see any reason for it to be preferable because in lowering one is also extinguishing, no less than completely. *I have a novel view on this issue which I don't wish to commit to writing.*

community rabbi was the third party), after I introduced myself, Reb Moshe remembered my name and remarked, "You are one of us [the yeshiva community], aren't you?" I believe the following ruling was affected by that fact, as many rulings are restricted to those who are familiar with the nuances of the ruling and thus unlikely to misapply it.

The prime problem was not about setting up a conversion court. Everyone involved was prepared for that. The problem was that the children's parental home was neither Sabbath-observant nor kosher. Both parents, however, very much wanted the children to continue in the school and were prepared to follow the Rav's ruling, if it didn't require them to change their own very Jewish but nonobservant inclination. Furthermore, the mother was insistent that she would not permit the conversion court to draw blood from her son for the halakhic conversion. Reb Moshe asked our opinion as to whether the children were likely to remain halakhic Jews after they left their parents' home. Our feeling was that they would so remain, and Reb Moshe ruled to convert them currently, even though they would not be able to observe all the mitzvoth, until adulthood, when they would have left their parents' home. He also ruled that it was unnecessary to draw blood from the boy, since the original circumcision had been done with the thought that it would bring him into the Covenant of Abraham.

A third interesting experience took place when a friend and I visited him in a hotel in the Catskills. He was sitting on the lawn when a bowl of vegetable soup was brought to him. He looked up at us and said, "You know that in the Shulchan Aruch there are two opinions about the proper blessing for such a soup." We said, "Yes, it is either *borei pri ha'adamah* or *she'hakol* (either "He who created fruit of the ground," or "He who created everything with His word)." He then took a spoonful and said his berakah[2] so softly that we couldn't hear what he said! We were very surprised but assumed that he was saying that the choice is subjective and didn't want to prejudice our own subjective choice. His son-in-law, Rabbi Moshe Tendler, however, when many years later I related the story to him, said he assumed that Reb Moshe was following his practice of not ruling on something upon which the Shulchan Aruch reports two opinions without choosing one above the other. If the Shulchan Aruch did not choose, Reb Moshe was not going to give us the impression that could be a standardizer and give

---

2 *berakah* (blessing)

a binding ruling. To me, this was an example of the modesty and greatness that he exhibited in all of his halakhic rulings.

There is also the well-known story of Reb Moshe's controversial *psak* (ruling) regarding artificial insemination by an anonymous donor, which led to a troubling backlash in the form of violent disagreement with Rebbe Yoel Teitelbaum, Grand Rabbi of Satmar. False notices were published that Reb Moshe had died and a hearse was sent to his house, among other disgraceful behaviors. The Rav never retracted his ruling. He did, however, publish a subsequent letter that one should consult his local rabbi before acting on this ruling.

Rabbi Yaakov Kamenetsky

Rabbi Yaakov (1891–1986) headed Mesivta Torah Vodaath in Brooklyn from 1948 to 1968. While I was strolling with him once, he told me that if he could have his way, he wouldn't have students begin the study of Gemara in fourth grade. Rather, he would have them complete Tanakh and Mishnah before they moved on to Gemara. It was important, he felt, for the student to have an overview of all the written Torah and Mishnaic rulings before he could understand the give-and-take of Gemara study. He bemoaned the fact, however, that he couldn't buck the trend of the other yeshivas by himself.

The Rav had been a neighbor of my first father-in-law, Rabbi Elisha Kohn, before he moved to Monsey, New York. They were friends, and we decided to visit him in his suk-kah shortly after the return from my 1967 visit to Israel. Knowing the

Wikipedia

Rabbinic tradition that the presence of God's Glory (the Shekinah)[3] remains attached to the Western Wall of the Temple even during its destruction,[4] and having just returned from a very moving visit there, I wondered if I had "experienced" that Presence. I asked the Rav if he could help me understand what that experience is and how one recognizes it. He said, "I can't tell you exactly what it means, but when one is there, he feels a closeness to God that he doesn't feel in most

---

3 *Shekinah* (lit. "dwelling" or "settling" and denotes the apparent dwelling or sensation of the Divine Presence)

4 מדרש רבה (וילנא) פרשת שמות פרשה ב- א"ר שמואל בר נחמן עד שלא חרב בית המקדש היתה שכינה שורה בתוכו...אף על פי שהוא חרב הרי הוא בקדושתו...הא- להים אינו זז משם, א"ר אחא לעולם אין השכינה זזה מכותל מערבי.

(Midrash Rabah Exodus 2) Rabbi Shmuel Ben Nachman said, "Until the Temple was destroyed, the Presence of God dwelled there... even when it was destroyed, it remained in its holiness...The [Presence of] God didn't move from there." Rabbi Acha said, "Forever, the Presence of God doesn't leave the Western Wall."

other places." I said, "If so, then I too experienced the Shekinah, because I too felt especially close to Him when I was there."

His son, Rabbi Shmuel, who heads the Talmudical Yeshiva of Philadelphia, was a good friend of my brother Yitzchak; they had studied together in the Lakewood Yeshiva. Another son, Rabbi Noson (Nathan), in 2002, published "Making of a Godol,"[5] a work about the early years of his father and many other rashei yeshiva of the twentieth century. The book raised quite a furor among leading rabbis and was immediately banned by a group of ten leading rabbis in Israel—primary among them was Rabbi Yosef Shalom Eliashiv of Meah Shearim, a leading religious posek. They issued an official letter banning the book, claiming that it was disrespectful to the rabbis whose lives it describes. There was speculation in the yeshiva world that an episode in the book about Rabbi Kotler prompted a grandson of his to urge Rabbi Eliashiv to ban the book. Obviously, Rabbi Noson's book was not thought by his father to be unpublishable, but in light of the "halo effect" that some wished to place on the heads of these religious greats, some felt that such public information might corrupt the minds of yeshiva

---

5   Hamesorah Publishers, 2nd ed. Jerusalem: 2005, 1,429 pages.

students who might ask questions similar to those that these giants had asked in their earlier years.

Rabbi Noson observed that none of the ten Israeli signatories had personally read the book. All but one were unable to read English. He believed that there is no need to hide anything, because knowing the truth about the gedolim only increases one's respect for them (due to their subsequent vast accomplishments, despite facing trials and being human).[6] Though the book also contains episodes about his father, neither he nor his father thought that the book would harm anyone's religiosity. He wrote an improved edition, hoping that the changes would appease the original objectors, but it did not. Likely because of the ban, a used good hardcover copy of the improved edition sells today on Amazon from $2,500 and up.

Interaction with Rabbi Meir Kuznetz regarding the Upper Pool of King Hezekiah

Meir was a friend from the years that we spent together in Yeshiva Chaim Berlin. Later in his life he acquired a degree in engineering. From his youth, he had dreamed and seen himself as destined to help build the third

---

6   Mark B. Shapiro, "Of Books and Bans," *Edah Journal* 3:2: Edah, Inc., 2003.

Beit Hamikdash. He was employed by the Ministry of Religious Affairs and assigned to be engineer for the area of the Temple Mount. In that capacity, he named one of the excavated rooms in his daughter's name.

Among the subjects that interested him was the location of the escarpment (Hebrew: *tzuk)* from which, in Temple times, the scapegoat (Sa'ir L'Azazel) was thrust, during the Yom Kippur service. Applying the Talmud's identification of the location as exactly 12 *mil* from the Mount, he pursued a number of suggested measurements of the mil (approximately one kilometer) and drew concentric circles from the Mount, representing each of these suggestions. He concluded that a location near the community of Geva Binyamin (Benjamin Hill), originally known as Yishuv Adam at the edge of Wadi Kelt (Nahal Prat), meets this criterion. The Hebrew word צוק (tzuk) is used in the Mishnah[7] to describe the location.

He depicted to me the first time that he came there with his children. Standing at the edge of the cliff, his children noted that they were standing between the villages of Michmash and Geva, a location that, in the Book of Samuel,[8] is called מָצוּק (*matzuk*). At a later occasion,

---

7   *Mishnah* (first major Rabbinic legal code, compiled by Judah ha-Nasi)

8   ד) וּבֵין הַמַּעְבְּרוֹת, אֲשֶׁר בִּקֵּשׁ יוֹנָתָן לַעֲבֹר עַל-מַצַּב פְּלִשְׁתִּים, שֵׁן-הַסֶּלַע מֵהָעֵבֶר מִזֶּה, וְשֵׁן-הַסֶּלַע מֵהָעֵבֶר מִזֶּה; וְשֵׁם הָאֶחָד בּוֹצֵץ, וְשֵׁם הָאֶחָד סֶנֶה. ה) הַשֵּׁן הָאֶחָד מָצוּק

when I visited the locality, I found it to be a windswept cliffside, full of stones split by frozen water—exemplifying ארץ גזרה, "a land of split [stones]"—another one of the terms used in the Torah to describe the site. A friend of ours, a professional French-Jewish documentary photographer, made a video of the location for a French program on Jewish topics, at our suggestion.

Another experience with Meir involved a total stranger who had come to him and asked if Meir was interested in knowing where the בריכה העליונה (The Upper Pool)[9] was located, alongside of which some kings of Judah were anointed during the First Temple era. The pool was closed by King Hezekiah during the siege of the King of Ashur, Sennacherib.[10] He responded to the stranger, "Everyone is interested in that location; the

---

מֵצְּפוֹן, מוּל מִכְמָשׂ; וְהָאֶחָד מִנֶּגֶב, מוּל גָּבַע. (שמואל א, יד, ד-ה)

And between the passes, by which Jonathan sought to go over unto the Philistines' garrison, there was a cliff on the one side, and a cliff on the other side; and the name of the one was Botzetz, and the name of the other Seneh. The one cliff rose up [matzuk] on the north in front of Michmas, and the other on the south in front of Geva. (Samuel 1, 14,4-5)

9   וַיֹּאמֶר ה' אֶל-יְשַׁעְיָהוּ, צֵא-נָא לִקְרַאת אָחָז, אַתָּה וּשְׁאָר יָשׁוּב בְּנֶךָ: אֶל-קְצֵה, תְּעָלַת
הַבְּרֵכָה הָעֶלְיוֹנָה, אֶל-מְסִלַּת, שָׂדֵה כוֹבֵס. (ישעיהו ז, ג)

Then God said to Isaiah: "Go forth now to meet Ahaz, you, and Shear-Yashuv your son, at the edge of the conduit of the upper pool, in the road of the launderers' field." (Isaiah 7, 3)

10 He failed to capture Jerusalem—it is the only city mentioned on Sennacherib's Stele as being besieged and of which a capture is not mentioned.

archaeologists think that it is in the area of Solomon's Pool near Bethlehem." The stranger proclaimed that the pool wasn't there at all, and if Meir wished, he would show him the exact location—near the Begin Center in Jerusalem. Thereupon, he took Meir to a paved street in that area, pointed to a spot on the road, and said, "Here! When they paved the street I knew that they were covering the well, but it wasn't the right time yet for the location of the pool to be revealed."

His interest piqued, Meir decided to ask some of the Torah giants if they thought it proper to continue the quest to find and reopen the pool. This, despite the fact that according to tradition, the well was not to be reopened until the times of the Messiah. After approaching several people who declined to rule on the matter, he reached Rabbi Yaakov Kamenetsky, who said that if what he was doing doesn't contradict any kind of halakhah, he may follow the guidance of kabbalah[11] and pursue the search. Before doing anything further, he elected to speak further to the man who had given him the information. Thwarted, he discovered that the

---

11 See: Encyclopedia.com: David ben Solomon ibn Avi Zimra (Radbaz). "Although he was a kabbalist, he introduced Kabbalah in decisions only when not in contradiction with the Talmud, or where no definite decision is laid down in the Talmud. When Kabbalah conflicted with the Talmud preference was to be given to the latter."

stranger was no longer living, but was known as having been a scholar of kabbalah. He went to his grave to pray and, to his surprise, found that it was then, exactly, the anniversary date of his death.

As the engineer responsible for archaeology under the aegis of the Ministry of Religious Affairs, he received permission to dig open the road surface. He undid one corner of the intersection, then a second, then a third—but found nothing. When he opened the fourth corner, however, he found the walls of a plastered well, in the middle of which was the drainage pipe of the Khan Theatre.

He requested and received further permission to divert an existent drainage pipe around the well. When the excavation reached the bottom of the well, he went down and scanned its surface. What looked like a little hole caught his attention, and he stuck his pen into it. It went right through, with no obstruction, and so he got a hammer and broke the hole open just enough to stick his arm in—again he found no obstruction. Consequently, he broke open an area large enough to identify what was there and found that it was a paved passageway. Water dripping from the wall of the well, which he had tested for purity, was found to be clean.

He was now quite excited and decided to scrape some of the plaster and send it to the most prestigious lab that deals with dating such plaster. The lab was in

London and run by an Israeli. The response that he received was that it matches plasters only from the time of the Second Temple. This was disappointing, and he did no further digging and left for America on a business trip.

On his return flight he found himself sitting near Teddy Kollek, then mayor of Jerusalem, and started chatting about his findings. The mayor advised him that he could not leave the street open any longer and must have it repaved—which the city did.

About two years later, totally unexpectedly, the London lab contacted Meir to tell him that new digs on the Island of Crete had revealed wells from the times of the First Temple that matched the plaster he had sent. That is the point at which Meir's interest was piqued again, but he was no longer actively in pursuit of the matter. Subsequently, from time to time, I would ask him to reopen the well and do more digging. He always said that he thought I was right, but he didn't do anything about it—and now, sadly, Meir is no longer among the living. The spot is on the street that leads to the entrance of the Begin Center in Jerusalem.

Rabbi Aharon Kotler

Rabbi Aharon Kotler (1892–1962) was my brother Yitzchak's rosh yeshiva. He was already a prominent leader of Orthodox Judaism, in Lithuania. In 1943, after he immigrated to the United States, he founded the Beth Medrash Govoha of Lakewood, New Jersey. Yitzchak, who with me had attended Rabbi Shurkin's class for dropouts at Torah Vodaath, as mentioned above, returned to the yeshiva world at the same time that I did. While I left for Yeshiva Chaim Berlin, he left for Lakewood and joined the yeshiva's second entrance class.

Geni

Reb Aharon, as he was known in the yeshiva world, was orphaned at the age of ten and adopted by his uncle, Rabbi Yitzchak Pinnes, a dayan in Minsk. He studied in Slabodka Yeshiva in Lithuania under the "Alter (Elder) of Slabodka," Rabbi Nosson Tzvi Finkel, as well as under Rabbi Moshe Mordechai Epstein. After a period of learning there, he joined his father-in-law, Rabbi Isser Zalman Meltzer, in the Slutsk Yeshiva, also in Belarus.

After World War I, the yeshiva moved from Slutsk to Kletsk. With the outbreak of World War II, the Rav and the yeshiva relocated to Vilna, then the major refuge of most yeshivas from the occupied areas. Reportedly, the Rav, as so many others of the yeshiva world, was begged by Rabbi Zerach Warhaftig to flee[12] but demurred. He reportedly encouraged his yeshiva to stay in Vilna despite the approaching Nazis. Most of his students were murdered in the Holocaust. Some did not listen to the Rav and escaped to China, together with the students of the Mir Yeshiva.

Reb Aharon was brought to America in 1941 by the Vaad Hatzalah rescue organization, which he eventually guided during the subsequent years of the Holocaust. He helped establish, and became a prime mover of, Chinuch Atzmai, an independent religious school system, in Israel, and was chairman of the Moetzes Gedolei HaTorah (Council of Torah Giants) of Agudath Israel. He also chaired the rabbinical administration board of Torah Umesorah and was on the presidium of the Agudas HaRabbonim of the United States and Canada.

In 1943, he founded the beit midrash in Lakewood, with fifteen students. By the time of his death, the yeshiva had grown to 250 students. He was succeeded

12 As reported above, during World War II, Rabbi Warhaftig was among those who had convinced the Japanese Vice-Consul in Kovna to issue transit visas for the entire Mir Yeshiva. After succeeding in this task, he went from yeshiva to yeshiva trying to convince them also to leave for Shanghai with such a transit visa. Unfortunately, he was not successful with a number of them—including Rabbi Kotler.

by his son, Rabbi Shneur. At the time of this writing, the yeshiva has grown into the largest institution of its kind in America, with over 6,700 college-age and advanced-level students. The surrounding Lakewood community supports a network of fifty other yeshivas and over one hundred synagogues with more than 100,000 residents, two-thirds of whom are associated with the devout community—and is still growing. Menashe's son, Yitzchak Mordechai, was a student of the Lakewood Yeshiva until the day of his death at age seventy-four in 2016 and authored *The Legacy of Maran Rav Aharon Kotler.*[13] He was very proud of the fact that he had a chair in his home that had been used regularly in the beit midrash by Reb Aharon, upon which Yitzchak Mordechai kept Torah books—but never sat. Significantly, Yitschak Mordechai died on the day of the yahrzeit of Rabbi Kotler.

Our family has a large contingent in Lakewood. In addition to Menashe's family, it includes many members of the Zecharia Fendel family and their extended families. Reb Aharon's personal doctor was the father of my nephew by marriage, Dr. Aryeh Zinkin, who grew up in Lakewood. I have often suggested to my Lakewood nephews that they try to move the whole

---

13 Yitzchok Dershowitz, *The Legacy of Maran Rav Aharon Kotler: A Portrait of the Qualities, Teachings, and Accomplishments of the Venerable Rosh HaYeshiva*, 2nd Edition, Spring Valley, NY: Feldheim Publishers, 2006, 637 pages.

Lakewood community and establish a new town in Israel. I have not yet succeeded, but imagine what it could do for the religious character of the state!

I frequently spent Shavuot in Lakewood and was always impressed by the fact that after being awake all night,[14] together with all of the students, Reb Aharon was always the first to return to the beit midrash after the morning meal. Furthermore, as opposed to others who delivered Torah lectures (*magidei shiurim*), I never saw anyone succeed in contradicting anything Reb Aharon said. He was always stimulating and complete. The conclusions he developed were his true conclusions, leaving no place for disagreement.

His son-in-law, Rabbi Dov Schwartzman, was a close friend of Yitzchak and catalyst for his move to Israel. I once asked him why the yeshiva world didn't accept the authority of the chief rabbinate in Israel. He replied that since the rabbinate is appointed by a committee that includes politicians, who do not feel themselves personally bound by the rabbinic rulings of the chief rabbinate, their chosen candidates are not necessarily the most authoritative *poskim* in Israel.

Rabbi Avraham Isaac HaCohen Kook, the first Ashkenazi chief rabbi, who was instrumental in

---

14 It is a custom in the yeshivot and in many Orthodox communities to remain awake all night studying Torah, on the Eve of Shavuot.

establishing the chief rabbinate and its method of appointment, intended that secular Jews should also feel a sense of connection to the rabbinate. Unfortunately, however, the panel has much politicking and is probably overpopulated with its current 150 members. Rabbi Kotler is buried on Har HaMenuchot in Jerusalem.

He is credited with having planted the seed for the contemporary Torah community of the United States. His students opened schools, yeshivas, and kollels across the globe and became socially active in their respective communities: 14,000 alumni of Beth Medrash Govoha have established 1,050 institutions across the globe, educating future generations from the youngest kindergarten children studying *aleph-bet* to mature scholars, for whom members of the alumni expound on Rabbi Kotler's deep Torah novella on intricate Talmudic concepts.

Rabbi Menachem Mendel Schneersohn

The main headquarters of Chabad Lubavitch is in the Crown Heights neighborhood of Brooklyn, where I lived as a youngster. It was well known that they had a second shaharith prayer service, much later on the Sabbath morning than any other neighborhood synagogue. For me, as a teenager who sometimes

Facebook

lingered in bed on the Sabbath, this offered a wonderful alternative synagogue that I attended on occasion. Rabbi Menachem Mendel Schneersohn (1902–1994), the last Rebbe of the Lubavitcher dynasty, also prayed with that minyan. He would be studying *hasidut* from very early in the morning until the 10:00 a.m. minyan started. Thus, I often prayed with him before he was crowned as the seventh Rebbe of the Dynasty. He made no airs and acted just as any other member of the minyan; we all sat together, around a very large table.

Furthermore, as mentioned above, I knew that my Rebbi had had a connection with him from the days of their studies with Rabbi Chaim Heller in Berlin. In fact, it is reported that my Rebbi said about the Lubavitcher Rebbe that as he was listening to lectures in engineering school, he had his Gemara open in front of him, learning throughout the lecture—and still got the highest grades in the course. My Rebbi's connection with Rabbi Schneersohn, however, continued only in private, away from the eyes of us, his talmidim. In fact, as mentioned above, when I once said to him something praiseworthy of Chabad, he shouted at me and called me a *plut* (idiot). I know that he didn't object to a connection with Chabad for others of his talmidim, but for me, apparently, he felt that it was wrong to have such an association.

I did, however, once contact the Rebbe's secretary to ask if I could bring my university mentor, Professor Herman Witkin, to one of his *farbrengens*.[15] In the course of my doctoral work, I had mentioned that to the Eastern European Jew, a person's head was very important, whereas the body was far less significant. In fact, I suggested that if we were to conduct an experiment in which we would take a large number of pictures of unknown people and sever the heads from the bodies, then ask subjects to choose the appropriate head for some of the bodies, Jews would tend to pick a larger head to match the body than would other subjects. Professor Witkin, himself the son of a shohet, asked, "How, then, do you justify all the heartfelt dancing done by Hasidim and yeshiva students?" I responded, "They are dancing with their souls and not with their bodies," and to prove my point suggested we go to a farbrengen with the Rebbe at Chabad headquarters.

The Chabad secretary arranged for my wife and me to visit, as well as Professor Witkin, his wife, and another couple, friends of the Witkins. When we made our way

---

15 Lit. A joyous gathering (usually on holidays and the like). The term is primarily used by Lubavitch Hasidim. It may consist of explanations of Torah subjects, with an emphasis on Hasidic philosophy. It always includes lively Hasidic melodies, with wine and other alcoholic drinks being served to enhance the happy spirit of the occasion.

to the farbrengen, we found the beit midrash packed from corner to corner. We were guided to the back of the building, where, by climbing over a pile of boxes, we reached a back door that entered directly onto the stage where the Rebbe sat. Chairs had been prepared for us on-stage. The Rebbe directed a bottle of wine to each couple, while we watched the "dancing." Of course, since the beit midrash was so crowded, no one was able to really dance; rather, it was performed while sitting. Led by the Rebbe's hand motions, the Hasidim sang, swayed their bod-ies, and occasionally stood up. When we left, Professor Witkin admitted that what he saw was not body dancing, but rather spiritual dancing. He added, "You don't know what spark you may have reawakened in me!"

Earlier, he had inscribed my copy of his book, *Psychological Differentiation*, with the following:

For Rabbi Dershowitz,
With warmest regards and with appreciation for your work and what you have done to stim-ulate my own interest in this fascinating area.

Interestingly, several years later, when I was chairman of the School of Education at Bar-Ilan University, Professor Witkin was invited by the dean of the social studies department, Professor Yaakov Rand[16] (who had also done his doctorate on Witkin's theory of psychological differentiation), to visit and give lectures. The dean and I, as well as other people from the department, met him at the airport. As we escorted him out, he began to speak in Yiddish. His wife exclaimed, "Hymie, why are you speaking Yiddish?" To which he replied, "I am in Israel!"

Knowing his background, I presented him with a tallit at his lecture. Unfortunately, he died very soon after this visit, and we will never know what memories these exposures aroused in him.

As mentioned above, The Rebbe and Chabad honored Senator Jesse Helms on the occasion of an Education Day, USA, reception.[17]

---

16 Professor Rand and I were coauthors of a study that led to the government's encouragement of children of Sephardic tradition studying in Ashkenazic religious schools to pray in their own tradition in separate quorums.

17 In 1984, when Professor Alan Dershowitz heard that Senator Helms was being honored by Chabad at a reception in Washington, he wrote:

I was surprised and disappointed. In my naiveté, I had the "chutzpah" and wrote a letter to the Rebbe, respectfully asking why he chose to honor a man who was, in my view, against Israel, against integration, against social rights, equality for all.

The Rebbe replied with a very poignant and powerful letter. He explained that Senator Helms was not being singled out for an honor, but was simply one of many U.S. Senators and U.S. Representatives who came to the Education Day, USA reception. Until he retired from the Senate in 2002, in his later years, as chairman of the Foreign Relations Committee (1995–2001), Helms couldn't do enough for Israel. He even exempted the nation from his fervent opposition to foreign aid.

Rabbi Aaron Soloveichik

The first Soloveitchik to establish
this family's great legacy was Rabbi
Yosef Dov (also known as the Beis
Halevi), a student of Rabbi Chaim
Ickovits (also known as Reb Chaim
of Volozhin),[18] whose book נפש

Picture credit, Chabad

Then Rebbe wrote a long and beautiful P.S., explaining how one
influences other human beings. All people—but especially politicians,
who often act out of expediency more than conviction—should be
engaged in a positive way. That way, we can try to influence them.
He said I should watch carefully to see whether or not we have had an
influence on Jesse Helms.

Sure enough, very shortly after he was honored, Senator Helms
assumed a very influential role on the United States Senate Foreign
Relations Committee and became one of the strongest supporters of
Israel and of other Jewish causes as well. So obviously the Rebbe had
had an enormous influence on persuading Jesse Helms that, even
with his very conservative values, he could become a beacon for the
Jewish people and the Jewish state. The Rebbe had an enormous
influence on persuading Jesse Helms to become a beacon for the
Jewish people.

This showed me how the Rebbe's influence transcended Brooklyn,
and even the Jewish community. Here, he was able to influence the
conduct of a Southern Christian who had a love for Israel that was
somehow buried. But the Rebbe was able to bring it out, and Senator
Helms was able to use his own Christian background to recognize the
need to be supportive of Israel. It really showed how far the Rebbe's
influence reached beyond his own community. ("Influencing the
Future" By Alan Dershowitz, Chabad, *The Rebbe. Org*)

18 Rabbi Chaim Volozhin's grandson, Rabbi Zvi Meltzer, is the maternal
grandfather of Shimon Peres, who served as both president and prime
minister of Israel. Wikipedia.

החיים[19] became a major source for the musar movement and for kabbalah literature. The latter, in turn, had been deeply influenced by the writings of the Gaon of Vilna and incorporated the methods of the Gaon in the Volozhin Yeshiva that he had founded in 1803, and that remained in operation for nearly ninety years until 1892. It became known as the "mother" of all Lithuanian-style yeshivas. The Beis Halevi was the father of the world-renowned Reb Chaim Halevi (Reb Chaim Brisker), the grandfather of Rabbi Aaron and Rabbi Yosef Dov of Yeshiva University.

My personal connection with Reb Aaron (1917–2001) had been developed during the years that I was dormitory supervisor at Chaim Berlin, and Reb Aaron was a young *maggid shiur*. From as early as when he was twelve years old, he had had a relationship with my Rebbi, as Reb Aaron's father, Rabbi Moshe Soloveitchik, had appointed him to mentor the young scholar. Reb Aaron always looked at my Rebbi as one of his main *mashpi'im* (people of influence). One of my friends suggested that we invite Reb Aaron to join the two of us for lunch in my dormitory room rather than

19 Rav Chayyim Of Volozhin, Eliezer Lipa (Leonard) Moskowitz (English Translator), *The Soul of Life: The Complete Neffesh Ha-chayyim*, Paperback, New Davar Publications.

eat in the regular dining room with all the others. As supervisor, I had a relatively large and spacious room. Reb Aaron accepted our invitation, and we had lunch together for a year. We used that time for a wonderful hour filled with all kinds of Torah discussion.

During one of our visits to our son, Nachum, and family in Chicago, Nachum asked me to introduce him to Reb Aaron. He wanted to meet with him because of the Sephardic Rabbis' Conference that was scheduled to take place at Yeshiva University. Nachum and his wife, Schulamith, wanted the conference to devote attention to the issue of the descendants of the Anusim being reabsorbed into the Jewish Nation.[20]

---

20 When we came to Rabbi Soloveichik's home, we saw the great discomfort and pain he had walking down the staircase, and I wished him a *refuah shleima*. He asked whether I was regularly praying for him. When I heard that, I decided that from then on I would pray for him. When I got back to Israel, I found that the 7:00 a.m. *minyan* in which I davened had stopped making a *mi-she'berach* (May He bless . . . with a full recovery . . .) for the ill. When I inquired why they had stopped, I was told that Rabbi Simon Dolgin had shouted at the gabbai when he made the *mi-she'berach* prayer. Since the rabbi at that time was already suffering from a serious speech disability, I doubted that the gabbai had understood him properly and checked with the 6:00 minyan and found that they were still saying the prayer. Our gabbai, however, refused to retract, and I took it upon myself to recite the prayer publicly—which I am still doing. Though unplanned, Reb Aaron became the catalyst for all the prayers for the sick that my minyan has been saying on Mondays and Thursdays all these years.

After I introduced him to Reb Aaron and his wife, Ella, Nachum related what he knew about the Anusim and explained what he wanted from Reb Aaron. He gave the Rav all the relevant information and explained that they were personally involved in the matter because, among other reasons, Schulamith was of Sephardic stock, felt a great affinity to Anusim, and was an expert in the subject. Both Nachum and Schulamith felt that Sephardic rabbis were much warmer and more receptive of the need to accept Anusim into our communities with open arms than Ashkenazic rabbis. They felt that the Sephardi conference about to take place in Yeshiva University was a good venue for giving publicity to the needs of the Anusim. Schulamith, however, had unsuccessfully tried to convince Rabbi Marc Angel, president of the Union of Sephardic Congregations, to add the subject to the agenda of the meeting. Reb Aaron stated his opinion that all Anusim who claim to have descended directly from pure Sephardic stock should be welcomed and treated like all other Jews when they come into our synagogues and communities. They should be counted for a minyan, called to the Torah, and given recognition in exactly the same way we welcome other newcomers. He added that if, however, they wished to marry out of their community, i.e., with non-Anusim, they needed to go through "full conversion [to cover all opinions]," to dispel any doubt. At a later meeting, in which Schulamith also participated, she asked if he would furnish a letter to this effect. He immediately responded positively and composed the letter shown here.

With his intervention and with this letter, the subject was indeed included in the agenda but was, in Nachum's words, assigned to a "relatively unknown" member rabbi from Chicago. Divine providence, however, led to its being assigned to the rabbi of the synagogue in which Nachum prayed. Nachum briefed him fully on the subject, enabling him to give a meaningful talk, backed by adequate evidence of the Jewishness of these unfortunate secret Jews who were just beginning to "come out of the woodwork" and admit their Jewishness and secret practices of these last five hundred years.

Rabbi Eliyahu Bakshi-Doron, the Sephardic chief rabbi of Israel at the time, was the overseer of conversion for the chief rabbinate and had sent a representative on his behalf to the conference. The representative was well impressed by the talk and conveyed its message to the chief rabbi. When Nachum and Schulamith returned to Israel, Schulamith met with Rabbi Bakshi-Doron to follow up on the matter and found him to be most receptive and agreeable to giving returnees a "Certificate of Return" rather than a "Certificate of

BRISK RABBINICAL COLLEGE 2965 W. Peterson Ave. • Chicago, IL 60659 • (312) 275-5166

Rabbi Aaron Soloveichik
Rosh HaYeshiva
Rabbi Yitzchok Giffin
Dean of Administration

Rabbi Moshe Soloveichik
Associate Rosh HaYeshiva

Rabbi Eliyahu Soloveichik
Associate Rosh HaYeshiva

1 Nisan 5754

To whom it may concern:

I am taking the liberty to write about the alleged anusim in the Americas who claim to be descendants of the marranos of Spain and Portugal.

Generally, they must be treated like full Jews in every way (counted for a minyan, given aliyot, etc.).

However, if anyone of these anusim wants to marry a Jewish man or woman, then he or she must undergo full conversion. A woman must undergo immersion in a mikveh (without the blessing) and full acceptance of mitzvot or commitment to the Torah. A man, if he is uncircumcised must undergo acceptance of mitzvot, immersion and circumcision. If he is already circumcised, then he has to undergo hatafat dam brit, immersion and acceptance of mitzvot.

Hoping that this will clarify the solution to this problem, I remain—

Respectfully yours,

Rabbi Aaron Soloveichik
Rabbi Aaron Soloveichik

Photo courtesy of Schulamith Halevy (Dershowitz)

Conversion." Psychologically, this is far more satisfying for the Anusim.[21]

I am convinced that I merited to be part of Reb Aharon's lunch break only because, eventually, I would be the instrument for helping obtain this letter, which plays such a significant role in all the work that is currently being doing with and for the Anusim.

Additionally, it is interesting to note the influence that Reb Aaron had one of his students, my colleague and friend, Professor Alex Blum of the philosophy department of Bar-Ilan University. As a future philosopher, he was always asking deep and provocative questions that were getting him into trouble with his rabbis. Being extremely displeased about this, he somehow got to talk with Reb Aaron about his unfulfilled inquiries. Reb Aaron was wholly receptive and caring about Alex

---

21 From a post by Professor Nachum Dershowitz: "Most programs for conversion to Judaism will not distinguish between returning *Anusim* and Gentile converts. Schulamith Halevy [Dershowitz], who researches crypto-Jewish traditions, has been advocating the reinstitution of the 'return' ceremony as an alternative for *Anusim*. This return process is akin to contingent conversion (in that it usually involves circumcision for males and immersion) . . . and a certificate of return (*teudah lashab ledarkhei abotav*), rather than of conversion. One can also retain one's parents' names as patronymic and metronymic. Mordechai Eliyahu (former Sephardic Chief Rabbi of Israel), the Chicago rabbinical council, and some Orthodox and Reform rabbis have adopted Halevy's procedure."

and his efforts. Alex says that Reb Aaron was his savior during these years and all through the rest of his life.

Rabbi Joseph B. Soloveitchik

Rabbi Yosef (Joseph B.) Dov (1903–1993), or the "Rav," as he was called by his students, was born in Pruzhan, Poland, the eldest son of Rabbi Moshe Soloveitchik (first cousin of Rabbi Moshe Feinstein). His students often described the classes that he taught at Yeshiva University in preparation for rabbinic ordination as extremely demanding. They often sat in terror, lest he call upon them when

From Makor Rishon

they were not properly prepared. His style in the classroom was threatening, and if a student presented an incorrect answer to one of his probing questions he would often berate him for his incorrect interpretation. At a public yahrzeit lecture, I heard him say to his many students who were present, "Don't think that just because you have received semikah you know how to *pasken* a *shailah* (be a decisor)!"

While serving as rosh yeshiva of Yeshiva University, he continued living in Boston, Massachusetts. In 1951, when I was principal of the Malden Hebrew Day School, in a Boston suburb, my wife and I made a courtesy call on him and his wife, Dr. Tonya Lewit, in their home. During our visit he was very pleasant and we chatted in an easygoing social manner. In the day school, I had occasionally faced a problem with non-kosher sandwiches that some children would bring for lunch. Having heard that he personally allowed Kraft (non-Jewish) cheese on his own table, I asked him the halakhah regarding the kashruth of such non-Jewish cheese produced in America.

His mood changed immediately, as if I had touched an electric switch. He went into an exhilarating, excited, and electrified discussion. He began by quoting the various opinions among the geonim and then stated his conclusion that since there was government supervision in the production plants and farms, and there were no non-kosher milk-bearing animals on the farm, the cheese is permissible.

Several years later, when there were already many varieties of kosher cheese on the market, I inquired of his son-in-law, Rabbi Aharon Lichtenstein, if the Rav was still using non-Jewish cheese in his home. He responded that ever since his wife had passed away, he had taken upon himself additional personal stringencies. Although he still ruled that government supervised non-Jewish cheese was permitted, he, personally, no longer ate those cheeses.

During my stay in Malden, I had been told that the Rav had ruled, originally, that it would be permissible for one to use a microphone in the synagogue on the Sabbath. At a later occasion, he changed his mind, having realized that glowing [or "burning"] elements are ignited when the microphone is used.[22] In view of this, the Zomet Institute, relying on halakhic authorities, Rabbis Shaul Yisraeli, Isser Yehuda Unterman, and Haim David HaLevi designed microphones for use by doctors in hospitals that use only transistors, such that, when turned on before the Sabbath, continue to only "Use the electric current that is continuously in the system."

During the time that we were in Malden, I called upon the Rav many times to rule on halakhic questions.

---

22 We note here the statement by Rabbi Ari Shvat on his website, Yeshiva, on Nisan 5, 5779, on the subject: "I asked Rav Aharon Rakefet who was very close with Rav Soloveitchik . . . and he said that he never heard . . . his opinion on the issue. He added that the Rav's famous *psak* on not hearing even shofar in a synagogue where there's no gender curtain separation, was a huge *chiddush* (a novel interpretation or approach) and it's hard to believe . . . [other than that it should be prohibited] regarding microphones, without [having heard him] publicizing it." Nonetheless, Rav Rakefet added that "the Orthodox synagogues in Baltimore in that era were using microphones on the Sabbath. . . . Rabbi Simcha Levy of the RCA and others permitted certain mikes."

On one such occasion, we asked a question and related it to what we had seen in the *Chayei Adam*.[23] His response was interesting: "I don't have the Chayei Adam in my home, but if he says this, you may follow his ruling."

I arranged to spend a Sabbath at Onset Beach on Cape Cod, where the Rav usually vacationed during the summer break. I knew that he went to a small synagogue where he had arranged that the reading of the Torah, when he was present, would be done only by him or a member of his family. He was very stringent about the proper punctuation and cantillation of the reading. He, himself, was the reader on the Sabbath that I was there. It was enlightening to see that in the middle of his reading, he turned to the gabbai[24] and asked (in English) what was the proper cantillation of the next few words. Only after he heard the answer did he continue with the reading.

While serving as principal of the Malden Day School, I was also serving as rabbi of the local Young Israel synagogue. Before Pesach, I was called upon

---

23 *Chayei Adam*, by Rabbi Avraham Danzig, was intended primarily "for the cultured layman," as opposed to rabbinic scholars, and the work is thus presented in a readily accessible form. Wikipedia.

    Rabbi Danzig is among the three authorities upon whom Rabbi Shlomo Ganzfried based his *Kitzur Shulchan Aruch*.

24 *gabbai* (sexton)

to prepare a contract with a non-Jew for the sale of hametz[25] in the homes of my community members. Never having done this before, I called the Rav numerous times to have him explain aspects of the contract. One of the points that he made was that I should require a written signature on the contract granting me each householder's permission to rent out the closet (or other hametz storage place) in which he was storing the hametz sold to the non-Jew. I followed his instructions.

On the day before Erev Pesach, I received a telephone call from the Rav's brother-in-law, asking me to include his hametz in my contract, and that the Rav had instructed him to tell me that he had also real hametz in his dentistry. Surprisingly, on the morning of Erev Pesach, I received a call from the Rav himself to also include his hametz in my contract (the non-Jew with whom he usually dealt was incapacitated, he said, thus could not be a partner to the contract). When I asked him how I could do so since the Rav was not available to put his personal signature on the contract as he had instructed me, he responded, "Well, it's better to do it the way I advised you, but it is not really a necessity." What he didn't say, but which I found out years later,

---

25 The owning or eating of hametz is prohibited on the Pesach holiday. This restriction includes cooked and baked foods containing the grains; wheat, oats, rye, barley, and spelt, when not prepared in the proper Passover manner.

was that in any event, the Rav personally never kept hametz in his home on Pesach.

Nonetheless, obviously, the contract that I wrote was valid for halakhic hametz too—I had included a liquor dealer's store in my contract—as per the Rav's permission. Interestingly, my congregant, the store owner, was still going to be selling his wares on Chol HaMoed (the intermediate days of the holiday) to non-Jews, as an agent of the non-Jewish purchaser on my contract. I found it gratifying that the Rav chose to sell his hametz through me, though I was not a student of his, while there were many of his students who had congregations in the Boston area.

In 1970, his son-in-law, Rabbi Aharon Lichtenstein, at the invitation of Rabbi Yehuda Amital,[26] became a co–rosh yeshiva at Yeshivat Har Etzion, with a large

---

26 It is significant to relate an interaction that I had with Rabbi Yehuda Amital when my lifelong study partner, Rabbi Meyer Fendel, and I went to him to adjudicate a number of theological questions about which we differed. We both felt that his opinion would be very agreeable to both of us. The most outstanding matter upon which he offered an opinion was the concept of דעת תורה (Da'as Torah—according to which, halakhic Jews should seek and follow input from rabbinic scholars not just on matters of Jewish law, but on all important life matters—on the grounds that the scholar's vast knowledge of the Torah aids everything in life—and obligates his devotees). When presented with this question he exclaimed, "A bluff!" In his view there was no justification for feeling obligated by an opinion that any great scholar may have if he cannot present the halakhic justification for that opinion.

number of their students attending a *hesder*[27] program with the Israel Defense Forces. In their promotional literature, the mission of the Yeshiva is described as "The pursuit of personal growth . . . intimately bound up with a dedication to serving Israel and the Jewish People." He and his yeshiva are, in some respects, an oddity in Israel. He

Wikipedia

defined much of his centrist philosophy of high-level secular education as an adjunct to Torah education, in a broad-based article,[28] some of which I quote:

> looking back . . . one recalls that, quite apart from the obvious instance of mori ve'rebbi Rabbi[29] Soloveitchik, the daughter of mori ve'rebbi Rabbi Hutner received a doctorate, as did the daughter of Reb Aharon Kotler. At least one of Reb Moshe Feinstein's daughters

---

27 Our son, Simcha Hillel, attended this program at Yeshivat Har Etzion.
28 *Centrist Orthodoxy: A Spiritual Accounting*, Rabbi Aharon Lichtenstein, Adapted by Rav Reuven Ziegler. Yeshivat Har Etzion: The Israel Koschinsky Virtual Beit Midrash.
29 *mori ve'rebbi* (my teacher, my master)

went to college and, if Reb Ruderman's and Reb Kamenetsky's did not—I do not recall offhand—it was surely not out of principle. Today, of course, no self-respecting Bais Yaakov girl, be her father a businessman or a programmer, would risk attending college, lest her prospects for a shidduch be impaired.

. . . Speaking for myself, however, I can emphatically state that my general education has contributed much to my personal development. I know that my understanding of Tanakh would be far shallower in every respect without it. I know that it has greatly enhanced my perception of life in Eretz Yisrael. I know that it has enriched my religious experience. I know that when my father was stricken blind, Milton's profoundly religious sonnet "On His Blindness" and its magnificent conclusion, "They also serve who only stand and wait," stood me in excellent stead. I also know—and this has at times been a most painful discovery—that many of these elements are sadly lacking among the contemnors of culture on the Right.

. . . Centrism at its best encourages a sense of complexity and integration, and this in several respects. First, inasmuch as a person of this orientation looks to the right and to the left, he is more likely to reject the kind of simplistic, black-and-white solutions so appealing to others. Second, again by dint of his basic position, it is more complex, because it encompasses more of reality. It relates to more areas of human life, to larger segments of our communal and personal existence. Third, not only in quantitative terms but qualitatively, a Centrist approach is more inclined to perceive shadings and nuances, differences between areas and levels of moral and spiritual reality; more inclined to understand, for instance, what the concept of devar ha-reshut (optional matters) is all about; more inclined to reject the popular myth that the answer to every single problem can be found in the Shulchan Aruch if only one knows how to deal with it. For those who lack a certain exposure, these insights are often more difficult to come by.

A large number of his students describe themselves as Dati Leumi (national religious) and are followers of Rabbi Kook's philosophy. Rabbi Lichtenstein himself, however, felt that Rabbi Kook's approach was too optimistic and should be tempered by more reality. Serving in the army, he thought, should be viewed more as sharing in the social burden of the country, rather than as an ideal in its own right.[30]

This follows my own Rebbi's approach—of whom Rabbi Lichtenstein was a student—to the Holocaust, where he wrote that the Holocaust should be seen as a social phenomenon, an attempt at the destruction of Jewish Europe, not qualitatively different from similar acts of persecution and destruction against other Jewish communities in the past. The Holocaust, he taught, should surely be seen as a catastrophe of horrendous magnitude that included vast cruelty and efficiency, but not as an exceptional, isolated occurrence in Jewish history.

Finally, it is, in my opinion, historically noteworthy that just recently, Rabbi Lichtenstein's son, Rabbi Yitzchok, has been welcomed and inaugurated as the new rosh yeshiva of Torah Vodaath, despite its contrary orientation, more in line with Agudas Yisrael, than is his father's yeshiva. As Rabbi Yitzchok Gottdiener, Executive Director of the Yeshiva, remarked at Rabbi Lichtenstein's inauguration:

---

30 Udi Abramowitz, *Religious Zionism of Another Type*, Shabbat Supplement of Makor Rishon, April 4, 2020, p. 7.

We were searching, waiting to see whom the Ribono Shel Olam [Master of the world] had in store for us, someone who will live and breathe Yeshiva Torah Vodaath . . . With much siyata diShmaya [Heavenly help], we are honored to have *Rabbi* Lichtenstein join our hanhalas hayeshiva [yeshiva directorate] to serve as rosh yeshiva[31] . . . Rav Lichtenstein joins Yeshiva Torah Vodaath with notable commendations and an illustrious background. A talmid of Rav [Meshulem] Dovid Soloveitchik and a tremendous talmid chochom proficient in many miktzaos haTorah [facets of Torah learning], Rav Lichtenstein embodies mesoras hatorah [tradition of Torah transmission] while possessing the ability to understand the challenges of, and to connect with, today's bochurim.

The above-mentioned *Rav* Meshulem Dovid Soloveitchik (generally known as Rav Dovid) of the Brisk Yeshiva of Israel was a son of Rabbi Velvel,[32] an

---

31 *rosh yeshiva, pl. rashei yeshiva* (title given to the dean of a senior level yeshiva)

32 My nephew, *Rabbi* Yitzchak Mordecai Dershowitz of Lakewood, studied under him. He affirmed the remarkable story of Rabbi Velvel's escape from the Nazis in WWII with the help of his concentration on, and internalization of, the concept: אין עוד מלבדו (there is nothing else

ardent anti-Zionist. Nonetheless, despite their different political orientations, Rabbi Velvel gave great respect to his cousin, Rabbi Meir Berlin, after whom Bar-Ilan University is named.

They say of Rabbi Yitzchak Lichtenstein that he lives and breathes the Torah of Brisk. He is quoted as having said, "The Brisker *mehalach* [way] is not exclusive to any specific group, or any specific *bais medrash*." He continued, "*Reb* Chaim . . . elevated the *ramah* [level] of *limud hatorah* in the world. *Ameilus b'Torah* [deep painstaking Torah study] is all the same [wherever you study]. Within the *bais medrash*, the future and the past intertwine. The Torah goes from Moshe Rabbeinu *ad sof kol hadoros* ['till the end of time]. There does not have to be any change to anything we have been learning for thousands of years."

The fact is that Rabbi Yosef Dov Soloveitchik—though also initially firmly anti-Zionist—fundamentally changed his perspective, after the impact of the Holocaust and became a leader of the Mizrahi movement. He went so far as to state that he can't fathom non-Zionists after the Holocaust.

---

in the world, besides Him and His will). See Nefesh HaChayim, op. cit., Shaar 3, Chapter 12.

POSTSCRIPT

AS I REACH the end of this literary journey, recalling my family and its involvement in Jewish life for the last century and a half, I feel humbled by the thought that so many important steps in the advancement of our People from the diaspora of Poland to the Land of Our Destiny have been accompanied by actions of members of my family and myself.

I have no doubt but that I have neglected many important events that are not known to me at this time. Nonetheless, I believe that it is important to record incidents and insights so that a future generation does not think that what they have and what they are reached them without the sweat and prayer of our ancestors. It fell to me, the youngest of my nuclear family, to have been born at a time when so many dramatic things were developing in the Jewish world, to record what

I remember hearing, reading, and personally experiencing during these nine-plus decades that have, until now, been part of my sojourn on Earth.

The Talmud explains a passage from the High Holiday prayers:

רבא בתר צלותיה אמר הכי: א-להי, עד שלא נוצרתי איני כדאי ועכשיו שנוצרתי כאלו לא נוצרתי, עפר אני בחיי, קל וחומר במיתתי, הרי אני לפניך ככלי מלא בושה וכלימה. (ברכות יז א)

Rava, after his prayers, would say: My Lord, before I was created, I was not needed [on this earth], and now that I was created, it is as if I hadn't been created. I am dust during my lifetime and certainly during my death. Thus, I am standing before You, filled with shame. (B'rachot 17a)

Rabbi Kook explains the passage.[1]

לפני יצירתי, ודאי כל אותו הזמן הבלתי מוגבל שמעולם עד יצירתי, לא היה דבר בעולם שהיה צריך לי, שאם הייתי חסר לאיזה תכלית והשלמה, הייתי נוצר. וכיון שלא נוצרתי עד אותו הזמן, הוא אות שלא הייתי כדאי עד אז להבראות, ולא היה בי צורך. כי אם לעת כזאת שנבראתי, מפני שהגיעה השעה שאני צריך לעשות [איזה דבר] להשלמת המציאות.

1 עין איה / ברכות א / פרק שני- מאמר מ"ו. על ברכות יז/א

ואם הייתי מיחד מעשי אל תכלית בריאתי, הנני עכשו כדאי. אבל כיון שאין מעשי [הולכים] לתכלית הטוב, כי אם לבצעו ולשרירות לב, הרי לא הגעתי אל התכלית. אם כן איני עדיין כדאי, כמו קודם לכן.

Before I was created, certainly all of that eternal time until I was created—there was nothing on earth that needed me, for if there were some purpose and improvement that needed me, I would have been created [then]. . . Now, the time has come during which I am needed for some improvement in the world. If I dedicate my actions exclusively to the purpose of creation, I am worthy to be here. But, since my actions don't go for that good purpose, rather only for my benefit and the stubbornness of my heart, I have not attained that goal. Therefore, I am not yet worthy enough to having been put here, rather than during the times that I had not yet been put here.

May it be the will of the Almighty
that He judges me as forwarding my mission
on Earth
by having written this book.
May He who makes peace in His heights,
make peace upon us and upon all of Israel.

Appendix 1
Emperor Franz Joseph

FRANZ JOSEPH WAS born on August 18, 1830, in the Schönbrunn Palace in Vienna, the oldest son of Archduke Franz Karl and his wife, Princess Sophie of Bavaria. His uncle, the Emperor Ferdinand, had abdicated the throne as part of a plan to end the Revolutions of 1848 in Hungary, allowing his nephew, Franz, to ascend to the throne. Largely considered to be a reactionary, Franz spent his early reign resisting constitutionalism. He chose to be known by his second as well as first given name, i.e., Franz Joseph, to bring back memories of the new emperor's great-granduncle,

Emperor Joseph II, who was remembered as a modernizing reformer.

Hungarian became the official language of administration, jurisdiction, and education of the kingdom. The diet of the Kingdom of Hungary turned into a diet of the Hungarian ethnicity; the minorities—Croats, Serbs, Germans, Vlachs, Ruthenians, and Slovaks—felt alienated, didn't read Hungarian newspapers and books, and didn't feel part of the sentiment toward a reformed, modernized Hungary.

In April 1848, the "April Laws" were passed. Civil rights were enacted, including equality before the law and the abolition of serfdom. The privileges of the Catholic Church and of nobility were abolished. The Ausgleich of 1867 granted greater autonomy to Hungary, transforming the Austrian Empire into the Austro-Hungarian Empire, where Franz Joseph ruled peacefully for forty-five years. He was greatly liked by the Jewish population.

After the earlier period of religious fanaticism against the Jewish population, a period of relative leniency began. Between 1848 and 1938, the Jewish Austrian population enjoyed prosperity. This dissolved gradually, however, after the death of Franz Joseph and, of course, stopped completely with the annexation of Austria to Germany by the Nazis.

As a token of appreciation, the Jewish population wrote prayers and songs about the emperor that were printed in the siddurim. In 1867, the Jewish population formally received full equal rights. Two years later he visited Jerusalem and was greeted with admiration by the Jewish population. He established a fund to finance the establishment of Jewish institutions and established a rabbinical school in Budapest. During the 1890s, several Jews were even elected to the Austrian parliament.

In 1895, Vienna elected an anti-Semitic mayor, Karl Lueger. The emperor was opposed to the appointment, but after Lueger was elected three consecutive times, the emperor was compelled to accept the election results, according to the regulations. Lueger removed Jews from positions in the city administration and forbade them from working in factories in Vienna. This situation continued until Lueger's death.

Austria's Jewish population contributed much to Austrian culture. They were lawyers, journalists (among them, Theodor Herzl), authors, playwrights, poets, doctors, bankers, businessmen, and artists. Vienna became a Jewish cultural center, as well as a center of education and Zionism. Theodor Herzl studied in the University of Vienna and was the editor of the special section (feuilleton) of the *Neue Freie*

Presse, a very influential newspaper at the time. Other notable influential Jews included composers Gustav Mahler and Arnold Schoenberg; authors Stefan Zweig, Arthur Schnitzler, Karl Kraus, Elias Canetti, Joseph Roth, and Vicki Baum; psychologists Sigmund Freud, Viktor Frankl, and Alfred Adler; philosophers Martin Buber and Karl Popper; and many others. The Jewish sports club, Hakoach Vienna, was established in 1909. Regrettably, with Jewish prosperity and equality, several Jewish scholars converted to Christianity out of a desire to assimilate into Austrian society.

The assassination in Sarajevo of Franz Josef's nephew, Archduke Franz Ferdinand, on June 28, 1914, resulted in Austria-Hungary's declaration of war against the Kingdom of Serbia, which was Russia's ally. This activated a system of alliances that resulted in World War I.

My neighbor in the faculty housing of Bar-Ilan University, Professor Baruch Kurzweil, had a picture of the emperor hanging in his home. He always said, perhaps tongue in cheek, that he was in favor of restoring the monarchy in Austria. Franz Joseph died on November 21, 1916.[1]

---

1   A variety of sources were used for this account, primarily from the Jewish Virtual Library, Wikipedia, and recollections of descendants of Pilzno residents.

Appendix 2
Pilzno after the German Occupation

THE FIRST JEW killed in Pilzno by the Germans was Aron Chilowicz, age twenty-five. His brother, Maurice, reported: "Aron was shot in the synagogue on September 13, 1939, *Erev Rosh Hashanah*. We buried him in the cemetery the next day. At night that same day, the synagogue and Talmud Torah were burned and the *gabbai*, Moses Beer, age 50, was burned [alive]." He had tried to carry the Sepher Torah out of the burning synagogue. He was shot by the German soldiers and thrown back into the flames.

In June 1942, a ghetto was structured in Pilzno at the old market. Into this area, about one thousand Jews were squeezed in primitive conditions. The ghetto did not last long, and in July 1942, most Jews were taken to Belzec, and the remainder were taken to the ghetto in Dembitz.

The Germans separated the elderly, disabled, and others who were not able to work and on June 12 put them on a wagon and shot them to death at the Jewish cemetery. Among them were: Chaim Spierer, age seventy; Zachary Szmoya, age seventy; Lazar Korn, age seventy; Max Korn, age seventy; Joel Adler, age seventy; Duwet Flam, age seventy; and Duwet Herbst, age fifty-five. Herbst was a war veteran who had lost his leg in World War II. He waved his crutch as he was taken and yelled: "Poland has not gone yet."

On February 19, 1943, the German police shot four Poles for offering shelter to Jews and at the same time shot the six Jews whom they had sheltered. On October 9, they shot five members of the Rebisiow family and the twelve Jews they had been hiding, and then burned down the whole farm. Josef Bobrowskiego was discovered to be hiding two Jews; he was shot, as were the Jews. Josefa Rysinska of Pilzno was given a medal by Yad Vashem after the war for her role in helping Jews during the occupation.

In November 1944, the German area commander posted a decree that any Jews found in Pilzno would be shot, and anyone who helped them would also be shot. By the end of July, Pilzno was cleansed of Jews, except for those few who were in hiding. Nonetheless, many Poles chose to help the Jews. One of these was Mieczyslaw Ryba of Slotiwej. From August 1942 to the summer of 1944, three Jews were hidden on his father's farm: Benjamin Deresiewicz (settled in New Jersey after the war, but it is not known conclusively that he is a relative, see below), Abraham Einspruch, and Israel Hamel. In the spring of 1943, two more came, brothers Hyman and Mendel Reiner of Pilzno. As the front got closer, all five moved to another farm and survived.

We also have a report of an Abraham Einspruch and Benjamin Dereszewicz (likely the same as mentioned above), who arrived at the home of Szczeoan Bradlo of Lubeza, near Tarnov, asking for shelter for thirteen people. These thirteen stayed in an underground hideout in a hayloft until liberation, some twenty-six months later.[1]

---

1   From an article by Mordecai Paldiel in the *Jerusalem Post*, February 25, 2019.

Helen Bochner Cohen was interviewed on Pilzno by Sharlene Kranz in June 1999 for *kehilalinks, jewishgen*. She reported that her mother married Benjamin Deresiewicz, whose father was Avram Leib Deresiewicz. Benjamin had been married before the war, and the Germans killed his wife and five children as well as his parents and siblings. As noted above, in Chart 1, Zecharja had a brother, Abraham Lowe, who was born in 1864. Perhaps this Avram Leib is his descendent.

Helen reports, further, that the Poles who hid them:

> were very brave to do it. But also, they did it for money. They were very poor. They had a farm, and after the war my mother [and others] . . . continued to send them money and goods. . . . They took a big chance on hiding us, but they got something out of it, too. I wouldn't go back

The soldiers took the most beautiful Jewish girls for sex, and then killed them, including: Schneidle Spierer, twenty-five; Gitle Katzner, twenty-one; Jute Turk, twenty-five; Reizle Szmaje, twenty-four; Chaya Nord, twenty-two; Ruchl Tannenbaum, twenty-one; Esther

Weinbach, nineteen; Rivke Chilowicz, nineteen; Sara Stern, eighteen; and Hanna Deresiewicz, sixteen.

Laya Reich, twenty-two, was shot in 1943 by the "navy blue policemen."[2] An informer turned her in. Pinkas Rosenbaum, twenty-five, who was hiding in Dulczowce, was found and shot in October 1943. Moses Tannenbaum, who was hiding in the woods near Jaworza, was found and shot. Gitl Warowicz, hiding in Lekach Dolnych, was also found and shot. Necha List, born in 1924, and Gedalie List, born in 1913, were also found and shot. The Wurzel family, Shlamy and Rywy, and their three little children, including a baby born in hiding, turned themselves in to the police on November 25, 1943. They couldn't hold out any longer; they were shot at the cemetery. Leizer Spierer was in hiding but turned himself in out of despair and was also shot by the blue policemen. Finally, the Steplow family was found and shot.

---

2 The so-called Blue Police were the local police forces in German-occupied Poland of World War II. They were subordinate to the German Order Police.

Appendix 3
Mother's Family: Steinhardt/ Maultasch

THE HOMETOWN OF the Steinhardt family is Tarnobrzeg/ Dzików, Poland, about eighty-five kilometers from Pilzno, the place of birth of my father. Dzików is famous as a private property of the Tarnowski family. We have family records there that go back to the mid-nineteenth century, as detailed below:

My mother was born in 1888 and probably had older siblings who didn't survive. I believe that I heard something to this effect when my mother explained why she had only one brother—my Uncle Joe (Joseph Eli). My maternal grandparents, Rochma Bleema (1861–1932) and Izak Leib Maultasch (1858–1918), like most immigrants of the time (including my paternal grandparents), followed the well-known procedure of the father landing first, so as to earn the fare for his wife and children. Rochma Bleema and their two children—my mother, Ida (Eidel), then age nine, and Eli (Joseph), age three—are listed as having arrived on the SS *Statendam* on December 18, 1899. The document states that she was joining her husband, who had arrived in January 1896. My mother had been brought to the Dzikówer Rebbe for a berakah before the family's departure.

Izak's September 1906 petition for United States citizenship declares that he was living at 47 Sheriff Street in Manhattan. Some of the details declared there differ from statements he made in his first "application papers." Earlier, he had declared that he was born on January 6, 1860, rather than in 1858, and that he had immigrated to the States in January 1891, rather than in 1896. He had also stated that he was a plasterer, unmarried, with no children. Since it was common that new immigrants did not have official birth certificates, it was not at all rare for them to make up dates that they felt would give them imagined advantages.

My mother's maternal grandfather, Aaron Menashe Steinhardt, married Rechel Eidel Schwartz. She is listed in the 1880 census of Tarnobrzeg/Dzików. Aaron Menashe may not have been alive by 1880, since his name does not appear in that census. It is likely that the couple lived in the Steinhardt home, in Building 394. My grandmother, Rochma Bleema (Rose), was born to them in 1861, according to the information on her tombstone. My grandfather, Izak Leib Maultasch, son of Yaakov Aryeh, was from Baranow, about fourteen kilometers from Tarnobrzeg/Dzików.

Five additional Steinhardts are listed as living in that building: Schmerl, Rafael, Boruch, Abraham Jankiel, and Cyrla. Cyrla may be Sara Steinhadt (who married Pinkas Blum), and whose children were Chaya Laya (born in Tarnobrzeg/Dzików on March 2, 1877) and Yechiel. After the death of her first husband, Sara married Jossel Weinberger from Zboro. This second marriage took place after Sara's daughter, Chaya Laya, had married Jossel's son, Solomon, on March 10, 1898. Both young people had brought a widowed parent into their relationship, and after a while, these parents decided to marry. When her mother was again widowed, Sara and Solomon moved with her to Zurich, where she died on March 29, 1921. She is the great-grandmother of Lilly Leah (named after Chaya Laya), who married Abraham Blum[1] (no relative of the afore-mentioned Pinkas Blum), and lives today in Rishon LeZion.

I know little more of these Steinhardts, but my mother often told me that "all Steinhardts are relatives." While she may have believed so, it seems that this was true only for the Tarnobrzeg/Dzików (or Galician) branch of the family. Steinhardt websites have claimed that there are about six thousand Steinhardts world-wide today.

My mother, Ida/Eidel, was probably named after her grandmother, Rechel Eidel, and my oldest brother, Yaakov, was probably named after my grandmother's younger brother, Abraham Jankiel (in Galician tradi-tion, the first child is named by the mother for one of her relatives). My third oldest brother (also tradition-ally named by the mother) was called Aaron Menashe, likely after my maternal great-grandfather, Aaron Menashe.

My guess is that Zeide Yitzchok (Izak) stopped using the name Leib when my mother married, because

---

1 Whose family is known to have come from Rozwadow, as also did Inacio Steinhardt's family. The Rozwadów suburb of Stalowa Wola included a thriving Jewish shtetl prior to World War II, closely associ-ated with the Jewish communities of Tarnobrzeg/Dzików and other nearby shtetls including Ulanów, Mielec, and Dzików. Wikipedia.

my father's Yiddish name was also Leib. "Alter" was possibly added to Zeide Yitzchok's name sometime later during some illness—perhaps the accident with the runaway horse that caused his death on Aug. 1, 1918. On the manifesto of the boat on which she arrived in the United States, Rochma Bleema is listed as aged thirty-eight, making her born in 1861 instead of 1855; this is a more reasonable year of birth, because the latter date would have made her as much as three years older than her husband. In other United States Federal papers, they are both listed as born in 1861. From the age of Yitzchok (fifty-eight) as listed on his tombstone (see picture), I conclude that he was born in 1860. Apparently, Bubba and Zeide Alter Yitzchok moved out of Sheriff Street at some point, since his address at death is listed as 77 Marcy Avenue, Brooklyn. The 1920 census, two years after his death, lists Rose (Rochma Bleema) and Joseph Maultasch as living at 870 Driggs

Photo courtesy of Zecharia Dor-Shav

Photo courtesy of Zecharia Dor-Shav

Avenue. Bubba died on December 20, 1932, at the age of sixty-five. I remember her death, as a seven-year-old at the time. Based on the papers that list her year of birth as 1861, she would have been seventy-one, as indeed is confirmed by the date of death on her tombstone in Bayside, Queens (see picture).

Also, of the Steinhardt family we know of Yaakov Weisenfeld of Tel Aviv. My mother spoke often of him as her cousin. At least one other descendant—Szyfra (Shifra)—lives in Caracas, Venezuela. Her parents were Szyja (Shiya) and Ryfka Syma (Rivka Sima) Weisenfeld.

Photo courtesy of Zecharia Dor-Shav

One Jakob Leib (Aryeh) Maultasch, also of Baranow, married Ruchla, also called Ruchie (perhaps of Tarnobrzeg/Dzików) and, seemingly, had a child, Chaja, thirty years later, on Nov. 30, 1891, named Jakob Wolf. Besides the improbability of a birth thirty years after marriage, it is also highly unlikely that Jakob Wolf would have been given one of the names of his father—Jakob—unless the father had died before Jakob Wolf's birth. Jakob Wolf is also reported as having had a sister, Selda, who also is not likely to have been a child of Jacob Leib. Therefore, I assume that Jakob Leib and

Jakob Wolf are not father and son, but, rather, cousins by way of my great-grandfather, Yaakov Aryeh (Leib).

Itala Schlissel, whom I knew in Williamsburg, was the daughter of Yaakov Aryeh Maultasch's sister, Saril Tema, who was the first wife of a Parnass. After Saril Tema's death, Itala married her sister's husband. Itala's daughters, Rochma and Rivsha, were the mothers of the Parnass and Kurtz families of Williamsburg. A cousin of theirs, and ours, was Pesha Goldman, who lived with her husband 'Chi'el and family as our tenants, at 870 Driggs Avenue. Their children were Renee Saperstein, Rhoda (Ruchama Bluma) Weiss, and Hinde Gittel Kornreich. Renee Saperstein introduced me to my first wife, Netta Kohn. Roslyn (Steinhardt) Greenberg of Boca Raton, Florida, was once taken to visit her aunt (?) Itala in Williamsburg.

In the copy of an Ellis Island ship manifest, Channe Steinhardt is listed as arriving as a widow in 1907, at the age of thirty-three (born in 1874), and going to her uncle, Isaac Moltasz, at 54 Sherifst Street in Manhattan. Since the US census of 1910 lists Isaac Molltasch at 47 Sheriff St. (which is just a transcription error of Sherif Street). I have no doubt that Molltasch and Moltasz is the same person: my grandfather, Alter Yitzchok.

On that manifest, Channe's father is listed as Sissel, probably Zissel or Ziskind Steinhardt, making him a brother of Rochma. The fact that such a name does not appear on the Tarnobrzeg/Dzików population census of 1880 is not a big problem, because there are other inaccuracies in the census.

The only one of the Steinhardts in their home in Tarnobrzeg/Dzików old enough to be Channe's father is Schmerl, born in 1840. He may have had a second name, or nickname, Zissel.[2] That would make him thirty-four when Channe was born. He may have been in another city, or he may have been trying to "stay off the radar" of the authorities to avoid military conscription.

On the other hand, since the next Steinhardt listed is Rafael, eighteen years younger, it is likely that there were other children, probably married, between Schmerl and Rafael who were already out of the house in 1880. One of them may have been Zissel. In either event, Channe was a niece of Isaac, one of Rochma's brothers, and my mother's first cousin. She moved to Roswadow—a satellite of the Tarnobrzeg/Dzików community.

Others that we know of include: Hersz Mendel (Zwi Menahem) Steinhardt—born in 1876, two years

---

2 Which is Yiddish for "sweet." As mentioned above, my mother also called my father Leib Zissel (see above).

after Channe; also, Berl (Bernard) Steinhardt, who died very young and whose name was added to Hersz Mendel, the grandfather of Inacio Steinhardt (formerly of Portugal and currently of Tel Aviv), of Tarnobrzeg/ Dzików descent. Inacio's father is Kopel Steinhardt.

Roslyn (Steinhart) Greenspan of Boca Raton, mentioned earlier, is eighty-one years old at the time of this writing. Her father, Nathan, died in 1984 and her mother, Gertrude, in 2003. Nathan's mother was Gitila and her father, Rafael, seemingly a brother of my grandmother, Rochma Bleema (Steinhardt) Maultasch. Nathan's older brother, Morris, as a fourteen-year-old, had come to the United States earlier and had been taken in by Alter Yitzchok, my grandfather. It was he who later sponsored the immigration of Nathan.

Alter Yitzchok's sister, Serel Tema, immigrated to the United States and married Moshe Yosef Dienstag, whose granddaughter, Sylvia Dienstag, married her second cousin, my brother, Herbert (Heshy). On the next page is a tentative family tree for the maternal side of the author: The Maultasch, Steinhardt and Schlissel branch of the family.

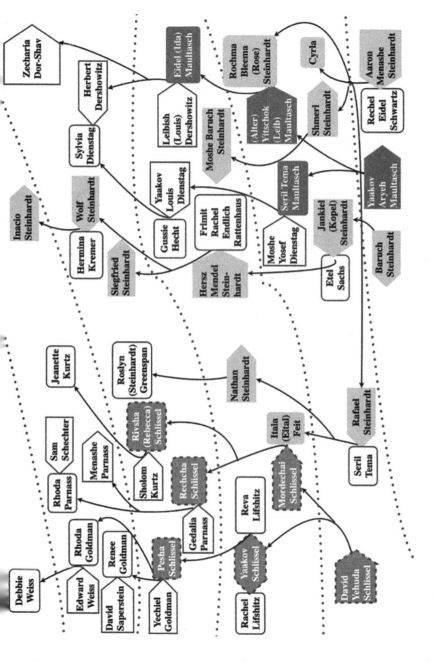

Appendix 4
A Tribute to Rabbi Zvi Dershowitz
by United States Congressman Brad Sherman
(D-Sherman Oaks, Cal.)

ON THE OCCASION of his eighty-fifth birthday.

On this happy occasion, it is a privilege for me to honor Rabbi Dershowitz, whom I came to know through his leadership in the Los Angeles Jewish community and whose lifelong contributions have made their mark in so many areas: Jewish youth and adult education, the struggle to free Soviet Jewry, advocacy on behalf of Iranian Jewish immigrants fleeing Iran, and more. Through his years as teacher, camp director, rabbi, counselor, and human rights advocate, he has touched many thousands of lives.

Perhaps it was his own experience as a refugee that influenced so much of the work Rabbi Dershowitz would later engage in on behalf of those fleeing oppression. When Zvi, whose Czech name was Hugo, was ten years old, Germany invaded Czechoslovakia. Young Zvi's grandfather, Shulem, and his father, Aaron, gathered the family and said, "Children, Europe is no longer a place for Jews." The family left the country on the last day of 1938, thirty-three days before Hitler's forces marched into the industrial city of Brno, the city where Rabbi Dershowitz was born and enjoyed his childhood. On February 2, 1939, with his parents Aaron and Ruth and sister, Lili, the family moved to Williamsburg, where he grew up, learning English, studying, and playing kickball.

Zvi spent his spare time working to support the nascent State of Israel. In 1949, he spent a year of leadership training, working, and studying in Jerusalem. Zvi helped refugees from Yemen and elsewhere settle into the newly independent State of Israel.

Inspired by his parents' love for Israel and Judaism, Zvi came back to Brooklyn and attended Mesivta Torah Vodaath and received his rabbinical ordination in 1953.

Rabbi Dershowitz held several pulpits, at Congregation Beth Shalom in Kansas City and Temple of Aaron in St. Paul, Minnesota. During that period, Rabbi Dershowitz was recruited to become director of Herzl Camp in Wisconsin. One of his campers was Bobby Zimmerman, who later changed his name to Bob Dylan. Rabbi Dershowitz laughs when he recalls telling the teenage Bobby to "stop banging on the piano." Years later, Dylan would become a guest at Rabbi and Tova Dershowitz's family Passover seder.

At camp, Rabbi Dershowitz's philosophy was to focus on creating an atmosphere in which campers would feel the joy of Judaism. The number of campers at Herzl Camp doubled during his tenure. In 1961, he accepted an appointment from renowned educator Shlomo Bardin to direct the Brandeis-Bardin Institute in Simi Valley.

Once in California, Rabbi Dershowitz pursued his love of Jewish education particularly with young people, at Camp Ramah in Ojai, where he served as director from 1963 to 1973. During that period, he was invited to build the adult education program at Sinai Temple in Los Angeles, one of the most well-known synagogues in the country. He eventually became associate rabbi at Sinai Temple, a post he held for some three decades and where he now serves as rabbi emeritus. Rabbi

Dershowitz's tenure there witnessed much growth and vibrancy, but also leadership transitions. Throughout these challenging years for the synagogue, Rabbi Dershowitz was the glue that held the congregation together, and he saw it through many achievements.

Rabbi Dershowitz has contributed to Jewish communal life in diverse ways, including serving often-neglected populations. For several years he led services, singing and discussions with Alzheimer patients at an old-age home, bringing joy and meaning to a special population. To this day, Rabbi Dershowitz conducts religious services at a home for the elderly while maintaining a hectic schedule, which includes teaching weekly classes at the University of Judaism, now American Jewish University.

Rabbi Dershowitz and Tova have traveled to many places around the world. At each place, they would meet with the Jewish community, become enriched by their experiences, and seek to do whatever they could to be helpful. One visit, however—to the former Soviet Union—was different from their other travels. It was on this trip that they took in a large load of books that would help Jews in Russia learn Hebrew, something that at the time was not permitted. Rabbi Dershowitz's advocacy in support of Soviet Jews continued for many years thereafter.

During his time at Sinai Temple, the synagogue witnessed an influx of Jews fleeing the Iranian Revolution. Many Jews had difficulty getting out of Iran, but Rabbi Dershowitz worked with Congress and the Executive Branch and helped secure visas for countless Jews who today make up a significant and wonderful part of the synagogue. For the work he did to help them enter this country and for the work he continued to do to help integrate them into the Los Angeles community, he has become well-known and well-loved among the Persian Jewish community.

Appendix 5
Bipartisan Tribute to Professor Alan Dershowitz

A Letter from President Bill Clinton:

In a personal letter from President Clinton, on official White House stationery, dated November 3, 2005, inter alia, the president writes:

> Hillary and I are delighted to congratulate you
> . . . honored by the Jewish National Fund . . .
> with the Tree of Life Award.

. . . through your writings, your teaching, and your fine example, you have inspired countless people around the world to value the basic dignity of all human life. Whether defending the State of Israel with the written word or the rights of an individual citizen in a courtroom, you have challenged assumptions, changed minds, and opened hearts—and our world is better off for it.

Senator Ted Cruz of Texas: A Tribute[1]

Mr. CRUZ. Mr. President, I would like to take a moment to honor a great teacher today. His name is Alan Dershowitz. For half a century he was a professor at the Harvard Law School. He retired in December of 2013.

From all those students who were so fortunate to learn from him, including myself, let us say thank you.

Professor Dershowitz joined Harvard Law in 1964—at the tender age of twenty-five—and during his time there, he trained more than ten thousand students in more than one hundred semesters to be critical thinkers, lawyers, judges, and leaders.

---

1   Congressional-record/2014/11/18/senate-section/article/S6085-3.

Aside from being an incredible teacher, he is known for his many faces: advocate, columnist, novelist, and intellectual. He is a passionate liberal, and yet he pressed all his students—conservative and liberal alike—to make the very best arguments they could, based on logic, reason, and precedent.

Like Professor Kingsbury in *The Paper Chase*, he didn't suffer fools. If you couldn't back up your position in his class, if you emoted rather than reasoned, you were in trouble.

He and I became friends, ironically, because we disagreed so much. In class, he would offer withering critiques of opinions authored by conservative Justices, Scalia and Thomas especially, and I was often moved to disagree. Heated arguments followed, which Professor Dershowitz always seemed to relish.

I am grateful for his patience and indulgence. As with countless law students before and after, Professor Dershowitz made me a much better lawyer.

He didn't just teach; he also practiced, in trial courts and the Supreme Court, taking on "impossible" cases and winning one after another. Truly, it was a privilege to learn from someone practicing at the very top of his field.

Although a man of the left, he did not shy away from disagreeing with his liberal colleagues when principle compelled it. A passionate advocate for free speech, he fearlessly took on the political correctness of campus speech codes. No conformist, he.

And there has been no fiercer advocate for Israel. His passion, his persuasiveness, his willingness to take on all comers, has made him an incomparable voice for the Jewish State.

Professor Dershowitz is an intellectual powerhorse[2] who could have done anything in his life, and he made the deliberate decision to teach. He chose to share his brilliance and pass it on. He chose to invest in the future of others instead of only himself.

I am so grateful that I could be among the thousands of students Professor Dershowitz taught. He has made and continues to make a real difference.

Courage and principle are rare today. Professor Dershowitz has them both.

---

2 This might be a typographical error in the Congressional Record. Perhaps, Senator Cruz said or meant, "powerhouse."

Appendix 6
Obituary of Doctor Aryeh Zinkin

At the Establishment of the Aryeh Zinkin Yeshiva Wrestling Award[1]

הוא [הלל הזקן] היה אומר אם אין אני לי מי לי וכשאני
לעצמי מה אני ואם לא עכשיו אימתי (אבות א יד)

[Hillel, the Elder] said, If I am not for myself, then
who will be for me?
And when I am only for myself, what am I?
And if not now, when? (Ethics of the Fathers 1, 14)

---

1   Wittenberg Invitational Tournament Pamphlet of Yeshiva University
    Wrestling Association, 2018.

WRESTLING IS THE purest of sports. It is just you against your opponent—direct, immediate, and inevitable. When you step onto the mat, there is nowhere to turn for help, nowhere to hide, no teammates upon whom you can lean, and no equipment upon which to rely for protection or advantage. You face your adversary with nothing more than your mental preparedness and your physical training . . . *If I am not for myself, then who will be for me . . . ?*

But wrestling is also about Team. It exists at the nexus where "I" becomes "We," as it takes a *We* to create the *I.* A coach to train, teammates with whom to spar, each member contributes to the success of the whole, epitomized by the betterment of the individual. A wrestler cannot reach the top alone; he cannot be the best without the help of others. As in life itself, wrestling is a symbiosis of self and community, where each becomes stronger by harmonizing with the other. Wrestler and Team. Individual and Community . . . *And when I am only for myself, what am I . . . ?*

Aryeh "Captain Lou" Zinkin was the consummate wrestler. From an early age, he stood as a solitary figure on the mat, forced to learn from experience, to fight for all that would become his. As a child, with minimal support and direction, he grappled with life . . . With no background in Jewish observance, he chose a life of Torah . . . and put himself through a Jewish High School, Jewish summer camps, and, eventually, Yeshiva University.

But Aryeh also understood that no man stands alone . . . friends and colleagues recognized and admired his strength, his decisiveness, and his leadership. They chose him to be captain of their wrestling team at Yeshiva University . . . He became a surgeon, sent his children to Jewish day schools and *yeshivot*, and became a pillar of his community . . . a model husband, father, and *kovei'a itim*—one who designates regularly scheduled hours to learn Torah, despite the demands and obligations of life.

. . . Aryeh was enormously involved with his shul, serving as its president during two separate critical junctures in the shul's history. He actively considered how he could elevate his Shabbat and Yom Tov table to be an inspiration for his family and guests. Every Shabbat, without fail, he would find time, from his flourishing medical practice and community involvement, to savor the incoming Shabbat by doing the grocery shopping, helping to cook, and setting the table. Shabbat meals were filled with *zemirot* and *divrei torah*, and while everyone retired to couches or to play after the meal, Aryeh was sweeping the floor and clearing off. Then, ever conscious of the example he was setting, he would demonstrate his love of Torah by opening a sepher and inviting his grandchildren to learn with him. His Pesach seder was a model for how to creatively integrate children into the rituals through questions, games, and riddles. From his wrestling days, Aryeh understood that the flashy moves and grand gestures might attract applause, but discipline and perfection of the fundamentals would bring him the win. For those of us who were honored to know him, it was Aryeh's consistency and his daily commitment to Jewish life that made him such an outstanding individual.

. . . He led by example, a soft-spoken man of action with a wry sense of humor and an easy, warm smile. Aryeh lived each day, even his last days, by the dictum אימתי, עכשיו לא ואם—"*If not now, when . . . ?*" When Aryeh was diagnosed with pancreatic cancer, being a physician himself, he was keenly aware of the brutal realities of his prognosis. Yet, the morning following his diagnosis, Aryeh awoke at 6 a.m.—as he always did—said *Modeh Ani* and picked up his talit and tefillin—as he always did—and walked to shul for minyan—as he always did. He continued to live his life the same way he always had for the previous 71 years.

Lewis Zinkin YU Wrestling Team 1966

BOTTOM, left to right: Barry Levy, Milton Sonneberg, Steve Dostis,
Mike Groob, David Carr. SECOND ROW: Allen Friedman, Shelly
Katz, Howie Poupko, Neil Ellman, Jeff Troodler. STANDING: Arnie
Weiss, Manager; Joel Levitz, Assistant Manager; Lewis Zinkin, Captain;
Mr. Henry Wittenberg, Coach; Elihu Romanoff; Burt Kaufman.

Appendix 7
Getting Kosher Food to Rav Hutner in Captivity

MY REBBI WAS among the passengers who were being held hostage by Palestinian terrorists in Jordan following a hijacking in 1970. Below[1] is an account by one of the hostages of the attempt to get him kosher food.

Allenby Bridge across the Jordan River, 11:30 AM: A lone United States embassy official

---

1 From Raab, David, *Terror in Black September: The First Eyewitness Account of the Infamous 1970 Hijackings.* New York: Palgrave Macmillan, 2007.

walked up to the Allenby Bridge, an unimpressive, steel and wooden structure spanning the Jordan River at a narrow point between Israel and Jordan. He carried a box marked "Special foods for [the Red Crescent] Amman." Inside were canned Israeli goods and a note that read "Kosher food for Rabbi Hutner." Two days earlier, the American embassy in Amman was told that Rabbi Isaac Hutner, "a strict adherent to the dietary laws of Judaism, has refused to accept food which he believes to be not kosher." In fact, eight other hostages, including [David] Raab, were doing the same. The embassy asked other United States embassies in the region to "obtain canned kosher items and forward [them] to Amman as soon as possible for relay to the captors." The next day, the United States embassy in Tel Aviv offered to do so. The Amman embassy advised Tel Aviv to deliver the food in "inconspicuous packages" to the Jordanian police at the Allenby Bridge and request that it be turned over to the International Committee of the Red Cross (ICRC) in Amman. Despite a day-long effort, the American Embassy in Amman could not reach the ICRC to alert it to the possible arrival of the food.

Now, the official walked across the bridge hoping to find someone on the Jordanian side willing to accept the package. Finding no one at the Jordanian end of the bridge, he walked about a kilometer into Jordan where he finally encountered a group of Jordanian soldiers. The corporal in charge was sympathetic but had no clue what to do; he phoned an officer. Instructed not to accept the parcel, the corporal suggested that it might be possible to deliver it in a couple of days, perhaps on Sunday. So, the official returned to the Israeli side and entrusted the parcel to the bridge commander, one Captain Ilan, who agreed to hold onto it until new arrangements could be made. The food never reached Rabbi Hutner.[2]

---

2 David Raab told me personally how Rebbetzin Bruria (Hutner) David shared with him a piece of fruit that she and her family had taken with them on the plane, so that even in captivity, he too could feel a bit different on the Sabbath.

Appendix 8
The Feuerstein
Family of Malden

HENRY FEUERSTEIN CAME to America in the 1890s from Hungary and found work in New York City, sewing blouses. After losing his job twice, he turned to selling dry goods. From small pushcart to factory to wholesale outlets, young Henry prospered. When his real estate investments went badly in 1906, he answered a classified ad and invested the remainder of his fortune on a small mill—eventually developing into the company called Malden Knitting Mills in the historic town of Malden, about twenty-five miles north of Boston, Massachusetts.

By the end of World War II, his son Samuel (Sam) had taken charge of the family business, with his teen-aged grandson, Aaron, also working there. Sam became very prominent in supporting Torah education in the Boston area, supporting both the Maimonides School, led by Rabbi Joseph Soloveitchik, and the Malden Hebrew Day School (where I worked as principal), led by his daughter, Lilian. In 1943, when Rabbi Shraga Feivel Mendlowitz established Torah Umesorah, the National Society for the Development of Hebrew Day Schools, Samuel Feuerstein was appointed its founding president. He was also honorary chairman of the board of the Union of Orthodox Jewish Congregations of America (OU).

The very first day that I arrived in Israel in 1967, when visiting my brother in Bnei Brak, I was brought to see the Ponevezh Yeshiva, to which, as mentioned above, I had tithed my wedding's cash gifts. I found that the "Donor of the Day" was Samuel Feuerstein. During World War II, Sam was very active in helping Jewish refugees who had arrived in the Boston area from Germany and the rest of Europe.

Sam's son, Moses (Moe), after graduating from Yeshiva University and Harvard Business School, began working in the family business with his father and brother. Following the path of his father, he began working with Torah Umesorah and became chairman of the Executive Committee. He worked for more than three decades to make the day school movement a vibrant force on the American Jewish scene. His leadership skills were evident even as a young student at yeshiva. A visionary and a doer par excellence, he founded and served as the first editor of the *Commentator*, the official newspaper of Yeshiva College. He also served, from 1954 to 1966, as the first American-born OU president. He advanced kashruth certification, youth work (NCSY), political action, and synagogue services. Amazingly, he held prestigious positions in both of these organizations before his fortieth birthday.

Prominent in the business world yet deeply devoted to Torah and mitzvoth, Moe served as a role model for his generation, teaching young Orthodox Jews that one need not sacrifice commitment to Torah to be successful in the secular world. He maintained relationships with gedolim across the Orthodox spectrum. He was extremely close to Rabbi Joseph B. Soloveitchik, while at the same time he had a strong relationship with Rabbi Aharon Kotler and Rabbi Yaakov Kamenetzky.[1]

---

1 From *Jewish Action*, Summer 2009. (slightly modified)

Moe's son, Rabbi Mordecai, was Rav in Congregation Schara Tzedeck of Vancouver, British Columbia, Canada. We once spent a Sabbath in his home, and among the stories about Vancouver that he related to us was one based upon his open invitation to Jews stranded in Vancouver for one reason or another. In one case, he let a stranded man park and live in his trailer on the grounds of the Feuerstein home. He also gave him free use of his home during the stay. Unfortunately, the visitor stole and improperly used one of the family credit cards. Nonetheless, this did not stop Rabbi Mordecai from continuing his open home policy, following the very generous pattern of his father and grandfather.

Aaron was appointed factory supervisor after graduation from Yeshiva University in 1947 and began a long and distinguished career at the mill. On December 11, 1995, his seventieth birthday,[2] he watched his life's work go up in flames—at least the most visible part of it. They had been alerted by a telephone call and were joined by thousands of anguished residents watching and mourning the six-alarm fire on the bank beyond. Three key buildings of the eight buildings that made up Malden Mills, one of the largest employers in the region, were ablaze.

---

2   Also, exactly, mine. [Zecharia Dor-Shav]

Fire insurance payments could have assured the Feuersteins a comfortable retirement if they had just walked away from their losses. Others might have seized the opportunity to move their manufacturing to a developing country, where labor would be cheaper. But the couple was committed to the mill, and to Lawrence and the adjacent town of Methuen just across the river. They paid their three thousand employees in full for six months while the business was being rebuilt.

"We had a sensitivity to the human equation," said Mr. Feuerstein. "The average American wants industry, the modern CEO and modern corporate America, to treat the worker as a human being, with consideration and thoughtfulness. And we did." Reopening nearly two years later, he rehired most of his (former) employees. In an era of widespread corporate downsizing, these actions made Mr. Feuerstein a national icon of corporate sensitivity.

Among a stack of letters on Aaron's desk was one from a woman in the Midwest who wrote that she had bought three Polartec coats (one of the company's prime products)[3] as a gesture of solidarity. As he spoke of the letter, Mr. Feuerstein's eyes brimmed with tears.

---

3 Our cousin Sam Dershowitz worked as a chemist for the Malden Knitting Mills at the time and was involved in developing these new fabrics.

He estimated he had received close to ten thousand letters from people who were moved by the events at the Mills. Some sent checks for workers' families:

> "They write me long letters," he said, "about how terrible it is in most companies and how they get thrown out and how they can't find a new job and how it destroys their children's chances for college, and, oh, I can't tell you. They pour their hearts out.[4]

"Twenty years later, during a telephone interview with the *Eagle-Tribune*, when asked if he would do such a thing again, he declared emphatically, "The answer is yes." Aaron is often referred to as a mensch (a Yiddish word that describes a person of strong character and honor).[5]

Among those who were affected by Mr. Feuerstein's paternalistic devotion to Malden Mills was President Clinton, who invited Aaron to be his guest for the State of the Union address in 1996.

Aside from the coincidence that one of the members of the Feuerstein family who had lost two hands

---

4   From: Lynnley Browning, *Business Day,* Nov. 28, 2001.
5   From: *Portland Press Herald,* December 11, 2015.

during the Yom Kippur War was among the wounded soldiers I helped in Tel Hashomer Hospital, as mentioned above, a granddaughter of the family, Leah Feuerstein, married Rabbi Daniel Feldman, a nephew of my cousin, Rabbi Meyer Fendel.

Appendix 9
The Ethiopian Aliyah and the Role of the AAEJ

JACQUES FAITLOVICH, AN Ashkenazi Jew born in Lodz, had studied Ethiopian languages at the Sorbonne and had visited Ethiopia for the purpose of connecting the Beta Yisrael with world Jewry. In 1904, with support from Baron Edmond de Rothschild, he traveled and lived among them and became a champion of their cause. In 1923 he opened a Jewish school in Addis Ababa, the capital of Ethiopia.

During a grand tour of Europe in 1924, Haile Selassie, regent of Ethiopia from 1916 to 1930 and emperor from 1930 to 1974, visited Jerusalem. His first stop was the Holy Sepulchre, for which he had a particular attachment. He toured Jerusalem and its districts, and, as he wrote, "We visited and kissed all the holy places." He then spent ten days visiting other significant holy and historic sites in Jerusalem and the rest of the country.

When the Italian army conquered Ethiopia in 1936, Jerusalem became a sanctuary to the emperor and his royal family. In 1941, he returned home and eventually established diplomatic relations with the new State of Israel. Yitzchak Ben-Zvi, president of Israel at the time, was interested in the lost Ten Tribes and asked Haile Selassie to allow a few young Ethiopian Jews to visit Israel in order to strengthen their connection with mainstream Jews. His idea was that they would study rabbinic Judaism and then return to Ethiopia to teach it to the rest of the Jews there. Eventually, in 1955, two groups totaling twenty-seven students were sent to study in Kfar Batya in Ra'anana.

The American Association for Ethiopian Jews (AAEJ) was created after Graenum Berger, its creator, met a group of Ethiopian Jews in Israel in 1955. During the next decade he discovered that information about their history and current life was scarce.[1] While visiting Ethiopia in 1965, he observed the Beta Yisrael living in poverty, lacking sanitation, receiving substandard education, and suffering universal discrimination. Berger also discovered a reluctance to assist the Ethiopian Jews or bring them to Israel.

He undertook a personal campaign to educate and raise money for their health and welfare and in 1969 created the AAEJ to bring pressure on World Jewry

---

1   With the rise of Christianity in the fourth century, conversion was forced upon the Jews of Ethiopia, and those who maintained their faith and identity were persecuted, forcing them to withdraw to the mountainous region of Gondar. There they settled, built communities, and lived for the ensuing centuries.

    With the rise of Queen Judith in the tenth century, the status of the Ethiopian Jews changed drastically. She led Ethiopia in a popular revolt that overthrew the Axum dynasty and sought to uproot Christianity from the land. A new royal dynasty was established within which the Jews held much influence for the next 350 years—often acting as a balance between Christian and Muslim groups. In 1270, the Axum dynasty returned to the throne, ushering in nearly four hundred years of tribal warfare and bloodshed. The end of that war, in 1624, marked the end of Jewish freedom. Jewish forces were defeated in a final battle by the Portuguese-backed Ethiopians. A long period of oppression began. Jewish captives were sold into slavery or forcibly baptized; their lands were confiscated; their writings and religious books were burned; and the practice of any form of Jewish religion was forbidden. For several hundred years—despite some encounters with explorers and missionaries—the community remained fairly isolated. Slowly however, recognition of Jews living in persecution in Ethiopia came to their attention. (Information gleaned mostly from the AAEJ and Ethiopian Civil War in Encyclopedia.com.)

to save this unique Jewish subculture from extinction. The AAEJ's primary purpose was to make the rescue of Ethiopian Jewry a number one priority of the Government of Israel and of world Jewish leadership. The organization used a variety of means to get the Jews from Ethiopia to Israel. Students at the University of California–Irvine campus became extremely vocal on behalf of the cause, under Professor Howard Lenhoff. The activists were in constant contact with the AAEJ in the United States. The organization provided them with money, supplies, food, and medical assistance. One of these activists was the husband of a cousin of my first wife, Netta. And it was he who organized the meeting of the rescued and rescuers in my home in Herzliya.

The organization was officially incorporated in 1974, and AAEJ established its offices in Highland Park, Illinois. It was loudly critical of the Israeli government for its inaction regarding the plight of Ethiopian Jews. Based on Berger's long personal experience with repeated lobbying of Israeli officials regarding the cause of the Ethiopian Jews, they were suspicious of the Israeli government's intentions. Even after the chief rabbinate, in 1973, declared Beta Yisrael to be Jewish, Israel made little effort to bring them in. Eventually, however, the AAEJ provoked Israel sufficiently for

Miki Tsarfati

them to act on behalf of this imperiled minority. By 1985, thousands of them had arrived in the Sudan, living in refugee camps under very poor conditions and with high mortality rates. Continued pressure on the Israeli government led to Operation Moses.

In the absence of full Israeli diplomatic relations with Ethiopia, the Mossad contacted officials in Sudan, adjacent to Ethiopia, for help. Prior to Operation Moses in that year, about eight thousand people had made the dangerous journey by foot to the border with Sudan and waited there in temporary camps until flown to Israel. They hoped to make their way to Kenya and from there to Israel. About four thousand Beta Yisrael perished from disease or hunger or were killed by bandits.[2] News of the rescue leaked out to the foreign

---

2 See Evil Days—30 Years of War and Famine in Ethiopia, An Africa Watch Report, Washington, D.C, September 1991.

media, with the result that President Numeiri of Sudan halted the operation for fear of hostile reaction from the Arab states. After mediation by the United States, Numeiri allowed six American Hercules planes to airlift the last remaining Ethiopian Jews in Sudan. Their arrival brought the numbers of olim to around sixteen thousand. The second stage of their journey was made from Sudan aboard Israeli Naval craft, which awaited them in the Red Sea.[3]

That was the beginning of Operation Moses.

---

3 The Israeli Secret Service agents opened a fake diving resort on the Sudanese shores of the Red Sea, with the sole purpose of clandestinely rescuing Ethiopian Jews from Sudan and bringing them to safety in Israel. Over several years the resort was in operation, about six thousand Jewish refugees who had fled persecution, war, and famine in Ethiopia were spirited by boat and plane to a new life in Israel.

GLOSSARY

a"h (alav hashalom): may he rest in peace
aliyah: immigration to Israel
anusim: the coerced
Aron Kodesh: holy ark of the Torah scroll
baal tefillah: prayer leader
baal teshuvah: returnee to full observance of Judaism
baalei batim: lay persons
beit midrash: senior study hall
ben-Torah: Torah scholar
berakah: blessing
bochur, pl. bochurim: unmarried yeshiva student
brit/berith: covenant or circumcision
Bubba: grandmother
chavrutah: primary learning group of Talmudic students
chuppah: canopy
daven, davening: pray, praying
din torah: presentation before a religious court

Eretz Yisrael: the biblical Land of Israel

gedolim: great Torah scholars

gemarah: text of the Talmud

giyur l'chumrah: conversion requiring only immersion in a ritual bath

haftarah: a reading from the Prophets—frequently bestowed upon a bar-mitzvah celebrant.

halakhah: authorized Orthodox Jewish law

hametz: grains prepared with leavening agents

hared, pl. haredim: ultra-Orthodox

hashkafah: worldview/philosophy

Hasidism: a movement emphasizing: communion with God; transformation and elevation of evil to goodness; no place is empty of God; and enthusiastic worship versus Torah study.

hazan: cantor

Hesder: an Israeli yeshiva/military service program.

kabbalah: esoteric teachings meant to explain religious texts

kaddish: lit. sanctification; mourner's prayer for the dead

Kadosh Baruch Hu: The Holy One, blessed be He

kes, pl. kessim: Ethiopian religious leader

kiddush: small sanctification repast

kippah, pl. kippot: religious small head covering

maftir: an honorific usually given to a distinguished member of the congregation.

malachim: lit. angels. An ultra-pious Hasidic sect that insist they are not "Americans," but rather, *Yidden* (Jews). They also assume ascetic practices.

mashgiach ruchani: spiritual supervisor or guide

mesivta: high-school level yeshiva

Midrash, pl. Midrashim: a mode of biblical interpretation prominent in the Talmudic literature

mikvah: ritual bath

minhah: afternoon prayer service

minyan: prayer quorum of ten men

mitzvah, pl. mitzvoth/mitzvos: Jewish religious commandment

mori ve'rebbi: my teacher, my master

Musaf: additional holiday prayer service

olam haemet: the world of true life, i.e., after death

olim: immigrants

parocheth: curtain screen that covers the holy ark

posek, pl. poskim: Orthodox Jewish adjudicator; halakhah decisor

Rav: Rabbi

reb: an honorific traditionally used for Orthodox Jewish men.

rebbetzin: a title, generally used for the rabbi's wife.

rosh chodesh: first day of the Hebrew calendar month

seder: traditional Passover eve ceremonial meal

semikah: rabbinical ordination

shalosh seudoth: third and last meal of the Sabbath

sheva brachot: wedding week of seven blessings

shidduch: a system of matchmaking.

shiur, pl. shiurim: Torah lesson

shiva: lit. seven. Seven-day mourning period

shloshim: lit. thirty. The 30-day mourning period following burial.

shmoneh esrai: standard 18 blessings recited 3 times a day

shmus: lit. talk: colloquially used to denote a moralistic presentation

shofar: a ram's horn blown on Rosh Hashanah and in times of anguish and joy.

shohet: ritual slaughterer

siddur: prayer book

tallit katan: small prayer shawl, often worn all day long

talmid, pl. talmidim: student

tanakh: Hebrew Bible

tefillah, pl. tefillot: prayer

tefillin: phylacteries

Tishah B'Av: the fast of the Ninth of Av. A commemoration of the destruction of both Temples in Jerusalem.

treifa medinah: non-kosher country

tzaddik: righteous person

ulpan: adult education program

yahrzeit: annual memorial day

Yamim Noraim: Days of Awe, Rosh HaShanah and Yom Kippur

yarmulka: (see kippah)

yeshiva gedolah: post-high school yeshiva

Yiddish: a Hebrew/Aramaic/German language with local variations

yungeleit: mature married yeshiva students

Zeide: grandfather

zemiroth: Sabbath songs of praise

zt"l (zecher tzaddik l'vrachah): of blessed memory